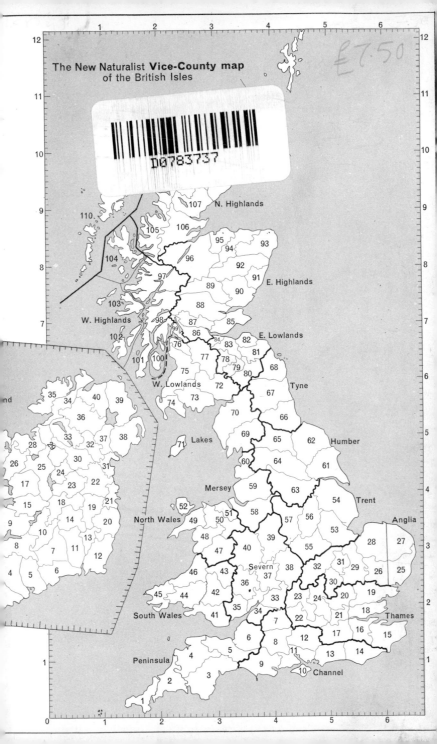

The Shell Bird Book

JAMES FISHER

The Shell Bird Book

EBURY PRESS and MICHAEL JOSEPH

© Copyright Shell-Mex and B P. Limited 1966

Designed and produced by
George Rainbird Ltd,
2 Hyde Park Place, London W2

Designer: Eric Hughes

Printed and bound by Jarrold & Sons Ltd, Norwich

Contents

Acknowledgements

We are grateful to the following individuals and organisations for permission to reproduce illustrations on the pages mentioned below:

H. G. Alexander (221, bottom); B. T. Batsford (32 top, and 37, from *Everyday Life in the New Stone, Bronze and Early Iron Ages*, and *Everyday Life in Roman Britain*, by Marjorie and C. H. B. Quennell); Trustees of the British Museum (48, 58, 59, 64, 184 right, 210 right); British Museum, Natural History, London (18 top); British Museum, Natural History, Tring (231 left); British Trust for Ornithology (131); Cambridge University Press (173, from W. H. Thorpe's *Bird Song*); Collins Publishers (79, from *A Field Guide to the Birds of Britain and Europe* by Roger Peterson, Guy Mountfort and P. A. D. Hollom); Crown Copyright (16, an H.M. Geological Survey photograph, and 29; reproduced by permission of the Controller of H.M. Stationery Office); Exeter Cathedral Library (43); I. J. Ferguson-Lees (221 top); R. Gillmor (101, 111, 153, 166, 215, 256); Eric Hosking (231 right); Linnean Society (71); Lundy Field Society (243); Museum of British Transport, London (19); National Portrait Gallery (65, 67 right, 180 left, 184 left, 185 right, 187 both, 188 left, 189 both, 190 both, 195, 198 both, 207, 209, 210 left, 211 both, 213, 225); Norwich Museums Committee (229 right); Oxford University Press (172, from E. A. Armstrong's *A Study of Bird Song*); Penguin Books (204, from David Lack's *The Life of the Robin*); J. Peterson (121); Plantin-Moretus Museum, Antwerp (178); Radio Times Hulton (50, 179); Brigid ni Rinne (47 right); Royal Society for the Protection of Birds (138 both, 107, 159, 200); Peter Scott (107 top); N. Wylie-Moore (256 top, 257, the latter reproduced by permission of Commander C. A. Herdman, R.N.); H. F. and G. Witherby Ltd (156).

The New Naturalist Vice-County Map on the endpapers is reproduced by kind permission of Wm. Collins, Sons & Co.

We would like to thank the libraries of the Royal Geographical Society and the Zoological Society of London for providing material for reproduction.

It is often difficult to ascertain whether or not a particular illustration is copyright. If we have unwittingly infringed the copyright in any picture reproduced in this book, we tender our sincere apologies and will be glad of the opportunity, upon being satisfied as to the owner's title, to pay an appropriate fee. Acknowledgement will also be made in any future edition.

Colour Plates

7

Illustrations

Maps

Preface

In 1934, as an undergraduate of Oxford University, it was my pleasure and indeed privilege to show some of the 309 other attending members of the Eighth International Ornithological Congress into their seats in Rhodes House and the Oxford University Museum. In 1966, as I write this, I am preparing – as a member, now, of the international committee and (not a very effective one, I fear) of the host committee, but feeling very much like a student again – to show three times as many members of the Fourteenth International Ornithological Congress into their seats again, some of them doubtless the very same ones they sat in a third of a century ago.

The world of ornithology, as this bird-watcher has followed it during the middle third of the twentieth century, has the attributes of all great sciences and hobbies. It is established. It is, indeed, big time, to use a modern phrase. It is evolving and proliferating so fast that in the first third of this century we saw the last of the ornithologists like Alfred Newton whose scholarship of birds could be globally more-or-less complete, and in the second the last of the living total encyclopedists of British and Irish ornithology, like W. B. Alexander. The next third may restore brains capable of digesting, in some way, the sum of ornithological knowledge; but the brains will be electronic. It is likely that some time before the year 2000 the ten-billionth word on birds will be printed; that is to say there will be about as many bird-words in the archives as individual living birds on the face of our planet.

Not many years ago my uncle, the late Arnold Boyd, laid down the latest of the deluge of bird books that the *Manchester Guardian* kept sending him for review, sighing "you can't see the birds for the words". A master of the nice economy of words himself, he did not much like a post-war school of nature-dramatisers who then had a (rather short) success, and despised people who proffered peeps at their powerful personalities in the guise of facts about their feathered friends. Largely because they were never in the mid-twentieth-century mainstream, the neo-Thoreaus (as some of them doubtless believed they were) have fallen by the wayside. Thoreau bush, Thoreau briar for Romps with Dame Nature is now out. Those who have tried it lately, under the misapprehension that nature writing still needs a Tone of Voice, or Slant of Pen, or (worst of all) a ponderous facetiousness, have not known what they were writing about, really. Thoreau, who piled some big, firm stones in the middle of our present untidy pyramid of nature understanding, has his niche in history. He is to be built upon, as are all the past heroes of our glorious natural history study. No old hero, called back to earth with his Elysian binoculars, would thank his followers for unthinking imitation of his style, his approach, his bias of investigation, his methods. He would be far more interested in seeing the new models, and enjoying the new things and the new subjects, and the new approaches, and the new tricks and tools, and perhaps most of all, new scholarship. The only thing that could upset a decent old hero would be to feel his followers climbing on his shoulders in hob-nailed boots.

All this makes it very necessary for me to apologise for this book, and explain what I have tried to do in it. If some readers recognise in it old themes and subjects, old ideas and old words that I have written about in old books now quite properly out of print, for instance *Birds as Animals*, *Watching Birds*, *Birds in Britain* and *A History of Birds*, they will quite rightly think it is something of a rehash. Why not? These old writings needed rewriting, as birds and their affairs change yearly. I have tried to make it a new soup with some old stock, some of whose ingredients have already been published in various articles, in *Country Fair*, *Woman* and *Punch* particularly. To the proprietors of these journals, and to the publishers of the old books (Heinemann, Penguin, Collins and Hutchinson) I am grateful for permissions. But a great deal of it is based on new analyses – mainly historical. I felt that it was time to write some sort of essay on the fossil birds of Britain and Ireland, pending a fuller analysis of them which awaits completion and the final searching of all the large array of archaeological and speleological journals—which makes one wish the long winter evenings were longer: and if what I have to offer lacks the scholarship of Richard Lydekker, who wrote the last such essay three-quarters of a century ago, I comfort myself that the available material he had to summarise was but a tiny fraction of the present published stuff. I felt it time, too, to follow after nearly half a century's gap, another hero of bird scholarship, J. H. Gurney, in analysing our birds of the Dark Ages and medieval times.

The birds of the present, in our reckoning of them, cannot be understood without an analysis of the past. A bird does not have a "distribution", notwithstanding all the field guides and textbooks and atlases which present such things in tidy descriptions or with crisp-looking maps. A bird has, of course, a "present distribution"; and except for a few rare species, or special social species all of whose breeding stations are known, nobody knows what that is. So much do bird distributions (and habits) change that every bird book or scientific paper is out of date the moment its writer starts writing it, let alone sees it in print. Birds, like all other animals, are in the process of evolution as we watch them.

All the instruments of research, involving trades other than strict ornithological zoology, are necessary to reach an understanding of birds' lives and status. It is necessary to see them through the eyes of palaeontologists, archaeologists, philologists, poets, historians and geographers to begin to understand what they are all about. Through the borrowed eyes of the scholars of these disciplines I have been happy to meet our Ice Age birds, the birds of Iron Age Glastonbury, the birds of Dark Age Northumbria, the birds of our medieval poets, in a form of bird-watching which is second-hand, but in some cases – so well have old digs been dug, old poems composed, old drawings drawn – like bird-watching from a Wellsian time machine, or like seeing a first-rate television bird programme.

I do not claim in this book to have done more than rubbed some different sciences together, to broaden the picture of our lovely birds, and demonstrate the various passions with which they have been, and are being watched. I have not thought it necessary to explain why they are being watched. Why climb Everest? Birds make their own watchers, of course; it is as simple as that. To put it as mildly as I can, they seem to generate a certain amount of enthusiasm.

The many sources of material, pictorial and textual, are duly cited in the appropriate place. I feel proud to have my words embellished in colour, once more, by Eric Ennion, Peter Scott, Donald Watson, Rowland Hilder, Roy Badmin, Richard Eurich, R. B. Talbot Kelly and Charles Tunnicliffe —the team who beautified Shell's bird sanctuary series of advertisements. Robert Gillmor and others living have contributed black-and-white images that match well, in my opinion, with the classics of Thomas Bewick and other old masters. Many friends have helped me with the text, too numerous to thank, though I have special gratitude to the editorial staff of Messrs George Rainbird, who have made contributions of time, research and collative skill well beyond normal duty. James Ferguson-Lees, the executive editor of that admirable journal *British Birds* (now older than all but a fraction of its readers), has checked and advised me on the list of British birds (Chapter 12, p. 296). John Flower has put a lot of work into the maps and diagrams. If text and maps contain errors, as doubtless they do, these errors are my responsibility, and none at all of those who have given me so much help.

JAMES FISHER

Ashton, Northampton, 14th June 1966

CHAPTER I

A Bird's Eye View of Britain

The readers, and the printers and publishers and illustrators and writer of this book, belong to a species of sophisticated ape, distinguished from other animals by a certain power to store and communicate experience, by certain skills with tools and engines, and by certain capacities for abstract thought, pure curiosity, spiritual values, and both altruistic and viciously aggressive behaviour.

Homo sapiens, as far as the palaeontologists can tell, has existed in his present species form for but a quarter of a million years or so. The earliest bone of him so far discovered is a cranium that belonged to a man who lived by the banks of the Thames at Swanscombe. Such is our present sense of history, and the value of research, that a National Nature Reserve now embraces the place he was quarried from, one of more than a hundred such reserves that adorn our kingdom, and prove that our peculiarly English Adam Swanscombe's descendants at least love nature, and value wilderness, wild places and the gloriously useless.

I shall have more to write about man's present love of nature later: let me just establish an objective fact concerning our islanders' love of birds. Birds, the most observable of the animals, are a litmus paper of a country's state of native culture. We are blessed with marvellously varied scenery, a good climate (and even, despite the old saw, good weather), a relatively unerodable soil. On the other hand, we are heavily industrialised and overcrowded. No other comparable country has dedicated, as we have (albeit rather recently), more than a tenth of its area as National Parks, Areas of Outstanding Natural Beauty, National Forest Parks, National Trust Areas, Nature Reserves, Geological Monuments, Greenways, Trackways, Wildfowl Refuges and Bird Sanctuaries. No other country has lived through so many decades of multiplying public enthusiasm for birds. Butterflies, of course; flowers, indeed; fishes and mammals, lizards and frogs, beetles and fleas, mosses, liverworts, ferns and seashore life. But, particularly, the birds. At least 456 species of birds have been seen alive and wild in Britain and Ireland since serious records began and by 1964. At least two dozen more lived in our fossil past, though only 23 of these have yet been named. The 125 land birds and 118 sea or water birds that play a really important part in the

England in the Lower Eocene. A diorama in the Geological Museum, of London Clay times, when the shores of the Wealden Island had a bird fauna of the first (known) tropic birds, herons, New World vultures and gulls, and members of extinct orders, including the big flightless *Dasornis* and *Odontopteryx*.

web of our wild life are the most written of, the most poeticised, the most sung of, dreamed of, observed, conserved, loved birds in the world.

The birds' eye view of Britain is a modest four hundred times (or more) as long as the man's eye view of Britain's birds – even if we assume (reasonably) that Swanscombe Man was a bird-watcher. When birds probably first lived around the planet-point represented now by England, Greenwich Observatory was near the shore of a vast inland lake that extended to the present shores of France, and the Woodwardian (now Cambridge) Museum was under a wedge-shaped arm of the sea that covered the present Midlands.

At the Cambridge Museum now repose some pieces of bird bone, the first of which was discovered by Lucas Barrett in 1858. Professor H. G. Seeley named two species from them and from other material – *Enaliornis barretti* and *E. sedgwicki* – Barrett's and Sedgwick's birds-of-the-sea, after his close colleagues. When found they were the oldest known birds, sea birds of the later part of the Lower Cretaceous deposits that geologists now believe to have been laid down in shallow waters some 100 to 110 million years ago, and are raised today to form the Upper Greensand beds near Grantchester. The pigeon-sized *Enaliornis*-birds are now believed by some to be ancestors of the present divers (themselves of a rather ancient family) and are today the third oldest known birds in the world : the oldest – *Archaeopteryx* of German Jurassic slate about 140 million years old – a real, toothed, bone-tailed but feathered link between the reptiles and the modern birds; and *Gallornis* of France about 130 million years ago, probably an ancestor of the flamingos. *Enaliornis* shared the coastal waters of Cambridge with other fish-eaters – big sea-serpentian mosasaurs and other reptiles like giant turtles and large flying pterosaurs.

Sixty million years or a little more ago, when the next known British bird lived, the sea had invaded nearly all of southern England, though a long island lay south of the present Thames. Here stalked *Gastornis*, a flightless bird as large as an ostrich (though in relationship held between the cranes and the waders), whose bones were discovered in Paleocene beds when the old Park Hill railway cutting was being excavated near Croydon. A slightly younger member of the same family, *Dasornis*, was earlier discovered by the Earl of Enniskillen at Sheppey in Kent. Other Sheppey finds in the Eocene London Clay of a little under 60 million years ago were a giant tropic bird *Prophaethon* (the first of its family known) ; *Argillornis* (between the gannets and the pelicans) ; *Odontopteryx* – a giant sea bird with bony tooth-like fish-grasping outgrowths of its jaw-bones, and sole representative of its family ; *Lithornis*, a peregrine-sized pigmy condor which is the earliest known representative of a family of vulture-like birds of prey now confined entirely to the Americas ; and *Halcyornis*, earliest known member of the gull family.

Lithornis, obtained by the great surgeon John Hunter before 1793, was the

first ancient fossil bird ever to have been collected and studied by scientists;
and *Halcyornis* was the first ancient fossil bird ever to be formally named (in
1838). The Eocene island of south-east England also held the world's first
known heron at this time: *Proherodius* was discovered during the excavation
of the Primrose Hill Tunnel of what was then the London and Birmingham
Railway; and another bone probably of the same species was found near
what is now St James's Park.

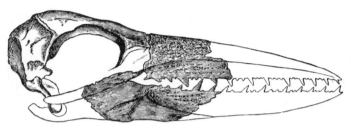

Odontopteryx toliapica; the skull of this false-toothed sea bird of the London
Clay of Sheppey, as figured with Richard Owen's original description of
1873.

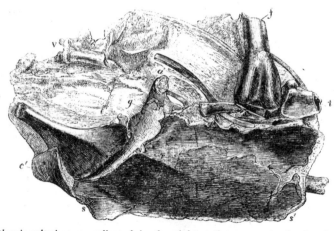

Lithornis vulturinus, as collected in the eighteenth century in the London
Clay of Sheppey; woodcut by W. Bagg, published in 1846 in Richard
Owen's *A History of British Fossil Mammals and Birds*.

During Eocene times England had a climate resembling that of the East
Indies. The great dinosaur-reptiles of the Cretaceous period had died out and
mammals had inherited the land-masses. The bird fossils of the Upper

Driven through Lower Eocene London Clay, the Primrose Hill Tunnel on what is now the main Midland Region line from Euston goes straight through the type locality of *Proherodius oweni*, the earliest known heron.

Eocene, a little over 40 million years ago, were mostly sea and shore birds, for most of Hampshire of the time was covered by a shallow sea. From the Hordle beds of this county come an early diver, *Colymboides*; an early cormorant, *Actiornis*; the earliest known ibis, *Ibidopsis*; *Agnopterus* of a pre-flamingo family, of which it was the earliest; the earliest true flamingo, *Elornis*; the earliest true hawk, *Palaeocircus*; two early cranes and another flightless Gastornithid. In younger (Oligocene) beds of the Isle of Wight *Agnopterus* was still represented.

From the early Oligocene of rather under 40 million years ago there is a gap in the British fossil record. Though the ages (Oligocene–Miocene–Pliocene) until the Upper Pliocene of about 2 million years ago were full of incident, including great volcanic activity and mountain building, few sedimentary deposits are preserved in Britain, and no bird fossils are known. We meet birds again when our islands had almost assumed their present shape, though England was quite broadly connected with France. Britain's only known Pliocene bird is an albatross – *Diomedea anglica*, the English albatross. It was discovered first in Suffolk rocks of rather over 600,000 years old (early Lower Pleistocene); then in the 2-million-year-old (or so) Upper Pliocene deposits in the same county; and over twenty years ago 9-million-year-old bones were found in Florida which Alexander Wetmore has referred to the same, obviously long-lived species. This may well have been the last native albatross of the North Atlantic, now probably climatically unsuitable to members of this ocean-gliding family.

The English albatross and 8 of the 9 fossil birds from Hordle in

Hampshire were described and named by the famous palaeontologist, ornithologist and mammalogist Richard Lydekker in 1891. The giant tropic bird of the London Clay was described by C. W. Andrews in 1899. Since then not a single further British fossil bird has been described and named by anybody; palaeornithology has become curiously unfashionable in the present century in the country where the first fossil bird was formally named. Most of the advances in our knowledge of early birds since Lydekker's list of British fossil birds of 1891 (the last attempt at a complete one until this present book) have come from a few students of the Pleistocene and prehistoric periods – the last million years or less. The literature of what has been found has been most sketchily cited in our scientific bird journals; and I have spent much of my free time during the last three years on a systematic search of the geologists', palaeontologists', speleologists' and archaeologists' publications in an effort to wring facts out of hundreds of different books and journals and assemble what is known; the work must go on for several more years before it is anything like complete, and the story of the birds of the Ice Ages and after, that follows, is based on but a biggish sample of the scattered material, and largely on the studies of comparatively few skilled and devoted (and disgracefully unquoted) bird-bone identifiers. Of the forty or so trained anatomists who have published competent identifications of British or Irish fossil and prehistoric bird bones in the present century I believe only four to be still alive; young ornithologists seem singularly disinclined to fossil work and unappreciative of the light that a study of past distribution can throw on the distribution of the birds of the present. I suppose that among the bones filed for years in several of our senior museums lie those of at least 5 unnamed good species now extinct. Possibly there are many more. Some have already been partly described, and need new study badly. In North America and the West Indies, where fine bird palaeontologists have been working hard for years, 444 species were known as fossils of the full Pleistocene period and prehistoric times (the last million years or so) by 1964. Of these 121, or 27 per cent, are extinct. Our British–Irish List for the same period is, by my own reckoning, 144 named species, of which only the English albatross and great auk are agreed to be extinct. Nobody can imagine that the Ice Age conditions in England and Ireland were about twenty times kinder to birds than they were in North America. Something is wrong with the British figures. It is true that the British last-million-year list has a greater proportion of more recent species (more likely to be living ones) than the American one. But its 142 still-living species should be, judging by the strong American sample, accompanied by perhaps over 30 extinct ones. Besides the English albatross and the great auk there are 4 others (at least) *obviously* waiting to be named. There must be many more than these in museums.

By means of a logarithmic scale (pp. 22–3) I have made an approximate model of the main events in Britain and Ireland of the Ice Ages and the later times to the Norman Conquest that gives more space to events as they get younger. It was during this quite exceptional state of planetary affairs that western Europe's present fauna and flora evolved. As far as can be detected, no series of Ice Ages had overtaken Earth since Permian times (interestingly, just about one rotation of our own galaxy, the Milky Way, ago). For the first time in about 250 million years permanent ice occupied substantial areas around the planet's poles. In the northern hemisphere these ice-zones fluctuated in size and an irregular, syncopated way; the advances and retreats of the ice appear to be linked with calculable variations in the sun energy received, from which they can be approximately dated. The main advances of ice in western Europe were four: to give them the names bestowed by the geologists of the Alps: Günz, Mindel, Riss and Würm. The Günz system had two distinct ice advances, the Mindel system two, the Riss system two (of which the second was probably the most extensive of all), the Würm system three. Between the named glacial systems were interglacials (Cromerian, Holsteinian, Eemian); between the advances within each glacial lesser retreats of ice known as interstadials. The longest interglacial (Holsteinian, or Great Interglacial) may have been interrupted by two minor advances; and there were minor ice advances, too, before Günz, probably dating back to over 800,000 years. But the main features are the nine principal advances, and the nine retreats. Since the last Würm glaciation ended about 10,000 years ago, and ushered in the rise of human civilisations, we have been in an interglacial; for though the Pleistocene may have its official end at the end of Würm, some geologists believe that we are still in it; and that the ice will sweep back a little in another 10,000 years – and a lot in 50,000 and 90,000 years from now, obliterating Scandinavia, and much of Scotland and Canada all over again.

Through the Pleistocene our islands varied considerably in outline, their land-masses at times hidden under vast ice systems which over 100,000 years ago obliterated the underlying land (except for a few mountain islands or nunataks) everywhere except in southern England. England was usually connected with France except in some interglacial times when the ice-melt raised the sea-level considerably. Ireland was connected with Britain at times by ice across which animals could travel, and probably by an ice-free land-bridge after the last Würm glaciation collapsed: this bridge did not last long, and was thought by some to have run between the southern Inner Hebrides and Donegal, but by later scholars between Wales and eastern Ireland.

In general our fauna and flora could advance and retreat with the warm and cold periods as one with that of western Europe, though Ireland, at

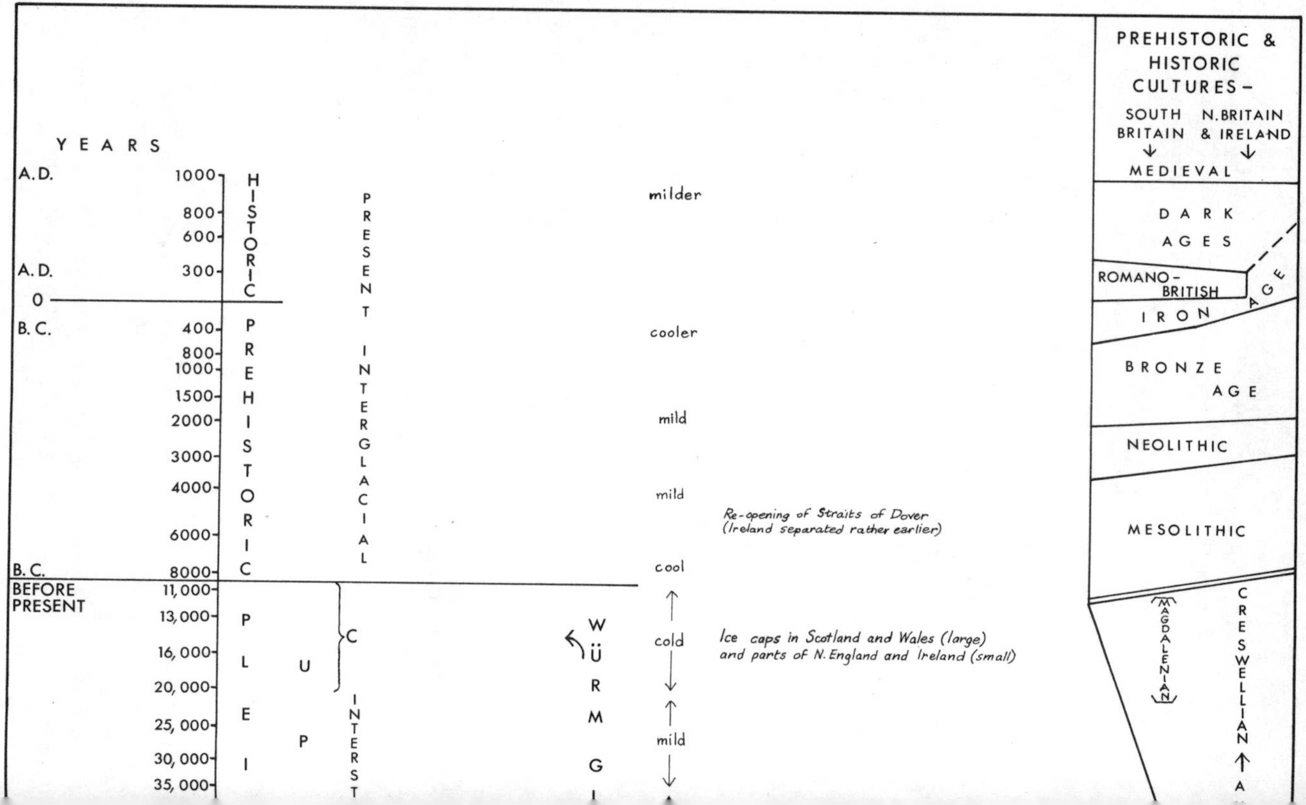
YEARS
A.D.
1000
800
600
A.D.
300
0
B.C.
400
800
1000
1500
2000
3000
4000
6000
B.C.
8000
BEFORE PRESENT
11,000
13,000
16,000
20,000
25,000
30,000
35,000
HISTORIC
PREHISTORIC
PRESENT INTERGLACIAL
C
U
P
INTERST
milder
cooler
mild
mild
cool
cold
mild
Re-opening of Straits of Dover
(Ireland separated rather earlier)
Ice caps in Scotland and Wales (large)
and parts of N. England and Ireland (small)
PREHISTORIC & HISTORIC CULTURES –
SOUTH BRITAIN
N. BRITAIN & IRELAND
MEDIEVAL
DARK AGES
ROMANO-BRITISH
IRON AGE
BRONZE AGE
NEOLITHIC
MESOLITHIC
MAGDALENIAN
CRESWELLIAN

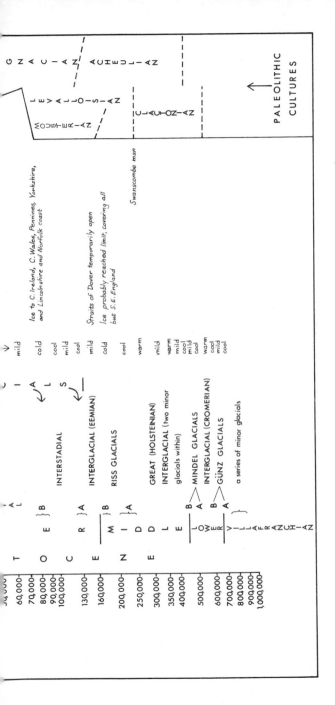

THE PLEISTOCENE PERIOD AND AFTER (TO THE NORMAN CONQUEST)
Note that time is on a logarithmic scale, the "present" time being taken as
A.D. 2000. Modified with Zenner, Godwin and other authorities.

times heavily glaciated and the least accessible to recolonisation, has ended in the present interglacial with a smaller animal list than the rest (snakeless, for instance, *pace* St Patrick's legend). Palaeolithic or Old Stone Age men could and did move freely into the present islands with cultures at first the same as those of France, though towards the end of the Pleistocene they developed their own peculiarly British style and technique of living, the Creswellian counterpart of Europe's classic Magdalenian culture.

It is time, then, for us to meet the early birds of the Pleistocene. How representative can fossils be? In old river-beds we find water birds and a few other big birds; a biased sample for such are more likely to be fossilised than little woodland birds. Caves give us a better sample – and our islands are full of bone caves. How did the bones get in? Hyenas and polecats, and in the later Pleistocene Old Stone Age hunters brought birds in to eat: they brought what they liked to eat, and no true random sample of the bird fauna. Old Stone Age hunters left the bones of what they hunted – as indeed also did the hunters of the Middle Stone Age (Mesolithic) and the farmers of the New Stone Age (Neolithic) and Bronze Age, and the sophisticated tribes of the Iron Age. The Romans leave us bones of the birds they domesticated, kept as aviary pets, or ate as gourmets. No "dig" in Ireland or Britain gives us a true cross-section: but some digs are big. E. T. Newton found over 60 species in the ancient (some over 100,000 years old) deposits of Chudleigh Cave in Devon, well over 30 in the Wye Valley caves of Old Stone Age hunters at the end of the last glaciation. Clare and Sligo's cave deposits go back to this time, too; and Scharff and Ussher list 57 and 37 cave birds from these counties. At Shetland's Jarlshof (Bronze to Iron Age) Margery Platt found 42, at Glastonbury's Iron Age lake dwellings Andrews 31, at Lagore's Dark Age lake dwellings in Co. Meath (A.D. 750–950) Stelfox 32.

Apart from the English albatross, we know rather few Lower Pleistocene British birds. The earlier ones come from the classic fossil beds of Norfolk and Suffolk, all about 500,000 to 600,000 years old. Some are undetermined; one is barn-owl like, another a guillemot (*perhaps* a different species from our common guillemot), another a goose, another a duck. But in the Forest Bed of Norfolk modern birds have been identified: cormorant, shoveler, pochard, greylag, capercaillie (? the modern species), eagle owl and crow. These birds shared the warm times of the Cromerian interglacial with mastodons, early forest elephants (straight-tusked) and the first mammoth; a British native monkey; many extinct kinds of horses and deer (some giant); sabre-tooths, cave lions, hyenas and several kinds of bear; the giant beaver; hippopotami and forest rhinoceroses.

In Mindel glacial times, cooler though it was, the same (to us exotic) sort of mammal fauna persisted, with northern additions like reindeer. The earliest biggish cave bird fauna of England – from Clevedon Cave – can possibly be placed here, around the middle 400,000's before the present. Buzzards and white-tailed eagles soared over the Somerset hills and shores of those days ; brent geese wintered on a neighbouring estuary ; mallard and other dabbling ducks doubtless nested around ; ringed and golden plovers, turnstone and whimbrel nested or regularly passed on their flyways ; the common gull probably bred on the moors. Swifts from Africa hunted insects in the summer ; herons and cormorants fished the lakes and estuary ; and the forests, glades and downs had a May-June-long L.P. of song thrush (perhaps also redwing, though a fossil cannot tell us whether it is a breeder or a winter visitor), blackbird, wheatear, robin, greenfinch and skylark. Ravens nested on crags or forest trees.

Our only known British Middle Pleistocene bird fossils come from the river-gravels of warm or mild Holsteinian times. The later ones – greylag, whooper swan and a possible wandering albatross from Ilford – are roughly contemporary with Swanscombe Man. The albatross bone should be re-studied ; perhaps it was the last of the English albatrosses. Some of the grey-lags from rather earlier deposits were smaller than the present ones, and some material referred to the bean goose suggests a bird larger than the present bean. We know, then, only of water birds – and rather mysterious ones at that until somebody has another look at the material – to go with a mammal fauna less different from the present one than that of the early Pleistocene. A native monkey was still with us, though ; cave hyena and cave lion, a hairy forest rhino like the surviving Sumatran rhino ; hippo, boars, giant deer, horse and forest elephant.

The Riss glaciations which brought the Middle Pleistocene (as most geologists now assign it) to an end may be represented by no known birds at all, unless the grouse and ptarmigan in Creswell's Pin Hole Cave in Derby-shire belong to this cold (or even coldest) horizon, which they well might. The Pin Hole and other Creswell deposits continue through the Upper Pleistocene and have taught us much of the native English Old Stone Age cultures. But for the birds of the early Upper Pleistocene we must look else-where – to Chudleigh Cave and Kent's Cavern in Devon, Hoe Grange Cave in Derbyshire and Kirkdale Cave in Yorkshire, where faunas are all pro-bably representative of the mild times of the Eemian interglacial. Mammals of those days: cave bear, cave wolf, cave lion, cave hyena, horse, forest rhino, giant deer, aurochs (the progenitor of our domestic ox), giant bison, forest elephant and mammoth. To match them, a mysterious duck from Kirkdale that may be an old new species (or a new old species) ; expectable water birds like red-throated diver (on a winter visit?), mallard, wigeon, shelduck, various geese ; game birds in force, including grouse, ptarmigan, blackcock, caper, partridge, quail and the only British record of the hazel grouse from

Creswell Crags near Worksop, Derbyshire, whose caves and fissures, first worked in 1875–79, disclosed evidence of the classic Creswellian Old Stone Age hunters, who were grouse and ptarmigan eaters. (*J. M. Mello*)

Chudleigh (the Channel was probably open at this time, but not long before England had been connected with France, as it was again soon after: today the hazel grouse still breeds west to Norway and eastern France), several waders, the little auk and puffin (Devon), a mysteriously large pigeon, snowy owl (another of several northern birds), little owl (extinct historically and now only present by reintroduction), and a surprisingly complete array of singing birds (a monument to the identificatory skill of the late E. T. Newton and others), at least 33 species strong. These include, rather interestingly, the house sparrow – and chough, redwing and great grey shrike which no longer breed in the area, though fossils cannot prove they did so then. Among them were tits, nuthatches, creeper, 9 members of the thrush family, whitethroat and hawfinch. The wren, which is the only member of its American family in Europe, was already present. Our jenny wren is of the same species as the winter wren of North America, which must have invaded the Old World, across the Bering Strait all the way to St Kilda and Iceland in Ice Age times; it is interesting to find it in the Devon of over 100,000 years ago.

The middle part of the Upper Pleistocene embraces the Würm glaciations A and B (cool and cold) and the mild interstadial between them. Stone Age hunters were becoming more sophisticated; the men who performed the formal burial at Paviland in Gower probably ate gannets and guillemots; and choughs nested around them, as they do in cliffs not far away today. Water and game birds are the common fossils of the caves of Brixham in Devon, of Yorkshire of this horizon, and of Inchnadamph in Sutherland.

Kirkdale Cave in Yorkshire's North Riding, first excavated in 1821, has fossil faunas of Eemian times; elephant, hippopotamus, rhinoceros and lion, with a number of birds, some of them still unidentified.

The bird fauna is on the whole northern, with long-tailed duck, scoter, eider, grouse, ptarmigan, black grouse, grey plover and puffin in the Highland cave. The Brixham cave deposits had a funny shelduck which may be of an undescribed species.

In the latter part of the Upper Pleistocene the mild interstadial between Würm B and Würm C was succeeded by the Würm C glaciation, less cold than Würm B but cool enough. During this time the human Creswellian cultures reached their peak of Old Stone Age skills, and hunted from a fauna which still included bison, horse and deer in the milder times, reindeer, mammoth, woolly rhino, varying hare and arctic fox in the cooler. Their bird fauna, from quite abundant evidence, was very like that of the present, with more northerly elements during the glaciation. A big eagle from Walthamstow Gravel of the warmer interstadial time may have been a super-white-tailed eagle close to its present relative, the huge Steller's sea eagle from Kamchatka. It needs re-examination, and possibly a new name. In the glacial time scoters, mergansers, smew and other northern ducks were hunted in the Wye Valley and Kent; ptarmigan lived in the present Forest of Dean (which may not then have been a forest at all) as did snow buntings; in Scotland the bird fauna was very like that of Lapland. Irish birds were northern, too; the crane is quite common in the caves of Clare and Sligo and may well have lived on the Irish bogs of those days, in the country of the still-living giant deer. The great spotted woodpecker and magpie lived in Clare, then; the former breeds in Ireland no longer, and the latter became extinct but recolonised Wexford (and later most of the country) in the 1670s.

When the last glaciation was over, and the humans of western Europe entered another phase of human culture, the Middle Stone Age, with more sophisticated hunting tools, Eskimo-like (in culture) Maglemosian hunters lived in Yorkshire and ate cormorant, mallard, goldeneye, swan and jay, and slew or took home kite and white-tailed eagle. In the succeeding Mesolithic and Neolithic times Azilian hunters and food-gatherers with even finer, polished stone weapons left traces of their bird meals in the kitchen-middens and some caves all round the north of our islands from Ayrshire and Bute to Antrim, Donegal, Argyll, Caithness and Durham. Sea-bird fowlers, they were, in a tradition that survived at St Kilda until 1930, and still survives at Ness at the north end of the Lewis. Their prey; gannets in strength, from colonies doubtless in some cases those inhabited today; cormorant and shag; sometimes the bittern; scoters, mergansers, shelduck, geese and swans; the white-tailed eagle and the peregrine (did they slay rival predators?), some game birds, waders and gulls, and many auks. Eight Azilian sites have great auk bones, sometimes in number : our only extinct British bird of the historic period obviously had a fairly wide range in 2000 or 3000 B.C. Razorbill, little auk, guillemot, puffin they ate too.

As the Neolithic peoples were the earliest British farmers, and not purely hunters, it would be interesting to know the birds of the farmland of their time (about 3000 to 1700 B.C.). Unfortunately, we have rather little information. The song thrush, and highly probably also mistle thrush and starling, sang while the clever flint-miners and knappers of Grimes Graves in Norfolk worked (and no doubt sang too) ; and the golden eagle ranged in those days to Wales. The surface peats of southern Britain, particularly those of the fenland, are the most rewarding source of Neolithic birds in England and Wales. Their deposition ran on into Bronze Age times, so we cannot be quite sure of the dating; but at least in the days of early prehistoric farmers the marshes and boggy moors and woods of the Humber, of London and Essex, Norfolk and the Isle of Ely and Cambridge, and Monmouth, housed (some doubtless winterers) the great crested grebe, the Dalmatian pelican, the bittern, mallard, teal, wigeon, red-breasted merganser, smew, greylags (some certainly domesticated by the farmers), pinkfeet, mute, whooper and Bewick's swans, black grouse, crane, moorhen, coot, great bustard and perhaps woodcock, bar-tailed godwit, rock dove (some certainly domesticated), woodpigeon, raven and song thrush. The bigger, more water-loving birds are the ones whose bones tend to get preserved in bogs, so this list can scarcely reflect the true fauna, which must have had a full song-bird assembly.

Some of these peat birds are of the very greatest interest. Pelican bones from King's Lynn in Norfolk and Burnt Fen in the Isle of Ely and Burwell Fen in Cambridgeshire proper certainly belong to the Dalmatian species, which today breeds no nearer to us than the Balkan Peninsula and Danube rivermouth. For years other East Anglian pelican bones have been referred to the white species (from Norfolk) or to a mysterious large species – the latter

Alan Sorrell's reconstruction of a working party of New Stone Age flint-knappers in the famous quarry of Grimes Graves in Norfolk; from a Ministry of Works publication.

based on the upper arm-bone of a young (not quite full-grown and thus presumably Fen-bred) pelican, either from Feltwell Fen in Norfolk, or more probably from Middle Bronze Age deposits at Wood Fen in Cambridgeshire. However, these bones have been lately re-examined and found to be within the size range of the Dalmatian species, and with the anatomical peculiarities that distinguish the Dalmatian from the white. It is most probable that Britain had but the one, modern, Dalmatian species – though a rather big upper leg-bone of a pelican from the peat dredged to make the King George Dock at Hull may be worth examining again.

The crane, which we already know to have been part of the Irish fauna at the end of the last Ice Age, features well in the early Fen fauna. We know it from the Neolithic–Bronze Age peats of London Wall in Greater London, of King's Lynn and Norwich in Norfolk and of Burwell Fen in Cambridgeshire. In Late Bronze Age times in Suffolk the lake dwellers of 1000 to 500 B.C. of Barton Mere ate crane on their artificial island, and doubtless found it as good as the ancient Egyptians did. Cranes were eaten, too, by the Late Bronze Age peoples of Ballycotton in Cork; by the sophisticated Iron Age folk of Glastonbury's famous lake village in Somerset; in Roman Calleva Atrebatum (Silchester in Hampshire) and Corstopitum (Corbridge-on-Tyne in Northumberland). Indeed, as a doubtless breeding member of the British–Irish bird fauna the crane continues into the Dark Ages and Medieval times, for the lake villagers of Lagore in Meath ate it in about A.D. 750–950; and a crane bone was found in the excavation of the foundations of Syningthwaite Priory (Walton Abbey), the Cistercian nuns' Yorkshire establishment founded by Henry I in the early twelfth century.

The crane has taken us beyond our time. Our Bronze Age began in about 1900 B.C. and lasted until replaced by the Iron Age between about 500 and 230 B.C. (England; some centuries later in Scotland). Only scanty Bronze Age bones are known to me, from Ireland (cormorant, heron, crane, common gull – typical hunters' birds); but one find in England is of some account. In 1851 Lord Londesborough opened a Bronze Age round barrow at Kelleythorpe near Great Driffield in Yorkshire. It contained the remains of a chief of some substance, buried in the usual crouching position but with the skull of a "hawk" lying between his wrists and knees. Among other typical Bronze Age relics in his grave were those of an armlet on his right forearm, made of a six-inch animal bone with perforations near each end, through which were thrust bronze rivets with golden heads, obviously for the attachment of a leather cuff which had been fastened by a small bronze buckle. Was this the arm-guard or bracer of a left-handed archer (as most modern archaeologists seem to think), or a falconer's sleeve or gauntlet, Bronze Age style? In the East, where falconry is thought to have originated at a time even earlier than any English Bronze Age, hawks and falcons are trained to fly to the right fist. Falconry is not thought to have reached England until about A.D. 860, or possibly up to two centuries earlier, depending on the dating of some Anglo-Saxon poems, by which time the western European fist fashion was left. Was the master of Kelleythorpe the first known European falconer? I believe so. The "hawk" skull has gone astray, but may turn up in some Yorkshire museum; it would be fine to know whether it was goshawk, peregrine or another of the rather few hawkers' main hunting birds. There are (too) many solvable mysteries about our early birds, and the Kelleythorpe "hawk" may be one of them.

In Scotland the (rather late) transition between Late Bronze and Early Iron Ages is well shown by one of the early cultures excavated at the classic site of Jarlshof in south Shetland. From Bronze Age horizons here we can log bones of great northern diver, gannet, cormorant, shag, heron, lapwing, white stork, swans, geese, eagles, falcons, herring gull and skuas – all to be expected and (with the exception of the stork – an unexpected find) birds of present Shetland, at least on passage. The later Iron Age Jarlshof birds take us from about the first century B.C. to the later wheel-house culture and eighth century A.D. (the Iron Age had its last British outpost here, by-passing the Roman culture and replaced only by the later Dark Age Viking and Norse cultures). They were much the same: divers, shag, storm petrel, turnstone, geese, curlew, great blackback, great auk – all huntable local birds. Similar bird faunas come from the broch cultures of Caithness and Orkney's pastoral fort-makers. The brochs were sophisticated fortresses that began to be built around the time of Christ against Southern Iron Age and Roman (? slave-) raiders. Keiss and Orkney's Broch of Ayre give us great northern diver, a shearwater (probably Manx), gannet, cormorant, shag, whooper swan, gulls, great auk and guillemot. A related culture in second-century-A.D. Fife caves shows red-throated diver, shag, geese and gulls.

Apart from these sea birds hunted by rather special, Late Iron Age peoples in Scotland, our knowledge of the Iron Age avifauna of Britain comes almost entirely from the great lake village of Glastonbury in Somerset's Vale of Avalon with a little support from an inhabited Irish cave at Ballynamintra, in Co. Waterford. The Glastonbury township had about eighty-nine human abodes, a marsh causeway and a high metal-working, textile-weaving and pottery-making culture which is held to have flourished in the later English Iron Age from about 250 B.C. (at the earliest, perhaps) to the time of the Romans. Among the bones impeccably excavated by Arthur Bulleid and H. St George Gray around the turn of the century, and identified by C. W. Andrews, are dabchick, a shearwater, the Dalmatian pelican, cormorant, shag, bittern, heron, mallard, teal and other dabbling ducks, scaup, tufted duck, pochard, red-breasted merganser, greylag, mute and whooper swans, goshawk, kite and white-tailed eagle, crane, corncrake and coot, barn owl, carrion crow and some small singing birds. The Avalon marshes may have been the last refuge of British breeding pelicans – for breeding birds these were, on the evidence of fledgeling bones. Clearly they had a classic marsh-bird fauna, probably fuller than that of any present place in Europe, though all Iron Age Avalon's species survive in Europe somewhere. The shearwater (? Manx) may suggest some foraging journeys to the near-by islets in the Bristol Channel of Steep Holm and Flat Holm which might well have housed breeding colonies then. Shags may also have nested on these islands and on Brean Down. Cormorants have bred lately on

Reconstruction of Glastonbury Lake Village in Somerset, home of Late Iron Age bird-hunters and pelican-eaters; by C.H.B. Quennell, from *Everyday Life in Prehistoric Times*.

Steep Holm and may well in old Avalonian days have also nested inland on marsh trees as they do in the marshland sanctuaries of Holland today.

Iron Age Ballynamintra gives us but kestrel, grouse (identified originally as ptarmigan, but probably wrongly so), domestic fowl (one bone identified originally as of black grouse, but certainly wrongly so : there is no evidence (yet) that the black grouse ever inhabited Ireland) and coot. The muddles

Ballynamintra Cave near Cappagh in Co. Waterford, Ireland, first explored in 1879, has remains of giant deer and bear and some birds, from Upper Pleistocene to Iron Age times. From the *Transactions of the Royal Dublin Society*.

Manx shearwater

Cormorant

Bittern

Heron

Shelduck

Mallard

Teal

Pochard

Moorhen

Coot

Common gull

Guillemot

in Ireland and elsewhere with the hard-to-distinguish bones of the game-bird families have plagued the literature for years, and deserve some digression, if only because only the end of the Iron Age brings Britain what is now the most numerous bird in the world, the domestic fowl, and the Romans brought us more fowls in great number and (albeit probably only for the period of their occupation), pheasants, and perhaps guineafowl, too.

The Irish "black grouse" cited above was a chicken. Irish "ptarmigan" have been identified in deposits back to the middle part of the Upper Pleistocene in Waterford and Sligo, as well as at Ballynamintra. All the "ptarmigan" material on re-examination was not found clearly to differ from bones of the very closely related red grouse. Yet another examination of it (the museum bones are well filed) may be necessary, pending which it should properly be referred to the grouse. While the ptarmigan *may* have inhabited Ireland in Pleistocene times there is no evidence of its existence there in historical times, except during unsuccessful attempts at introduction in the late nineteenth century.

The chicken story is even more confused. Alleged fowl bones have been identified from Chudleigh Fissure in Devon, where early deposits are early Upper Pleistocene (probably over 150,000 years old); from late Upper Pleistocene sites in Cork, Down, Derbyshire and Somerset, some of whose horizons are about 60,000 years old and none less than 10,000; and from Neolithic and Bronze Age sites of varying antiquity in Greater London, Ayrshire, Yorkshire, Derbyshire, Suffolk and Durham. The datings of all these deposits are well authenticated by palaeontologists and archaeologists on the faunas, floras and artefacts. Nevertheless, one of the greatest of all daters of the past, the late F. E. Zeuner, argued convincingly that the British fowl "had not had a long history when the Romans encountered it", and commented that British finds of *certain* pre-Roman, Late Iron Age, date are few. Those at Glastonbury (whose people's known mallard and greylags were also doubtless domesticated, or semi-domesticated) are acceptable. Perhaps those at Ballynamintra and some other Irish caves also have the Iron Age date. But the chicken bones recorded from *all* the earlier horizons are considered to have been confused with those of other game birds or (more likely) superficially deposited with the aid of foxes, speleologist-picnickers, farmers or the dying chickens' own wandering feet, and sometimes washed and slipped to earlier horizons, as cave bones indeed unfortunately can be. By virtue of its own habits, and the style of its human cultivation, the fowl can be an excavator's hoodwink. The hoodwink, *Dissimulatrix spuria* Meiklejohn 1950, is, by the way, a common and widespread British and Irish bird never yet collected, but whose habits are often discussed.

The pheasant, too, appears in the array of truly early Chudleigh bones, and is reported also from the late Upper Pleistocene of Merlin's Cave in Herefordshire, from prehistoric or historic Clare and Sligo, from a Neolithic (Azilian) midden at Ardrossan in Ayrshire, from the Late Bronze Age of Barton Mere in Suffolk, from Roman Silchester and Corbridge-on-Tyne, and from Norse Dark Age time (c. A.D. 900–1100) at Jarlshof in Shetland. We can ignore the Silchester and Jarlshof bones as provedly and probably misidentified, respectively. The Corstopitum (Corbridge) record is probably valid. The Romans were ardent domestic cultivators of pheasants, but there is no sign that such pheasant stock as they kept in Britain survived their occupation, or ever went wild (or became feral, as the pundits put it). The consensus of scholars' opinion is that the feral pheasant was a Medieval (just pre-Norman) introduction, which did not reach Ireland until about 1589; and the necessary conclusion is that all the above records save that from Corbridge were wrongly identified, or re-horizoned hoodwinks from Medieval or later times. The "Catacombs" Cave at Edenvale in Ireland's Co. Clare has several horizons from the late Upper Pleistocene on; and the pheasant bones are from an uppermost level where those of rabbit (post-Norman) and rat (post-Crusades) have also been found, and which might well date from after 1589.

Some time ago the late P.R.Lowe re-examined all the game-bird material in the Reading Museum from Silchester and some other Roman sites (though not Corbridge), and found all big game-bird bones to be of fowls. This puts paid, I fear, to Britain's only ancient guineafowl record, still occasionally quoted in the literature. It was first published by the late J.H.Gurney, though he had some doubt about the identification. The leg-bone was encircled by a metal ring; and at least we now know that even if the bone was a chicken's, the ring was the earliest example the world yet has of the marking band, one of the most important instruments ever devised for studying the migration and life span of wild birds.

The last game-bird fossil mystery is the turkey. No turkey reached Europe until post-Columbian times; the earliest date the scholars quote is 1523 or 1524; for England, 1541. Yet turkeys are reported from deposits with an otherwise late Upper Pleistocene fauna in the Lea Valley (Essex–London) and caves of Clare and Sligo. Some of these turkeys are doubtless re-horizoned hoodwinks first deposited in post-introduction times; and the possibility of confusion of some (or all) of the Irish bones, from the Edenvale, Newhall and Keshcorran caves, with capercaillie bones must not be over-looked. At the time when the material was identified it may not have been fully realised that the capercaillie was quite common in Ireland until the seventeenth century, and did not become extinct there until about 1790.

This digression about fossil game birds was necessary to show that our ornithology, which (despite scorn of the point from some of today's younger

ELTIC EARTHWORKS
ORUM & BASILICA
NN 4 BATHS
TEMPLES
CHRISTIAN CHURCH
AMPHITHEATRE

Reconstruction by C. H. B. Quennell of Calleva Atrebatum (Silchester),
founded in about 78–85, when Agricola was Roman Governor. Excavations
begun in the 1890s have found bones of at least 17 species of birds.

scholars) has the *history* of our birds as its foundation-stone; and that the
elucidation of our bird history needs careful and critical techniques. The
bird anatomists who can tackle the fossils and rub our glorious science and
hobby against the equally beautiful sciences and hobbies of palaeontology
and archaeology are far too few, or far too bored to do the work. Before I
over-ride a hobby-horse I must return to the Romans, and the traces of the
avifauna of their day (extremes *c*. A.D. 43 to *c*. 410; with its most stable
period in its first two centuries). Sixteen Romano-British sites at least have
yielded bird bones, but only Pevensey in Kent (Anderita), Silchester in
Hampshire (Calleva Atrebatum), Colchester in Essex (Camulodunum),
Caerwent in Monmouth (Venta Silurum) and Corbridge-on-Tyne in
Northumberland (Corstopitum) more than a few, as far as I can discover
from such archaeologists' (seldom ornithologists') records as I have been
able to consult. We find heron (Colchester); white stork (Silchester); ducks
at several sites including mallard, teal, wigeon and possibly pochard;
domestic greylag geese at three sites, and perhaps the wild form also at
Silchester; mute and whooper swans, and perhaps Bewick's swan at Colchester; buzzards at Colchester, Haddington in Scotland and perhaps at the
villa at Folkestone's East Cliff in Kent; red and black grouse at Corbridge
and in the Romano-British stratum of the Victoria Cave near Settle in
Yorkshire, which is probably as late as the fourth or fifth century A.D. – after
the Romans had gone, but before their coins had ceased to circulate.
Partridges featured in the faunas of Silchester and Corbridge, domestic

fowl in that of at least eight sites, the pheasant (as we have seen) in one. Crane bones were found at Silchester and Corbridge, traces of oystercatcher at Pevensey; and of other waders we have grey plover (Silchester), golden plover (Caerwent), woodcock (Pevensey, Silchester, St Alban's) and curlew (Mount Caburn in Sussex and Pevensey). Gulls were found at Exeter in Devon (great blackback) and Pevensey (common – not far from its only present breeding-place in southern England). Silchester and Caerwent had the domestic pigeon, Cranborne Chase in Dorset and St Albans in Hertfordshire the barn owl. Thrushes sang, and were probably also eaten, at Silchester and St Albans, dunnocks at Caerwent. The crow family was represented by the jay and carrion crow at Silchester, by the jackdaw at St Albans (Verulamium), by the rook at Richborough in Kent (Rutupiae; the Caesars' principal port of entry into Britain) and by ravens, which the Romans tamed and taught to talk, at least six settlements. From all this a Romano-British bird fauna emerges differing (as far as the rather small sample hints) rather little from the modern one, saving crane and white stork, and reflecting to an extent the Romans' well-known skill in bird domestication and taste for aviculture.

Very few Dark Age excavations have disclosed pre-Norman bird faunas. The best one was of the lake dwellings that were inhabited at Lagore in Co. Meath in Ireland from about A.D. 750 to 950. The bird bones of the Harvard University excavation, identified by A. W. Stelfox, show a fauna very much like that of earlier Glastonbury; wild food obviously provided a large amount of the protein of these pastoralists of the age of the Irish Saints. They ate or took red-throated diver (not very palatable, from my own experience), great crested grebe, cormorant, heron and at least 14, perhaps 16 species of wildfowl (mallard, teal, garganey, wigeon, pintail, scaup, tufted duck, goldeneye, red-breasted merganser, greylag, whitefront, ? bean goose, ? brent goose, barnacle goose and both whooper and Bewick's swan). They also took buzzard, white-tailed eagle and crane; corncrake, moorhen and coot. They kept fowls, took gulls, barn owl, raven, crow and possibly chough. The Lagorians do not seem to have bothered with the little birds, any more than the Dark Age Vikings and Norsemen of Jarlshof in Shetland did from the ninth to the eleventh centuries. These colonists took red-throated diver, Slavonian grebe, gannet, cormorant, shag and heron; kept domesticated mallard; ate shoveler, eider, shelduck and whooper; kept a little domestic form of the greylag, no more than pinkfoot size; took peregrines; kept fowls; ate oystercatcher, curlew, 4 gulls (great blackback, herring, black-headed, kittiwake), guillemot and puffin; took, ate or kept ravens and crows. All these live in or pass through Shetland today. Perhaps most interesting from Jarlshof are bones of Leach's storm petrel, black grouse and magpie, which may well have nested in Shetland then, though

Leach's petrel was found nesting there only lately. The two woodland birds, though not on the accepted historical list for Shetland, may indeed have been part of the Shetland fauna at a time when its south mainland was probably naturally wooded in sheltered valleys, in a climate benign enough, compared with that of today, to enable the same groups of Vikings and Norsemen as founded Jarlshof to colonise also Iceland and Greenland.

At the end of the Dark Ages, then, I close an account of the early birds whose bones alone we know. One Dark Age find, more, I must relate. On Hirta, the main island of St Kilda, the most remote archipelago ever to have been inhabited in our islands, an E-shaped underground dwelling was excavated in stages between 1876 and 1927. The house itself is probably of Early Iron Age date, or possibly even of much earlier Middle or New Stone Age (Azilian) bird-hunter culture. Though no artefacts have been found on which the House of Fairies could be culturally dated it shows that adventurous kayakers or oarsmen explored Hirta (it can be seen from the hills of the Outer Hebrides, fifty miles away) nearly a score of centuries ago, or more. The important material found in the house was, however, of Viking age, judging by an iron spear-head of ninth-century design. With it were the bones of gannets, fulmars and puffins, the staple protein diet of the mixed Norse-Gaels we know from historical records to have inhabited the islands from the sixteenth century and suspect (from their unique use of the old Norse-Icelandic world *fulmar*) to have lived there from Viking times, as the archaeological evidence confirms. The St Kildan fowling culture, on a par with or even superior to the sea-bird cultures that still survive in Faeroe and parts of Iceland, died out when the islanders finally left in 1930. The ancient annual cropping of the young gannets on the very remote rock of Sula Sgeir, north-east of the Butt of Lewis and north-west of Cape Wrath, goes back at latest to the sixteenth century. The fowlers from Ness in Lewis continue to this day to voyage there every August in a Norse-type boat and take the *gugas* for salting and eating by their families and relatives, with a special dispensation to do so under the Wild Birds Protection Act of 1954. This Act stopped the last English sea-bird fowling – the egging of the great guillemot chalk cliffs near Flamborough Head in Yorkshire by the Bempton "climmers". The only bird-hunting culture, in effect, now left in Britain, is the relatively new one of the sixpenny cartridge, the syndicate, the pheasant-rearing pen, the grouse-butt and the long wild-fowlers' wait dug in the estuarine flat at goose-flighting time. By what appears to be a paradox to some non-shooters (though I believe it to be nothing of the sort) our bird sportsmen include a powerful cadre of forward-looking and sensible conservationists, protectors of our fauna (including rival animal predators) and bird lovers.

The existence of present field sportsmen and hunters cannot be understood without a consideration of our Stone Age history, as well as the ballistics of explosively driven missiles and the present ecology and populations of game. I am about to give a somewhat delayed (the reader may think) statement of our present avifauna. I make no apology for a further slight postponement, for a recapitulation of our islands' history since the final retreat of the ice.

The semi-official date of the "end" of the Pleistocene period is about 8000 B.C. Already before that there had been a warm climatic oscillation, in which open vegetation gave way to woodland – the Allerød episode of Late Glacial times. It must have been a time of success for the later, more sophisticated Creswellians in a time when England, Wales and parts of Scotland had birch forests as their primary cover – between 9000 and 10,000 B.C. For a time, between 9000 and 8000 B.C., semi-tundra conditions returned, but these disappeared rather rapidly around 8000 B.C., and Britain had a quick succession from birch to birch and pine in the "Pre-Boreal" times of 8000 to 7000 B.C. Mesolithic culture now reigned. The plant carpet of about three-quarters of Britain (bogs, moors and alpine mountain zones alone excluded) became woodland. The woodland evolved; it was basically pine when Ireland had already probably severed from Scotland; pine and hazel with a significant element of oak by the time our ocean level's rise had broken the Channel bridge around 5000 B.C. With a quick improvement of climate around 4000 B.C. (probably the best climate Europe has had since the last glaciation), our islands settled down to alder, oak and pine, with a tendency for the pine to retreat to Scotland as oak took over the domination of England. By the end of Mesolithic times (see time-table on pp. 22–23), England and Wales had the richest jungle of oak, with alder, lime and some elm, that it has ever enjoyed. Beech came in later, not really until Iron Age times when for the first time forests began to shrink under the influence of the metal axe.

The forest clearance had, of course, begun earlier, with the sophisticated polished stone axes of the Neolithic pastoralists. But they scarcely affected the area of woodland jungle. Possibly the Bronze Age axes cleared enough woods to make fields to push the open land up from a quarter to a third. But with the iron axe, and the Iron Age, Roman and Dark Age farmers, the woodland shrank from perhaps 40 million acres (England, Wales and Scotland have 57 million in all) in Neolithic times, to between 30 and 35 at the end of the Bronze Age, about 25 at the end of the Iron, under 20 by the end of the Roman, around 10 at the Norman Conquest, and not much more than 2 million acres by the middle of the eighteenth century, when woodland clearance had become a national obsession (in Scotland particularly) and was operated far beyond its use for agricultural improvement. The climate since Iron Age times has not been so good (with fluctuations; it was quite good a thousand years ago) as it was in Mesolithic times. Birch, that signal tree of sharp conditions, and the dominant of the most northerly and montane forests, has returned in strength, particularly in Scotland. The climax forest of today is poorer than that of 4000 B.C., in the places where it can still grow. But it grows, now, only by courtesy of man. Re-afforestation of Britain and Ireland has been the rule of the late nineteenth and particularly the twentieth centuries; though Britain has recovered woodland only to the extent that it now has nearer 3 million acres, if we include scrubland: less than a tenth of what it enjoyed in prehistoric times.

I have gone into the consequences of this vast change more fully in Chapter 3 (p. 82). The present situation is that every spring about 120 million land birds take up territories, build nests and raise their young upon the 57 million acres of England, Wales and Scotland – a pair of birds to an acre, on an average. If we include the sea birds, and the land birds of Ireland, the spring bird population must be of the order of 200 million or more. In Britain the 57 million acres available are of about fifty-seven varieties, but can be divided into about 20 million acres of rough grazing, moorland, deer forest and alpine uplands; 18 million acres of rich grassland grazing; 12 million acres of arable crops; half a million acres of parks, orchards or gardens; over $2\frac{1}{2}$ million acres of towns and built-up areas; a further million waste, scrubland and swamp; half a million, inland waters: about $2\frac{1}{2}$ million, woodland and true forest. Besides the woodland, and despite the building of reservoirs and canals, Britain's wastelands have significantly receded since prehistoric times, as the consequence of drainage. In our Orwellian double-talk, we humans have called this drainage reclamation. But the marshes belonged to nature, and when we drained them for the first time we claimed them; we did not *re*claim them.

In the period of historical records (see pp. 58, 299) between 1600 and 1964, 456 full and valid different species of birds have been provedly seen in Britain in circumstances which have made them acceptable to the British–Irish List (in the case of the more recent "new" British birds, likely to be accepted). Two hundred and twenty of these have bred since 1600. In addition 3 still-living species were British or Irish before 1600, as the fossil records show, of which 2 doubtless bred. Twenty other species all extinct before 1600 are known only as fossils. The full species list is thus 479. Of the 456 species of the historical fauna no less than 133 are vagrants acceptably reported less than 21 times. Seventy-nine are vagrants with over 20 records; some of these are now logged annually or almost so. Twenty-five are regular winter visitors; 28 regular visitors on passage migration. Three are non-breeding regular summer visitors (the great and sooty shearwaters which breed in our winter in the summer of the southern hemisphere and some of which spend another summer round our coasts; and the spoonbill which used to breed with us). Fifty-four are regular breeding summer visitors. One hundred and thirty-three are steady residents. One old resident, the great auk, became extinct in Britain in about 1840 and globally extinct in 1844.

The simplest summary of a "British–Irish" List is thus 243 living regulars (of which 118 are water birds, 125 wholly land birds), and 212 vagrants. Owing to their borderline position in Europe, Britain and Ireland have more vagrants than have been recorded from any other country in Europe. Many of these – no less than 48 species – are strays that have been wind-borne across the Atlantic Ocean from North America (a number of small song birds included) and lived to be identified by one of our host of competent bird-watchers.

With 456 species, Britain and Ireland combined have the biggest modern bird list in Europe. The U.S.S.R.'s 704 contains over 150 species from its Asian part only. Italy comes next with 450, then France with 441, Germany with 435, Spain with 397, Poland with 370, Holland with 364, Sweden with 356, Switzerland with 347, Rumania with 345, Belgium with 343 and Greece with 339. Ireland on its own has 338, equal fourteenth with Austria and Bulgaria. Of countries of at least the order of size of Ireland, Iceland has the smallest list with 231.

The list of countries in the order of the numbers of species that have provedly bred is different, and reflects the fact that Britain's List is much swollen by vagrants. Excluding the U.S.S.R., whose (Eurasian) breeding list is 622, the champion country is France with 260. Next come Germany with 250, Rumania and Sweden with 240, Jugoslavia and Bulgaria with 236, Italy with 232, Poland with 230, Spain with 225, Norway with 220 and Britain and Ireland combined are eleventh with only 218; and Ireland alone is near the bottom of the major league with only 133; indeed only Iceland of the big-area countries has fewer with 76.[1] From all this our islands emerge as the hosts of many vagrant rarities; their *regular* fauna is in the weaker half of the European league. These rarities and vagrants, of course, have spurred our bird-watchers on; and the host of passengers and "annual vagrants" on our great migrant flyways are largely responsible for the fact that we have ever been pioneers in migration study, and have today the finest network of flyway Bird Observatories and manned migration watch points in the world. Some of this will emerge in Chapter 4, p. 120. Mean-while, a consequence of a big bird list is a big problem: the problem of knowing the birds. Field identification – the technique of recognition with-out destruction – has been refined by British pioneers as much as by any-body. It is to the naming and the knowing of the birds that I now turn.

[1] These comparative figures may be slightly over-generous to Britain–Ireland, whose figures embrace the season 1964. The figures for the other countries were *published* (by Roger Peterson) in 1963, and though they were pretty up to date then, must mostly be small by a very few species.

CHAPTER 2

The Naming of the Birds

þær ic ne gehyrde butan hlimman þe ifcalo ne
pæg hpilu ylfete þong· ꝺ·ꝺe ic me togomfhe ganſtꝼ
hleoþon ꝺhuilpan fþeg þone hleahton þꝺa mæp ſingꝼh
ꝺe þone meꝺꝺ ꝺnince ſtonmar þꝺſtan cliꝼu beoꞇun
þꝺhim ſtanin oncpeꝺ iꞁiꞁ pepꝺa ꝼul ofꞇ þæꞁin bꞁꝥl
uꞁiꞁ pepna

The West Saxon script, in the *Exeter Book*, of the "Bass Rock" passage in *The Seafarer*; written about 1000, this is the only known manuscript of the much earlier poem.

> Þær ic ne gehyrde   butan hlimman sæ
> iscaldne wæg   hwilum ylfete song.
> Dyde ic me to gomene   ganetes hleoþor
> & huilpan sweg   fore hleahtor wera
> mæw singende   fore medodrince
> stormas þær stanclifu beotan   þær him stearn oncwæð
> isigfeþera;   ful oft þ[æt] earn bigeal
> urigfeþra. . . .

which, as I translate, runs:

> There heard I naught but seething sea,
> Ice-cold wave, awhile a song of swan.
> There came to charm me gannets' pother
> And whimbrels' trills for the laughter of men,
> Kittiwake singing instead of mead.
> Storms there the stacks thrashed, there answered them the tern
> With icy feathers; full oft the erne wailed round
> Spray-feathered. . . .

My guess is that this scene, so tenderly described, was observed by a young Anglo-Saxon ornithologist in some year before A.D. 685, at the Bass Rock in what his present heirs call East Lothian, most probably between what we

"The earn"; the white-tailed eagle much as the Seafarer saw it nearly thirteen centuries ago. Painted by Joseph Wolf and lithographed in John Gould's *The Birds of Great Britain*.

would call 20 and 27 April by our calendar. Birds change their distribution, but not so much their season; just at this stormy time the winds can blow cold in the Firth of Forth, and the great whooper swans pass north to their breeding-grounds on the moorland wetlands, and the whimbrels utter their trilling titter, usually of seven beats, on their flight to the moorland drylands; and the common terns' main arrival is due; and the gannets and the kittiwakes and the white-tailed sea eagles hold their nest-sites on the ocean-facing cliffs. At least the ernes did: they have gone now, from the Bass, though a statement of the late, great Professor Alfred Newton of a century ago – a little vague as from so deep a scholar – indicates that the white-tailed eagles still has an eyrie on the Bass in our bird-historical times (that is, since 1600) a thousand years after the Seafarer saw them there.

This dating, and placing, of perhaps the first bit of true-sounding, wild-inspired field ornithological record since the Romans gave up their colony is of course no more than an (I hope) educated guess. The Bass is the only place I can think of within the Anglo-Saxon realm in the Dark Ages where all these birds could have been seen together under the circumstances which the unknown author of *The Seafarer* describes. There is, today, it is true, a small gannet colony on the chalk ledges of Bempton Cliffs in Yorkshire, with kittiwakes, where terns and whimbrels pass. But it is quite new. Nowhere else in England save on Lundy in the Bristol Channel have gannets nested since "Domesday Book" times; and the description of the Seafarer is no description of Lundy. The gannet colony of the Bass is one of the old, ancient ones. It was flourishing in 1447, and if a conservative, home-true bird like the gannet can throng a breeding-rock (only thirty, now (and probably never more at any one time in the past), are used by the North Atlantic gannet) for half a millennium, it can for a millennium and a half. "Hleoþor" is a very good representation of the *urrah . . . urrah* of the breeding gannet. The terns fit; to this day common terns nest on the Bass's skerry-neighbours Craigleith, Lamb and Fidra. Icy storm or no, their mantles ever have the sheen of ice. The erne fitted. The kittiwakes fit – and what a glorious bit of onomatopoiea the poet perpetrated with his "medodrince": just what these sea-mews were doubtless heard to say in Anglo-Saxon times, just as they are heard to say, and are called, kittiwake in Britain now, kishiefaik and killyweeack in Orkney in the old days, *krykkje* in Norway, *pikkukajava* by the Finns, *tâterâq* by the Greenlanders, tickle-arse by the Newfoundlanders. The whoopers fit; they are the singing swans of the north that doubtless nested widely in the Scottish loch-side bogs in the Dark Ages, and sometimes do so even now. The whimbrel fits, though scholars still dispute whether the Anglo-Saxon *huilpe* meant the whimbrel or its close congener the curlew. It probably meant both. Whimbrels nest in the northernmost Highlands to this day; curlews all over the Scottish moors. But the trill of the whimbrel is perhaps better laughter than the curlew's musical April bubble: at least I think so. *Huilpe*, it is true, becomes the Scottish whaup for curlew (1538 earliest in the *Oxford English Dictionary*) and the Dutch *wulp* for curlew (and *regenwulp* for whimbrel). But the whimbrel whilps as well as titters, and I favour it for the Seafarer's bird; and even if his bird *was* the curlew, the Bass must still have been the Seafarer's place.

His place, when? The Northumbrian Anglo-Saxons did, for a time, occupy the Firth of Forth. They had moved strongly into the Lothians by about 630, and established a supremacy even north of the Forth until the Battle of Nechtansmere in Angus in 685. Internal evidence suggests that *The Seafarer* was written by an elderly, nostalgic man, in whom the love and at the same time fear of the sea was strong; nostalgic for things past and unattainable. It is no wild fancy to believe that he wrote, after 685, of wild, naturalists' sea places once loved before that year. The *Codex Exoniensis* version of his poem in Exeter must have been copied long after the Seafarer was dead, possibly not till around the year 1000: it is the only MS. copy extant.

The Seafarer and *The Wanderer*, in most opinion the finest Old English poems apart from *Beowulf*, both contain evidence of classical scholarship and both pagan and Christian thinking. If, as many believe, they were originally written by the same man, then he was a Northumbrian scholar, though the *Exeter Book* copies are in the West Saxon dialect. The Northumbrian "little Renaissance" dates from the founding of the Wearmouth monastery by Benedict Biscop in 673, and practically coincides with the lifetime of Bede (*c.* 672–735), the greatest Anglo-Saxon scholar of all. Ecgfrith, the Northumbrian king whose death (with his bodyguard) at Nechtansmere at the hands of his cousin Bruid MacBeli, King of the Picts, was prophesied by Cuthbert, was succeeded by his half-brother Aldfrith the Learned, the first literate king of England. But when Aldfrith died in 705 the succession passed into rough hands and, as Bertram Colgrave writes, "the great social ideals of the Germanic peoples – loyalty to one's kin and loyalty to one's lord – were abandoned and forgotten". Towards the end of his life Bede wrote sorrowfully about the decay of social morals. Just such a climate is reflected in the nostalgia for stable times in the two great poems. Nobody has given more than a hunch-date for *The Seafarer*; mine is that the writer used the libraries in Lindisfarne, Wearmouth or Jarrow (or all three), and was probably a follower of Ecgfrith, if not a follower of Aldfrith, and that the deep sorrow in his poem (or poems) for the passing of the old leadership and scholars' patronage so overt in what he wrote dates his work to the turn of the seventh and eighth centuries, perhaps 705 or just after. The Anglo-Saxon rule was more or less strong in the southern Forth shore until the Scottish struggles (under Malcolm II onwards) from the early eleventh century: but the Seafarer's style and thinking is of the Bedan Renaissance.

Best observed as they seem to be, the Seafarer's birds were not the earliest of the Dark Ages. A Romano-British third- or fourth-century bronze image of a bird, reported from Corby in Northamptonshire in the present decade, looks very much like a robin. The robin can be certainly dated as in our

Robin; woodcut by Thomas Bewick, 1797. Bewick still used "ruddock", from the Anglo-Saxon, as the vernacular name for what has some claim to be the earliest bird in our historical record.

St Kentigern, or Mungo, believed to have performed a robin miracle in Fife in about 530. Like the account of the robin story, this portrait is reproduced from W. Stevenson's *Legends of St Kentigern*.

St Columba. It is possible (though I think unlikely) that the bird this saint and teacher succoured on Iona in *c.* 570 was not a crane but a heron, as in this modern ceramic relief by Brigid ni Rinne (1936).

fauna about A.D. 530, for around then St Serf of Culross in Fife had a tame one that was killed by roughness in play by his pupils, but miraculously brought back to life by the holiest of them, Kentigern, who later became St Mungo. This story was not written down until 1125. Nevertheless, the little tame bird now adopted as our national symbol by the bird conservationists has some qualifications as our "first" bird in post-Roman historical times.

An even greater Celtic saint, Columba, came to Iona in 563 to lay the train of Christian values and scholarship that gave us most of the light that shines on the life of the Dark Ages. According to one of his biographers,

St Cuthbert, who can be regarded as the founder of Britain's first bird sanctuary on the Inner Farne, Northumberland, in 676; from an edition of Bede's *Life of St Cuthbert*.

Adamnan, Abbot of Iona rather over a century later, by around 570 he was so familiar with the passage of the migrant cranes (then members of our fauna without doubt, and doubtless in this case not confused with herons) that he expected it, and nursed a particular exhausted bird for three days, after which "raising itself on high in the presence of its ministering host, and considering for a little while its course in the air, it returned across the sea to Ireland in a straight line of flight, on a calm day". This might be from the notebook of a Bird Observatory of today.

If the Seafarer lived when I believe he did, he was not then the only working ornithologist in the Anglo-Saxon kingdoms. The bishop of his diocese (as he later became), Cuthbert, soon to become also a saint had, in 676, established a nature sanctuary and holy place at the Farne Islands, only fifty miles to the south-east of the Seafarer's likely place of gannets' pother and erne's wailing. From near-contemporary accounts Cuthbert

Gannets; by Edward Lear, from John Gould's *The Birds of Europe*, published in 1837. These birds are first mentioned in Anglo-Saxon literature in the seventh-century *Beowulf*.

knew the white-tailed eagle perhaps earlier – at Melrose in Roxburghshire in about 662, and knew the carrion crow on the Farnes in 676 or after (tradition assigns the eiders of the Farnes to him as his favourite birds – St Cuthbert's ducks – but this is a Medieval refinement of his history).

Around 685 (or a few years later), another saint, and great bibliophile and scholar, Aldhelm of Malmesbury, knew from his (mostly Latin) writings and riddles woodpigeon, nightingale ("mean is my colour, but none hath scorned my song"), swallow (as a migrant, clearly) and chaffinch. Just before the end of the seventh century, perhaps in 699, another Anglo-Saxon saint, Guthlac, retired to the eastern English Fens to lead a Francis-like life, where "many kinds of families of tree birds blessed him, mingling their voices and showing by signs they knew the saint had come back". To Guthlac the cuckoo was familiar. Swallows perched on his shoulders. He knew the raven. He reminded a naïve visitor, the monk Wilfred, that "he who has lived according to God's will, him the wild birds and beasts hold as their friend".

In East Anglia, too, perhaps a little earlier, a young poet had watched the erection of an incredibly rich memorial to an Anglian king. The Sutton Hoo ship "burial", the greatest monument to Dark Ages life excavated in western Europe, is probably of 650 or later judging from the Merovingian coins in it. It may be a memorial to one of the Uffinga dynasty of East Anglian kings Anna (d. 654), Æthelhere (d. 654) or Æthelwald (d. c. 664). If the current scholar's collation of *Beowulf* and Sutton Hoo be sound (and most agree that it is), the poet later wove the ceremony and ritual into the greatest of all

Æthelbald, later to become King of Mercia, visiting Guthlac in the early
years of the eighth century. After Guthlac's death in 714 Æthelbald built
Crowland Abbey over the shrine of this nature-lover.

Old English poems, along with bird references of some originality (gannet,
swan, sea eagle, raven) that are not all just the eagle-raven "atmosphere"
citations that accompany nearly all fights in nearly all Anglo-Saxon poetry,
which is full of fights.

The total body of surviving Anglo-Saxon literature amounts to less than
a quarter of a million words, about which many millions of words have been
written. By the year 700, if *The Seafarer* and *Beowulf* were composed before
then, it had named for us a first English List of 16 species: robin and crane,
Cuthbert's sea eagle and carrion (or hooded) crow; Aldhelm's woodpigeon,
nightingale, swallow and chaffinch; Guthlac's cuckoo and raven; *Beowulf*'s
whooper swan and gannet; *The Seafarer*'s whimbrel, kittiwake and tern
doubtless seen before that year; and the quail from *Exodus* (*c.* 700), no mere
Biblical paraphrase but a piece from an unknown churchman well aware
of the pre-Christian English tradition.

By 800 the Bird List had reached at least 59 species, if a Latin to Anglo-
Saxon vocabulary in Corpus Christi College, Cambridge, can be assigned,
and the tender *Riddles* of the *Exeter Book* can (as scholars seem to think) be

Curlew

Whimbrel

Kittiwake

Raven

White-fronted goose

Ringed plover

Roseate tern

Little tern

Red grouse

Dipper

Great tit

Jay

The song thrush, a much-loved singing bird of the eighth-century Anglo-Saxons. One of Thomas Bewick's beautifully observed and drawn woodcuts of 1797.

mainly assigned, to the eighth century. The *Riddle* poems' answers have to be found by the readers today as then, and are naturally subject still to error, for the riddles are not easy. But from them we probably have mute swan (a lovely description of the organ music of its wings in flight), song thrush, barnacle goose, starling (though the runic clue, "higora", has been made into green woodpecker in most glossaries) and house martin.

If we accept 7 or 8 birds by Guthlac's time, the first doubling of the List was by the end of his century; the second and third by 800. The glossary of the great scholar Ælfric the Grammarian, compiled in *c*. 998, added 14 species and brought the total to 75 at the end of the first millennium.

The fourth doubling (114 by *c*. 1460) took well over six centuries, the fifth (228 by 1776, in Gilbert White's time) only a little over three, and the sixth (456 by 1964) less than two. There will never be a seventh; notwithstanding

The goldfinch, which the Anglo-Saxons knew as the thisteltuige (thistle-tweaker) in the eighth century. This is another woodcut of 1797 by Thomas Bewick.

Blackcap – probably the swertling of Ælfric the Grammarian's Latin to
Anglo-Saxon vocabulary of *c.* 998. From a woodcut of 1797 by Thomas
Bewick.

our network now of a few thousands of skilled identifiers, who have added
an average of a little over 2 new species a year since the end of the Second
World War, we are in the phase of diminishing returns, and unlikely (as we
shall presently see) to reach a list of more than 480 wild species by the year
2000, or more than 500 ever.

We must return to the past, though, at least to the Middle English past,
to celebrate a few heroes of the Medieval and Renaissance rise of
ornithology. One of them was Giraldus Cambrensis, who wrote at the end of
the twelfth century and brought the List to about 92 species in 1200 by
knowing of and naming (though not by present names) the white-fronted
geese that winter in Ireland; the capercaillie; the hobby and the merlin.

Geoffrey Chaucer rates as an ornithological hero. He knew at least
43 of the wild birds of Britain – and gives us 2 new ones in his *Romaunt
of the Rose* (*c.* 1369) and 2 more in his *Parlement of Foules* (1382), bringing
the List then to 100. His contemporary, William Langland, writer of *Piers
Plowman* and *Richard the Redeless*, much more a countryman, but much less a
bird-watcher, only seems to have mentioned about 16 already familiar
species. By 1500 the last Middle and first Modern English scholars had
pushed the List up to 118. Britain and Ireland entered the new Renaissance,
and revitalisation of art and science, with a Bird List well over the hundred.

If example be needed of the impact of the Age of Print and Science upon
the world, the transformation of the List in the sixteenth century is a good
one. As I have it in my collection of names, it rose from 118 to 150. Nearly
half the 32 new birds were contributed by William Turner, the father
of British ornithology, when *Avium Praecipuarum* was published in Cologne
in 1544 in Latin, the first printed bird book.

Coal tit; the colmase of Ælfric and later Anglo-Saxon glossarists, colmose
in a fifteenth-century English vocabulary. A woodcut by Thomas Bewick,
1797.

If we remove from Turner's 130 recognisable birds those which are
domestic or were not seen in Britain, we are left with 105 species (including
2 gulls and 2 grey geese where final identification is not possible) of which
no less than 15 have appeared as British birds in no previous document,
manuscript or printed, that I have seen or heard of. Turner recognised
for the first time rather difficult birds such as hen and marsh harriers,
woodlark, meadow pipit, whitethroat and brambling.

Turner was a reformer, and in about 1540 was imprisoned for preaching

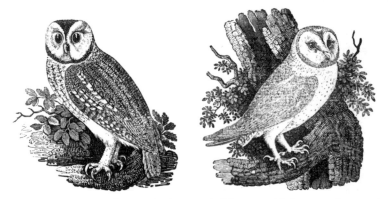

The tawny owl (*left*) and the barn owl. These two birds are perhaps not
clearly distinguished in literature until John of Guildford's poem *The Owl
and the Nightingale* of about 1225. Both these drawings are from woodcuts of
1797 by Thomas Bewick, who was clearly in no doubt as to the differences
between the two birds.

Swift; a bird not clearly recognised before Turner's *Avium Praecipuarum* of 1544. Published in 1840 in Yarrell's *A History of British Birds*. All the engravings in this book were drawn on wood by Alexander Fussell and engraved by John Thompson or his son Richard or another son.

without a licence; on his release he went to the Continent. Here he became friends with, and was much stimulated by Conrad Gesner of Zürich, and Gybertus Longolius of Utrecht, two other great naturalists of the scientific revolution. But when he was not in trouble with the established Church (and this changed a good deal in the times of Henry VIII, Mary and Elizabeth) Turner lived in England, where it is clear that he had much first-hand knowledge of birds, particularly marsh birds. He knew that the hobby was a summer visitor, and described exactly its habitat and some of its principal

The dunnock, engraved by Thomas Bewick in 1797. This bird appears as the sugga in an eighth-century vocabulary, and is later known as the hegesugge (hay-sucker) or hedge sparrow.

The great grey shrike is another bird not clearly distinguished before Turner's great work of 1544. The illustration above is one of Thomas Bewick's woodcuts of 1797.

prey; he had obviously watched closely the hen harrier and marsh harrier, the dipper, the common sandpiper, the black-headed gull, black tern, swallow, swift, martin, cormorant, great grey shrike, robin and redstart. He took the Aristotelian authority that had long been studied by the scholars, and for the first time turned it into meaningful and critical descriptions based on sixteenth-century reality and the *revision* of tradition.

Turner was by far the best ornithologist of the century, though a rather recent discovery of the late Hugh Gladstone shows that in about the year 1600 one Nicholas Carter annotated a copy of Gesner's *Icones Animalium* of 1560 and established for the first time yellow wagtail and redwing, and what

The redstart, probably the sæltna (dancer bird) of an eighth-century Anglo-Saxon vocabulary. The illustration above was published in Yarrell's *A History of British Birds* in 1838.

John Caius (or Kay), 1510–75, founder of Caius College, Cambridge. Though he was not responsible for naming any new species of British bird, he was a talented ornithologist and keen observer.

are presently connoisseurs' pieces – avocet and hoopoe – as British birds. Another real ornithologist of the time was John Kay, who founded Caius (Kay's) College in Cambridge in 1557 and published *De rariorum Animalium* in 1570. Rare animals notwithstanding, Kay seems to have found no new British bird; but his observations were rather original. He kept a puffin in his house for eight months and made good observations on the food of the jackdaw. He was a colleague of Turner's and like nearly all educated scientists of his time a correspondent of Gesner.

By 1600, then, the List was 150. By 1700 it was just over 200, thanks to a group of really modern-minded field zoologists.

If we tot up the first *publications* of new British birds of the seventeenth century we find that of the 52 novelties, no less than 33 come from John Ray, 8 from Christopher Merret and 6 from Sir Thomas Browne. This does not really reflect the shares of the field men who identified the material. Merret was a moderate naturalist, in whose *Pinax rerum naturalium* of 1666 most of the novelties came from Browne. Browne, who published little himself, was a fine East Anglian bird-watcher who sent copious notes also to Ray. Ray's great friend Francis Willughby supported him in a long saga of travel and investigation, as did a smallish group of other ardent naturalist-correspondents. For the first time a reputable British avifauna began to emerge with some detailed breakdown of distribution,

John Ray, 1627–1705, the greatest of all field naturalists, whose travels covered most of England and Wales and much of Scotland. Engraved by G. Vertue from a portrait by W. Faithorne.

status and season, under the guidance of Ray who, in the opinion I believe of most, was the greatest field naturalist that has ever lived, and the father of modern zoology.

In 1660 Willughby and Ray started their first journey together, to North England and the Isle of Man, visiting Browne at Warwick later in the year. From there until Willughby died in 1672 Ray hardly missed a season travelling with his great friend, or with his pupil Skippon: they went into most parts of England and Wales, and many of Scotland, and to the Low Countries, France, Germany, Austria, Italy, Sicily and Switzerland. It seems likely from the Willughby-Ray *Ornithologia* (1676; English version 1678) that they were aware of the difference between the chiffchaff and wood warbler, the redpoll and twite, the yellow and grey wagtails, coal and marsh tits, and among Ray's identifications in difficult families, supported

The tree sparrow, first recognised as being a different species from the house sparrow by Willughby and Ray in the seventeenth century. One of Thomas Bewick's woodcuts of 1797.

by *field notes* as well as collecting, are four warblers, the little and probably the Sandwich terns, the greenshank and the great blackback. Ray brought sophistication to the science of identification : his notes are so good that we even know that the pelicans that the Russian Ambassador brought to Charles II in 1662, shortly after the Restoration, to start the pelican tradition in the new royal waterfowl collection in St James's Park, were of the grey or Dalmatian species and not the white species – still not easy to distinguish in the wild by our field men of today.

The first century of modern bird-watching ended with the voyage of the Scot, Martin Martin, to our remotest inhabited archipelago, St Kilda, in 1697. The only "new" bird Martin added was the fulmar : but he made what almost amounts to a simple ecological survey of the sea bird life of these amazing islands, upon which the ancient Norse–Gael inhabitants depended for their primary source of protein. Martin had the notebook precision of almost an observatory-trained bird-watcher of today (and an observatory is indeed intermittently manned now on Hirta, St Kilda's main island). He noticed the St Kilda wren (though did not recognise it as a separate race), described with real accuracy the year-cycle dates of the fulmar (egg-date, incubation period, arrival and departure), made an estimate of the combined incubation and fledging period of the great auk (six or seven weeks) – which is the only one the world has of this now extinct bird which bred on St Kilda in the seventeenth century; and wrote a most interesting, amusing, and indeed moving account of the gannet – which has now, and doubtless had then, its largest colony in the world on the towering cliffs of Boreray, Stac Lee and Stac an Armin.

The next century was a time for consolidation and reappraisement. Ray had made ornithology a science : others came to make it a sport, an art and a discipline. The heroes of the eighteenth century only added 40 more birds. By 1st January 1758, when Carl von Linné of Sweden (Carolus

The house sparrow, drawn by Thomas Bewick for his series of woodcuts of 1797. Doubtless well known to the earliest Anglo-Saxons, this bird appears in the writings of Bede of *c.* 731.

Linnaeus) is held to have published the tenth edition of his *System of Nature*, the British–Irish List was 214; by 1780 it was 229; by 1800 240.

The Linnaean year of 1758 is, by international agreement, assumed as the starting-point of the binomial (now trinomial) system of scientific naming. Linnaeus in fact gave the first proper scientific names to 215 of the present British–Irish List in 1758 (some were not *on* the list by then, of course).

Scientific names are popularly called "Latin names", which is quite false. They are Linnaean names, by convention derived from Latin or Greek or in their style. Some bad (but unchangeable, by rule) names have Latin and Greek mixed up. In the original Linnaean definition the name of the species is of two words which make it only when together. The specific name is *not* the second of the two names, as is often thought; this is simply an adjectival description of the first, and must start with a small letter. The first word is the genus and there may be several species belonging to one genus, distinguished by the use of different adjectives (second words) describing it.

Upon the foundation of the Linnaean system of nomenclature the whole of modern international systematics is built, and no post-Linnaean innovation is more than a refinement. For the ordinary bird-watcher the Linnaean name is now no longer a bore: indeed all who travel abroad find no trouble now in naming birds since every nation uses the Linnaean system, without any attempt at transliteration by those (like Russia, China, Japan and many Eastern countries) that do not use the Latin alphabet.

In most branches of the animal kingdom a third name has now been introduced to be descriptive of geographical races of a species. These are known as subspecies. Various rules have been introduced and agreed upon, such as the citation of the authority who first gave the name with an adequate description in published print. This citation must always be used, with the date of first publication, when the name is set out in a *formal* systematic list (the one on pp. 300–38 is *not* in this sense formal). There is an International Commission of Zoological Nomenclature which is steadily improving the international rules of nomenclature, all of which are based on the Linnaean system.

Here are some Linnaean names of British birds:

Charadrius hiaticula Linnaeus 1758. Just as Linnaeus named it in the *System of Nature*; the ringed plover.

Charadrius hiaticula tundrae (Lowe 1915). In 1895 P.R. Lowe named this northern race of the ringed plover *Ægialitis hiaticola tundræ*. To the present name his authority is attached in parenthesis, because he applied the *tundrae* to a different genus, which he thought the bird should be put in (a view not shared now). His mistaken spelling of *hiaticola* is not preserved: Linnaeus's *hiaticula* is retained. His use of the *æ* is not now retained; diphthongs are discarded in modern nomenclature.

Oenanthe hispanica (Linnaeus 1758). Linnaeus's name and date go in brackets because Linnaeus originally described this species, the black-eared wheatear, as *Motacilla hispanica*, believing it to be in the same genus as the wagtails. The genus *Oenanthe* was named by Vieillot in 1816 for the black wheatear; and this and 17 other species are placed in it today. Not one single one of these was placed in *Oenanthe* when first described; all have now found their way into the genus by systematic revisions. The black wheatear was first described in 1789 by J.F. Gmelin as *Turdus leucurus*; since the acceptance of Vieillot's genus it of course becomes *Oenanthe leucura* (Gmelin 1789); note that the adjective changes its gender.

All this sounds complex; and some nomenclature problems can be very vexing. But the firmer the rules, the more easily are they learned; and there is now a profound measure of stability and agreement about the scientific names of European birds.

From this Linnaean digression we must return to the eighteenth-century British birds. The principal heroes of ornithology were William Derham, Eleazar Albin, George Edwards, Thomas Pennant, Marmaduke Tunstall, John Latham, Gilbert White and George Montagu. These were all good field men who had Ray to stand on, but they scored only 40 novelties (with some other friends) mainly because rather few distinctions of well-established native species remained to be made, and there were rather few observers to gather in the lucky sightings of rarities and vagrants.

The difference between the willow warbler and its other native congeners chiffchaff and wood warbler was suspected by Derham in 1718 and confirmed in 1768 by White. Today the Hanger and Common at Selborne, which house, in hanging beech woods, the direct descendants of the leaf warblers which White finally sorted out, are (p. 245) a Nature Reserve, with many happy spring pilgrims armed with binoculars (how White would have appreciated field-glasses!).

Other distinctions or recognitions cleared up in the eighteenth century, as far as our islands' List was concerned, include tree sparrow (from house sparrow), black- and red-throated divers; the arctic skua; the sedge warbler from the reed warbler; the Dartford warbler; the lesser whitethroat from the common whitethroat; the tree and rock pipits from the meadow pipit; the grey from the red-necked phalarope; the lesser black-backed and great black-backed gulls; the Slavonian from the black-necked grebe; the wood and purple sandpipers from others of their rather difficult family; the rough-legged from the common buzzard. The gun was the main instrument of determination; optical aids were crude and ineffective; only a few pioneers like White were using calls and songs for field distinction.

The systematics began to tidy itself up; though it has not yet reached full stability (the arrangements of the British Ornithologists' Union's *Check-List* of 1952 are rather different, for instance, from those of Charles Vaurie's *Birds of the Palearctic Fauna* of 1959 and 1965). Latham was an important general writer, though he did not use the Linnaean system until 1790. Thomas Pennant, energetic traveller and voluminous letter-writer, was the most important British-bird-sorter; his *British Zoology* first appear in 1766 and went into edition after edition. But undoubtedly the dominant figure of the century has proved to be the modest curate of Faringdon in Hampshire with whom Pennant and Daines Barrington and others corresponded, Gilbert White of Selborne; the man who started us all bird-watching.

I have (as have many better analysts) tried to find the reasons for the success of *The Natural History of Selborne*, first published in December 1788 – and of which, since then, there have been over 150 editions. Unquestionably White's gentle humour, wide scholarship and marvellous literary skill, which gives an impression of simplicity but is the fruit of the endless pains of a genius, are among these reasons : but he excelled as a field man, and his original discoveries (leaf warblers, lesser whitethroat, noctule bat, harvest mouse) remain as interesting, as exciting, even – to us as they must have been to him. This humane, tolerant, kindly and modest man must have delved into the nature of things with no other motive but that of inquiry or, as he probably thought of it, worship. There are many now who, in so far as they possess such motives, owe them to him. In White the nature-investigator

Portrait of G: Wh
penned by T. C.

Gilbert White, 1720–93, at the age of twenty-seven; the father of British field natural history. Sketched on the flyleaf of one of his own books (now in the British Museum) by his friend T. Chapman.

and the nature-lover were inextricably confused; and many believe that the pursuit of truth in natural history will continue to be successful only so long as this benign confusion is preserved.

We shall see later, in more detail (p. 176) that the observation of wild birds has two streams, the literary and the investigative that, depending on the climates of times, flow now together, now separate. The bird lore of the centuries comes hot and cold to us. Each temperature is valuable. It comes emotionally and unemotionally. Each attitude is valuable. The Seafarer, whom, with Serf and Cuthbert, I recognise as of the first detectable stream of bird-lovers, found "gomen" (or "gamen"), Anglo-Saxon delight or entertainment, from the "hleoþor" or pother or arragh or kurragh of his beloved gannets (and if some scholar tells me he did not *love* birds that scholar is no poet). Chaucer wrote of birds with love, as did all the Middle English poets who knew the sounds and smells of the countryside. Turner and Ray were rather dispassionate observers; only between their lines can we find (as we do) that they loved their work and its subjects. Gilbert White wrote in a harmonious combination of the passionate and the dispassionate. One or other of these attitudes has eluded many of his successors, despite the fact

Thomas Bewick, 1753–1828, whose two greatest collections of engravings of birds appeared in 1797 and 1804 and are together one of our best source-books of fine bird pictures. After the portrait by James Ramsay.

that both can disinter the truth. My personal heroes of ornithology are the scientists with the poet's heart, like White, and the poets with the scientist's heart, like Clare (p. 192). I do not know a top ornithological scientist of today who does not live in love with his subject; most of them do not mind saying so, and have.

Besides *The Natural History of Selborne*, the other work of the late eighteenth century with a comparable claim on the hearts of bird-watchers is Thomas Bewick's great picture-book, *A History of British Birds*, which began to come out in Newcastle-upon-Tyne in 1797. This must be primarily judged as a work of art. The first volume, of 1797, the *Land Birds*, had a text largely compiled from the works of previous authors. It is of no importance when compared with Bewick's woodcuts, and was written, as a matter of fact, by Ralph Beilby to whom Bewick was apprenticed to learn engraving in 1767. The text of the *Water Birds*, which appeared in 1804, was not only illustrated by Bewick, but entirely written by him. The words are of no better quality than Beilby's text of the first volume, and prove nothing except that Bewick was not a *very* good observer of natural history or a very original thinker on the subject. But when he died in 1828, at the age of seventy-five, he had done for nature art what Burns did for poetry – put a little honest humanity in it.

By modern standards of bird illustrations the birds in some of Bewick's cuts are unnatural; with those he watched himself as a boy, he is at his best. His fieldfare, for instance, is surely based on a field sketch. His blackbird, with his old house at Cherry Burn by Tyneside in the background, may have been sketched (p. 164) at the very spot on which it appears in the cut. Bewick at his best was perhaps the best woodcut nature artist since Dürer.

This digression on the subject of White and Bewick must be forgiven, for these heroes of bird-watching have had a special influence upon the development of ornithology, that has been felt beyond Britain. We must continue with the development of the British List, which stood at 240 species in 1800.

In our book *The World of Birds* (1964), Roger Peterson and I analysed the local and county and State faunas of several countries and showed how quickly a detailed knowledge of regional natural history developed in the nineteenth century. For England we showed that some sort of county avifauna listed in modern style (if only a list in an otherwise general natural history book) dates back to Dr Robert Plot's *Natural History of Oxfordshire* first published in 1677. We showed that all the major counties now have avifaunas of at least this status, and that half of them produced their first one in the seventy-two-year period 1829–1901.

I have made a rather deeper analysis here for England, Wales and Scotland. In Scotland many of the faunal works are based not on counties so much as on the principal drainage areas under J. A. Harvie-Brown's great and successful plan for *Vertebrate Faunas* of Scotland that began to come out in 1885. Counting these as counties, every county in the United Kingdom now has had at least one printed avifauna that is not just a bird list in passing in a general book, but a full avifauna with the treatment of species in some detail, headed as such in a scientific journal or, more often, a full book. Avifaunas of this sort really began in 1794, with John Heysham's *List of Cumberland Birds* in Hutchinson's *History of Cumberland*: the rest of the first ten are all also English – W. Marwick's *Aves Sussexienses* (1798), R. Pulteney's *Catalogues of Birds* in Hutchinson's *History of the County of Dorset* (1799), A. G. C. Tucker's *Ornithologia Danmonensis* – of Devon (1809), R. Sheppard's and W. Whitear's *Catalogue of Norfolk and Suffolk Birds* (1826), L. Jenyns's *Observations on the Ornithology of Cambridgeshire* (1829), P. J. Selby's *Catalogue of Birds hitherto met with in Northumberland and Durham* (1831), Mrs C. L. E. Perrot's *Selection of British Birds frequenting Worcestershire* (1835), P. Rylands's *Catalogue of Birds found in Lancashire* (1837) and H. J. Torre's *A List of Birds found in Middlesex* (1838). Of the eighty-four counties, or units of county (not vice-county, see p. 234) status from the ornithological point of view, all had at least one avifauna by 1958 – some finely worked counties like Norfolk have now had up to a dozen. Half the first ones for each "county" (actually forty-three) were published in the forty years 1864–1903, great years of the flourishment of collecting and field work and semi-competitive local logging. The "county" areas are mapped, and dated with their first proper avifaunas, on page 68.

Naturally, national avifaunas succeeded each other in quick succession. Leaving aside avifaunas concealed as parts of more general works, and developed in relatively little detail, the nineteenth century inherited, as we have seen, Turner's great *Avium Praecipuarum* of 1544, the Ray-Willughby *Ornithology* of 1678, Ray's *Synopsis Methodica Avium* of 1713, Eleazar Albin's *Natural History of Birds* of 1731–38, Edwards's *Natural History of Birds* of 1743–64, Latham's *General Synopsis of Birds* of 1781–82, with works also by W. Hayes (1775), J. Walcott (1789), W. Lewin (1789–94), T. Lord (1791), E. Donovan (1794–1819) and Bewick. In the nineteenth century at least thirty-three important British–Irish bird books were published, many of which went into second editions. Many others were produced on eggs, on breeding birds, on migrants, or on groups of birds (game birds, waterfowl, song birds, etc.). There are, among these, classics: George Montagu's pioneer *Ornithological Dictionary* (begun in 1802); the *History of British Birds*

(*Left*) William Macgillivray, 1796–1852, Scotland's first great scientific ornithologist; from J. A. Harvie-Brown and T. E. Buckley's *A Vertebrate Fauna of Outer Hebrides*. (*Right*) William Yarrell, 1784–1856, writer of the first scientific textbook on British birds of deep scholarship. From 1837 to 1899, in successive editions (the later ones edited by others), his *History of British Birds* was the great standard reference.

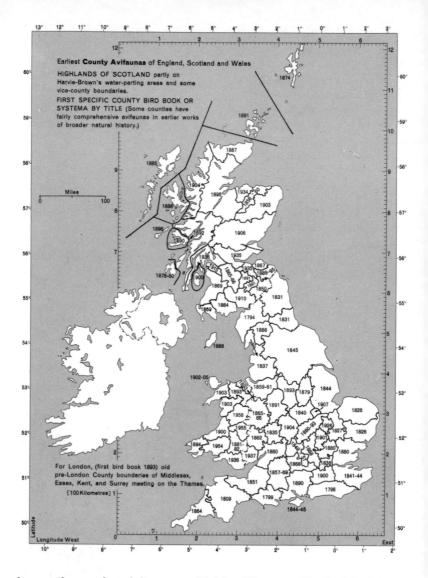

Earliest **County Avifaunas** of England, Scotland and Wales

HIGHLANDS OF SCOTLAND partly on
Harvie-Brown's water-parting areas and some
vice-county boundaries.

FIRST SPECIFIC COUNTY BIRD BOOK OR
SYSTEMA BY TITLE (Some counties have
fairly comprehensive avifaunas in earlier works
of broader natural history.)

Miles
0   100

For London, (first bird book 1893) old
pre-London County boundaries of Middlesex,
Essex, Kent, and Surrey meeting on the Thames.

[100 Kilometres]

Latitude
Longitude West
East

by a rather neglected Scotsman, W. Macgillivray, a friend of Audubon's
(1837–52); Yarrell's fine *History of British Birds* (1837, with very many subsequent editions); John Gould's magnificent *The Birds of Great Britain*,
issued in five volumes between 1862 and 1873 with 367 large folio litho-
graphs (these were coloured by hand from drawings by Gould and the
brilliant artists Joseph Wolf, H. C. Richter and William Hart); the first

British Ornithologists' Union official list of 1883; a book by another neglected scholar now perhaps coming into his own as an original thinker, Henry Seebohm – the *History of British Birds* of 1883–85; and Lord Lilford's great picture-book of 1885–97, *Coloured Figures of the Birds of the British Islands*, in which he commissioned, and indeed made famous, the young artist Archibald Thorburn. Thorburn was just about as good as Gould, and held his position as the leading British bird artist until his death in 1935. The B.O.U.'s *Ibis*, begun in 1859, is now the oldest ornithological journal in the world with an unbroken run, though the *Journal für Ornithologie*, the still-flourishing organ of the German Ornithological Society antedates it by six years.

The heroes of nineteenth-century British ornithology are of three main strains, all rather highly educated: the clergy, the landowners and their cousins the officers of the army and navy, who tended to retire early to their seats in those days, and the University dons and allied scholars. The clergy played, and play now, a special part in the proceedings.

For Gilbert White, for the natural knowledge that he unlocked, and for the existence and work of a regular school of his successors, we have to thank the system of bestowment of Church livings. No other, better system could have been derived for placing educated, simple, honourable, truthful and contemplative men in the places where they were needed most – dotted evenly all over the countryside, where they could record nature. Without the clergy our knowledge of nature in Britain at all ages, but particularly up to the end of the nineteenth century would, quite simply, have been poor instead of rich. To give an example, the clergy of nearly a thousand Scottish parishes were invited to give accounts of their areas in the *Statistical Account of Scotland* (published between 1791 and 1797), and again in the *New Statistical Account of Scotland* (published in 1845, but mainly written in the 1830s). Nearly a hundred of them, on each occasion, made quite a bit of the heading "natural history" provided for them; some of their accounts form the basis of our present knowledge of changes in the Scottish bird fauna; many of their writings are full of enthusiasm, and a love of nature doubtless descended directly from Serf, from Kentigern (or Mungo) and from Aldhelm, Cuthbert, Guthlac and other bishops and saints who loved birds long before Francis of Assisi.

A further pointer to the importance of the Anglican and Scottish clergy, as recorders of nature, is the fact that there was, *in the nineteenth century*, no detectable parallel movement in Ireland (and little in Wales). It is fair to say that we know relatively little about Irish natural history a hundred years ago. There were, of course, pioneers and stalwarts, not all Irish but many of them visitors from the outer space of England and Wales and the Continent. Giraldus Cambrensis, after all, made some Irish bird notes in 1187. Arnold de Boot, of Dutch extraction, sent some exiguous information to his brother

William Thompson, 1805–52. The bird volumes of his *Natural History of Ireland*, published in 1849–57, established him as the first deep scholar of Irish ornithology.

Gerard, Physician to the English King, that was published in 1652. One, Patrick Browne, published a poor *Catalogue of the Birds of Ireland* in the *Gentleman's and London Magazine* of 1774. Not until 1849–57 was a respectable Irish avifauna published, from the pen of William Thompson, a Belfast man who deserted the linen trade for science, but died before he was fifty. The integrity of the bird sections in *The Natural History of Ireland* puts him on a par with his equally unsung contemporary Macgillivray. John T. Watters, who had contributed a good deal of information to Thompson, published what almost amounts to a rehash of the essence of Thompson's book in Dublin in 1853. A.G. More, an English-Scottish immigrant, made a good *List of Irish Birds* in 1885. But, apart from those of Thompson and More, and the notes of a succession of travelling and holidaying gentlemen mostly from across the Irish Sea, the nineteenth century lacks a broad conspectus of the Irish birds. In the twentieth century, as we shall see, things have become very different. In the nineteenth century there were very few native Irish who took any interest in birds. The parish priests were not interested in wild animals, then.

The substantial rise of the British–Irish List from 240 in 1800 to 380 in 1900 was a pretty steady one. The early accessions owe much to George Montagu, that energetic army officer and field worker who in turn owed much to White's inspiration. "Your work produced in me fresh ardour," he once wrote to White. Montagu was always full of fresh ardour. In his efficient

George Montagu, 1751–1815, from a portrait belonging to the Linnean Society of London, with their kind permission. A man of enthusiasm and scholarship, and the compiler of the first dictionary of birds.

way, he swept up almost the last of our birds that were unknown because unrecognised, and usually unrecognised because undistinguished from some close relative. Others later picked up those unknown because rare or vagrant – a process, indeed largely responsible for the continued surge of the List in the present century. In 1800 Montagu distinguished the cirl bunting from the yellowhammer for the first time in Britain. In 1802 he was the first to identify and distinguish from the hen harrier, the harrier that now bears his name. In 1813, in the *Supplement* to his famous *Ornithological Dictionary* of 1802 he gave the first description ever, lay or scientific, of the roseate tern, and published the first British records of the little crake, the little gull and the gull-billed tern.

A few species that really belonged all along to our regular bird fauna remained unrecognised until later. Leach's storm petrel was first scientifically described in 1817 and discovered in Britain at St Kilda which is its nesting-headquarters in our islands, by William Bullock in 1818. In the next year, 1819, the fundamental difference between the arctic and common tern was at last scientifically cleared up by J. F. Naumann, and soon recognised by our field men.

In 1822 Laurence Edmonston, a fine native ornithologist of Shetland, identified the glaucous gull as a winter visitor from the north (it is the northern counterpart of the great blackback), and in the following year found that the very similar Iceland gull (which breeds not in Iceland but in

Greenland and is the counterpart there of the herring gull) was also a British bird. In the next year, 1824, William Yarrell identified Bewick's swan as a British bird : it had previously been confused with the whooper by even the best native talent.

The marsh warbler was not distinguished from the reed warbler in Britain until 1871, when Edward Blyth discovered it near London. Bird song was scarcely noted in those days except by a few disciples of White, and it is on song that the two must (except in very favourable conditions of light or by a knowledge of their preferred habitat) be distinguished in the field. There is, in fact, highly suggestive evidence that the marsh warbler nested in Hampstead (where it could scarcely nest now) in 1861–63 and in 1865.

The last of the "present but hitherto unrecognised" native breeding birds was the willow tit – also found in Hampstead. In 1897 the systematists Otto Kleinschmidt and Ernst Hartert were looking through a tray of skins labelled "marsh tit" in the Bird Room of the British Museum of Natural History, when they saw at once that two birds from Hampstead were undoubtedly willow tits. In the same year the Rothschild Museum at Tring – now part of the British Museum of Natural History – obtained two willow tits from Finchley. After that it took some years before it was finally discovered that the willow tit had an even wider distribution in Britain than the other very similar species. Incidentally, only recently has the willow tit been distinguished from the black-capped chickadee of North America with which, for a long time, it had shared the same binomial Linnaean name. Look-alikes often stay under the same names in museums, until their habits are finally studied ; and habits cannot be studied in museums.

The rise of the British–Irish List was still steep, though rather wavering, from the 380 of 1900 to the 456 of 1954. In a real way the evolution of ornithology in our present times from a hobby of the educated few to a mass-movement with considerable rules and disciplines derives from the take-over by trained zoologists of scientific ornithology towards the end of the nineteenth century.

By the end of that century an ornithologist, Alfred Newton, was in the Professorial Chair at Cambridge. The British Ornithologists' Union was a strong, progressive, learned body. The great collections were accumulating, still partly in private hands under the contemporary motto : "what's shot's history, what's missed's mystery" – but mainly in the Bird Room of the British Museum, and in the Rothschild Museum at Tring, and in certain go-ahead provincial museums with go-ahead curators. The textbooks were kept carefully up to date. The management of ornithological affairs was, generally speaking, in the hands of a body of University-trained men, to whom was attached a large group of highly educated, often wealthy lay enthusiasts.

The general trend of bird science was still in the directions of classification

"Shooting Kestrels in the Cathedral"; a sketch made by Henry Davenport Graham in 1852, from a portfolio (parts edited and published in 1890 as *The Birds of Iona and Mull*) entitled "The Birds of Iona; all shot upon that sacred island or in its vicinity" with naïve Victorian callousness.

and geographical distribution, reappraised and refined ever since the publication of Charles Darwin's *Origin of Species* in November 1859, and the British ornithologist Philip Lutley Sclater's *On the General Geographical Distribution of the Members of the Class Aves* in the *Journal of the Linnean Society* for 1858.

It is true that active bird protection had begun in Norfolk (with our first modern bird sanctuary) and with the foundation of what is now the Royal Society for the Protection of Birds; and active migration and behaviour studies were being pioneered by a few. But these affairs we shall consider later. The process of the List in the twentieth century was due to a revolution which involved a transition from the gun to·the rapidly advancing optical instrument (monocular or binocular) as the primary means of identification, and which enabled our ever-increasing army of ornithologists gradually to discover that among all the European countries, Britain and Ireland were those most blessed with rarities and vagrants.

The transition to the new integrity was not without event, even if some of the events concerned have turned out to be of the kind we have to be wise after. A student who consults the British Ornithologists' Union's last (and therefore still supposedly current) *Check-List* of 1952 will find no less than 16 full species (out of that *List*'s 426) which subsequent researches, whose results have been generally (and fully officially) accepted, have shown ought never to have been on the list at all, at that time.

It is true that of these "Hastings Rarities", as they are now universally called, not less than 10 have been restored to the *List* on other records subsequently accepted as valid. The rest, among those I cite, by meiosis, as "doubtful" in my 1964 British–Irish List (pp. 300–38), are the grey-rumped sandpiper, a Siberian species of which 2 were recorded in September 1914 at Rye Harbour, Sussex; the slender-billed curlew, a Siberian species of which 4 were recorded near Brookland, Kent in September 1910, 1 at Jury's Gap in Sussex in September 1914 and 2 at Pevensey Sluice in Sussex in May 1919; the black lark, a Siberian species of which no less than 9 were recorded in January and February of 1907 and 1915 at Pevensey Levels, Rye, Westfield and Hollington in Sussex and at Lydd in Kent; the masked shrike, a Balkans–Asia Minor species of which 1 was recorded at Wood-church, Kent in July 1905; Rüppell's warbler, a Balkans–Asia Minor species of which 2 were recorded in May 1914 at Baldslow in Sussex; and the snow finch, a high mountain species whose nearest breeding-places are in the Pyrenees and Alps, of which at Rye Harbour, Sussex, 2 were recorded in February 1905 and 3 in February 1916, and at Paddock Wood, Kent, 2 were recorded in December 1906. A few of these were sight records, but the majority, involving every species, were records of birds "obtained", "shot", "found dead", "examined in the flesh", etc. and as specimens these entered various collections, and were recorded in various journals of repute, and were accepted (or at least most of them) by the great authorities of the day, the B.O.U. and all.

In a remarkable number of our fine journal *British Birds* (August 1962), E. M. Nicholson and I. J. Ferguson-Lees, editors of the magazine, and statistician J. A. Nelder, boiled thousands of hours of research (over eight years) down to over a hundred pages of text, analysis and tables, and con-cluded that no less than 594 records of individual rare birds in Sussex and Kent within a radius of twenty miles from Hastings made between 1892 and 1930 were untenable in the British faunal analysis, subject to reinstatement when particular cases were made out. "We are satisfied", wrote Nicholson and Ferguson-Lees with some careful choice of words, "that deception was practicable as far as the origin of these birds was concerned, and the time which had elapsed after death."

Many of the Hastings specimens still exist, and as the *British Birds* editors write, "their identifications by the highest authorities are clear and un-disputed". The point at issue was the certainty with which the birds were freshly killed in the district. Statistician Nelder concluded that the rain of rarities around Hastings, compared with the normally observed rarity-fall in "control" neighbouring areas, was so exceedingly improbable that any hypotheses brought forward to account for it (and he considered all he and his colleagues could think of) were "exceedingly unlikely to be true and that the basic assumption of the validity of all the records must be questioned".

Besides the 16 questionable species, no less than 13 exotic races of other species were discarded during the clearing of the Hastings stables. As a task of scholarship the Hastings investigation has no parallel, save perhaps the exposure of the Piltdown.fraud (which occurred but twenty-four miles from Hastings in the same period) by J. S. Weiner, K. P. Oakley and W. E. le Gros Clark in 1953. "No trouble can be too great and no self-discipline and scrutiny too searching to ensure that the record is kept straight", wrote Nicholson when it was all over. Some, including doubtless the Hastings analysts, believe that some valid records have been emptied with the Hastings bath. Go they have to, until rehabilitated from new evidence.

Meanwhile, all must ponder on the motives of the Hastings group, if group there was, whose curious records and discoveries confused and deceived scholarly and disciplined collectors, authorities and local recorders of the highest integrity. An interesting taxidermist character appears in the transactions. So do collectors. Collectors of birds have been known to seek the "fame of the first", to vie in the scoring of rarities. Everybody loves a rarity. Not everybody realised, around Hastings, then, that (for instance) the then new techniques of ship refrigeration made it possible to deliver fresh bodies of birds to any chosen English spot. There is still a lesson to be learned from Hastings. The records petered out, it would seem, almost in direct proportion to editorial questioning, once editorial questioning was aroused. But it took some years for them to cease. The private *competitive* collection phase of British ornithology is three decades and more away from us now. We no longer want to own rare birds; though we still want to see them. The business is to see them straight.

Notwithstanding the Hastings interlude, the rise of the List in the present century has been largely a function of the multiplying number of orni-thologists, and a rapid refinement and sophistication of their instruments for, and techniques of identification. To the more elderly of our present bird-watchers every man who led the movement is still a living (albeit grey) eminence, or an Absent Ibis, as the British Ornithologists' Union annually toast those of their members they know who are away, or those they knew, and went birding with, who are dead.

I need not dwell on the major geographical works and field guides which have inspired the twentieth-century trend of the British–Irish List. They are summarised here in table form and are within the normal reading of most present bird-watchers:

The Book and Magazine Marks of the British and Irish Avifauna since 1900, with special reference to identification and records. Those marked * are fully cited in Chapter 11, pp. 234–95.

1900	R. J. Ussher and R. Warren. *The Birds of Ireland*. London.
1907	Foundation of the magazine *British Birds*, by the late Harry F. Witherby.
1908	R. J. Ussher*.
1910	A. L. Thomson. *British Birds and their Nests*. London.
1910–13	F. B. Kirkman ed. *The British Bird Book*. London, 4 vols.
1915–16	A. Thorburn. *British Birds*. London, 4 vols.
1920–26	T. A. Coward*.
1920, 1924	H. F. Witherby, E. Hartert, Annie C. Jackson, F. C. R. Jourdain, C. Oldham and N. F. Ticehurst. *A Practical Handbook of British Birds*. London, 2 vols (in 3 parts).
1928	E. V. Baxter and L. J. Rintoul. *The Geographical Distribution and Status of Birds in Scotland*. Edinburgh.
1933	Foundation of the British Trust for Ornithology, by H. F. Witherby and others.
1937	G. R. Humphreys. *A List of Irish Birds*. Dublin.
1938–41	H. F. Witherby, F. C. R. Jourdain, N. F. Ticehurst and B. W. Tucker*.
1941	H. F. Witherby*.
1952	P. A. D. Hollom*.
1952	British Ornithologists' Union*.
1952	R. S. R. Fitter and R. A. Richardson*.
1953	Foundation of the *Irish Bird Report*, by the Irish Ornithologists' Club.
1953	E. V. Baxter and L. J. Rintoul*.
1953–63	D. A. Bannerman*.
1954	Foundation of the magazine *Bird Study* by the British Trust for Ornithology.
1954	P. G. Kennedy, R. F. Ruttledge, C. F. Scroope and G. R. Humphreys*.
1954	R. T. Peterson, G. Mountfort and P. A. D. Hollom*.
1958	Foundation of the magazine *Scottish Birds*, by the Scottish Ornithologists' Club.
1960	P. A. D. Hollom*.

1963   R.S.R.Fitter*.
1965   B.Campbell*.

Of the perpetrators or founders of master-works cited here published before the Second World War, Sir Landsborough Thomson (A.L.Thomson) and N.F.Ticehurst are grey eminences (if they will forgive me for so citing them), still flourishing and working. Sir Landsborough, indeed, has just completed one of the most massive editorial tasks ever to have confronted an ornithologist, the editing of the classic *New Dictionary of Birds*, published for the British Ornithologists' Union in 1964 to celebrate its hundredth birthday in 1959.

Apart from these two living pioneers of modern ornithology in our islands, the Absent Ibises whom we all have to bless for developing the rules and discipline of field identification without collection are pre-eminently (among those cited), Harry Forbes Witherby, Thomas Alfred Coward, Francis Charles Robert Jourdain, Charles Oldham and Bernard William Tucker: also (not cited, as they never contributed to a major textbook as editors) Arnold Whitworth Boyd and Wilfred Backhouse Alexander. B.W.Tucker's field-identification contributions to the classic *Handbook* of 1938 and onwards were of the greatest originality and based on deep thought and the broadest field experience. Only a few living field men, like H.G.Alexander (W.B.A.'s brother), Roger Tory Peterson (the American who can outbird most Europeans in Europe) and P.A.D.Hollom, can match his amazing skill.

Many things have happened to ornithology in the present century; but not one fails to be built, just as the ascent of Everest was made on the shoulders of all previous expeditions, on the Tucker code of identification. I make no apology for presenting a code based upon it, to end this chapter with. The code is a mnemonic one, devised by Roger Peterson and the writer in our *The World of Birds* of 1964, but here somewhat developed. The mnemonic is **WHICH IS IT? DO IT!** – thus:

Primary Drill	*Secondary Drill*
Where and when?	**D**istance
Habitat	**O**ptics
Impression	
Comparison	**I**nstant of observation
Habits	**T**eam
Identification flashes or field marks	
Sounds	
Important details	
Tail and wings	

Now for the development: and how to fill in notes on a species of bird of uncertain kind, with the highest expectation of producing a precise identification, true and *acceptable to others* (i.e. recorders and editors and thus eventually science).

WHERE, WHEN AND WEATHER. Locality, date, time of day (use continental system, e.g. 1800 for 6.00 p.m.), altitude (from map on ground, estimated when bird or observer in air). Weather, including light conditions (see *Optics*, below), and wind direction and strength (use Beaufort scale, see table). In Britain and Ireland the 1-inch or ½-inch to mile maps which have the National Grids, enable an observer to code a locality correct to 100 metres (or yards) with a six-figure reference.

HABITAT. Not simply wood, marsh, meadow, estuary, mountain; but more detail if possible. In some cases supporting evidence needed to clinch an identification may be almost at the "microhabitat" level; e.g. with some marsh-living warblers whether in pure stands of reeds, or in mixed water-growing vegetation.

IMPRESSION – of the *general* kind; the general appearance of the bird at rest or in movement. W. H. Hudson used to say that each species of bird had its own, rather undefinable "jizz". The job, under this heading, is to *define* this "jizz".

COMPARISON. Here particularly note relative size, in comparison with species known. First note comparison with similar and familiar (i.e. certainly identified) species that the bird is in company with, if any – and be sure to note if the mystery bird is close to, or some (what ?) distance from these "controls". Secondly, note comparison with absent controls, even to the extent of noting whether your last check with a control was on the same day, on a previous day, or long before (a useful idea of D. G. Bell's, this).

HABITS. Note as many details as possible of your bird's style in every kind of movement you see: flight (including alighting and taking off); running; walking; standing; preening, etc.

Recognition plate of plovers by Roger Tory Peterson from the current *Birds of Britain and Europe* (with G. R. Mountfort and P. A. D. Hollom), showing the Peterson system of guide-lines to diagnostic field marks. By courtesy of the authors and Messrs Collins.

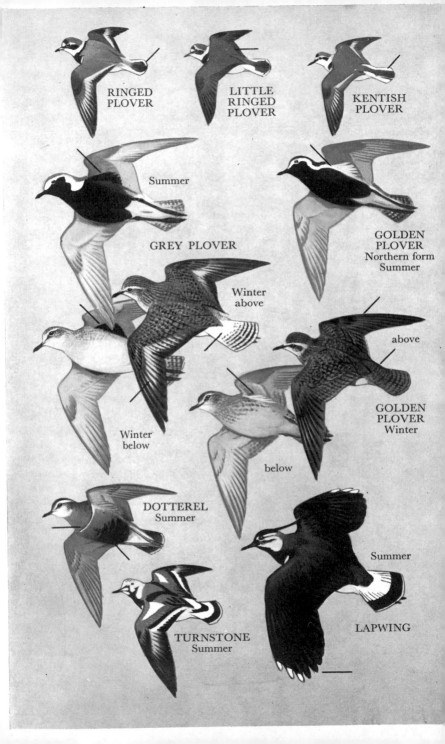

RINGED PLOVER

LITTLE RINGED PLOVER

KENTISH PLOVER

Summer

GREY PLOVER

GOLDEN PLOVER
Northern form
Summer

Winter above

Winter below

above

below

GOLDEN PLOVER
Winter

DOTTEREL
Summer

Summer

TURNSTONE
Summer

LAPWING

IDENTIFICATION FLASHES OR FIELD MARKS. Roger Peterson calls these the "trade marks of nature". Many birds have diagnostic patterns of plumage (some of which are often called "flash marks") adapted to signalling their identity mainly to others of their own kind. They are singularly valuable to the ornithologist, too. Here then notes on bars, patches and all contrast areas; tail and wings to be developed under the next headings. Is breast plain, streaked, spotted or striped? Is there a rump patch (see tail)? Note head, where diagnostic patterns often around eye which may have stripes over, "through" and under, a ring around crown may have stripes, patch and/or crest.

SOUNDS. Transcribe all vocal utterings you may hear into some sort of words, whether they turn out like Anglo-Saxon (quite likely), Gaelic, Welsh or English. Distinguish *if you can*, between what are *apparently* songs, call notes, alarm notes, etc., but do not overdo judgments on these points; they may be wrong.

IMPORTANT DETAILS. Here particularly note size (specially in the absence of "controls" — do the best you can), shape and colours not noted under *Identification flashes* above, or *Tail and wings*, below. Pay attention to colour and length of legs, structure of toes (web, etc. if any), colour, length, shape of beak.

TAIL AND WINGS. Some field men deprecate singling out headings for notes such as this, but I do not agree. Some bird men can forget to note a bird's tail as easily as they may forget to note that it can (usually) fly. Flash marks are *very often* on the tail and wings. Tails may have bands or spots, note where (across, down, corners, centre, tip, etc.). Wings may be plain, barred, patched, tipped or have special pattern areas, e.g. the "speculum" of ducks. Note, importantly, tail length, and wing length too, e.g. whether the wing projects beyond or not beyond the tail tip when it is folded in the normal position of rest.

It is not necessary that the following notes be made during the observation, but they should be promptly made as soon as it is over.

DISTANCE. How far from the bird, at what phase of observation?

OPTICS. Power of binoculars and telescope. Power and direction of the light.

INSTANT OF OBSERVATION. Not only time (see *Where*, etc. above) but *duration*.

TEAM. Names of any companions, with remarks (*not* to be exchanged until this point if possible) as to their experience of the bird, if any, and their measure of agreement or disagreement about it. This check is vitally necessary for the presentation of an acceptable record.

Further remarks will probably be inevitable; and if the observer is an artist, field sketches should be appended to or incorporated with the remarks under the above headings. *Not until this has been done* should the observer use his *Field Guide* or *Sound Guide* or other recognition book. If he uses this too soon, the book may suggest things to him that he did not see or hear.

The Beaufort Wind Scale

Beaufort Number	Strength	Knots	Observable Effects	
			Land	Sea
0	Calm	Under 1	None	None
1	Light air	1–3	Smoke bends, weather-vanes don't move.	Ripples
2	Light breeze	4–7	Wind can be felt. Weather-vanes and leaves move.	Small wavelets. Sailing ships can make way.
3	Gentle breeze	8–12	Leaves in continuous motion, flags begin to wave.	Large wavelets. Sailing ships may list.
4	Moderate breeze	13–18	Dry dust flies; little branches move.	Small waves, may break white. Sailing ships list well.
5	Fresh breeze	19–24	Small trees sway.	Long waves; white horses frequent. S.ss usually reef.
6	Strong breeze	25–31	Big branches move, wires whistle.	Large waves and white horse foam. S.ss should all reef.
7	Moderate gale	32–38	Big trees sway.	Big waves; foam blows off. S.ss heave to.
8	Fresh gale	39–46	Trees lose twigs; walkers bend.	High waves; foam in streaks. S.ss to harbour if they can.
9	Strong gale	47–54	Roofs may lose tiles; trees old branches.	High wave foam may block vision.
10	Whole gale	55–63	House damage; trees may fall.	Very high waves; whole sea white.
11	Storm	64–75	Widespread building and tree damage. (Headlines in papers.)	Exceptionally high waves; sea inchoate.
12	Hurricane	Over 75	Undoubted chaos. (Headlines in other country's papers.)	Sea totally inchoate.

CHAPTER 3

The Peculiarity of British Birds

THE CHANGING PATTERN OF THEIR LIFE

Thirty-nine living kinds of birds are found in Britain or Ireland, or both, and nowhere else in the world. A few more are found in our islands and in small neighbouring parts of Europe and nowhere else.

I wrote *kinds* purposely, for what I am alluding to are not full species, but the geographical races or *subspecies* accepted as valid by the latest authorities, particularly Charles Vaurie in his admirable *Birds of the Palearctic Fauna* published in 1959 and 1965. Modern systematists now usually apply the "three-quarters rule" in deciding whether, within a species, two populations occupying different areas differ from each other enough to merit a trinomial, or subspecific name (see pp. 61–62). For practical purposes the distinction must be based on museum material. If, in regard to one or more characters (size, shape, colouration, etc.) identifiable in a museum, 75 per cent of a series from region A differs significantly from 98 per cent of a series from region B, then the B population is deserving of a different third name from the A population. Names have often been given which, by this rule, are undeserved. In nomenclatural parlance (if the reader will forgive the expression) these are "relegated to the synonymy" – that is, regarded as meaning the same as another, earlier name for the population. Synonyms are quoted in formal systematic lists, but fall out of use in general works often for the very good reason that there is not room for them all. The 39 "good" British races of birds have been given about twice as many subspecific or racial names as they hold in a modern list like Vaurie's – simply because the systematists of the past have tended (as they always will) to split off and name races on material which does not prove any *real* distinction.

Many of the British–Irish birds which we now know to be good indigenous races were first described as full species. Britain and Ireland have, in fact, no living full species peculiar to them. For many years the red grouse was thought to be such a bird; but even this has been lately dropped to racial status, being clearly no more than a geographical representative of the willow grouse (a widespread and successful bird with 16 different races all round the northern hemisphere) which, unlike the other races, does not go white in winter. A few systematists like to hold our red grouse a full species still.

The threshold is always difficult to decide between island forms. But national pride, and the desire to have at least *one* full bird of our own, must, I fear, give way to the tidy and severe naming practices of the twentieth century. If the red grouse is to be a full species, then by the same token so might be the pied wagtail, the British dipper, the St Kilda wren, the Dartford warbler, the British long-tailed tit, the Scottish crested tit, the Irish and British coal tits, the British tree creeper, the British twite, the North British bullfinch and the British chough. All these were originally named as full species.

Here is a chronological list of races of birds, that are purely British and Irish, accepted by modern systematists as good ones. Those marked * are not as well differentiated as others but can be regarded as scraping home under the three-quarters rule.

1 (British or Cornish) chough, named *Upupa Pyrrhocorax* Linnaeus 1758, from England. "England" becomes the "type locality" that must now be cited by the first namer, or designated by a later reviser if the early namer did not do so. Becomes *Pyrrhocorax pyrrhocorax pyrrhocorax* in trinomial nomenclature, as the "typical" race of the species, i.e. the race to which the type of the species as first described, belongs. Seven other races of the chough are now accepted, in Europe, Asia and northern Africa, including Las Palmas, Canary Islands. Note that Linnaeus in his *System of Nature* put it in the genus of the hoopoe; the genus *Pyrrhocorax* was named for the "Cornish chough" by the English ornithologist Marmaduke Tunstall in his *Ornithologia Britannica* of 1771.

2 (British) twite, named *Fringilla Pipilans* Latham 1787, from the Derbyshire Peak. Now accepted as *Acanthis flavirostris pipilans*, 1 of 8 races of the twite, first named *Fringilla flavirostris* Linnaeus 1758. The genus *Acanthis* was named for the redpoll by Borkhausen in 1797, and the common consent of present systematists refers the twite to it, also.

3 Dartford warbler, named *Sylvia dartfordiensis* Latham 1787, type Bexley Heath, Kent. Now regarded as 1 of the 3 (or 4) races of the bird first named *Motacilla undata* Boddaert 1783: as *Sylvia undata dartfordiensis*. The genus *Sylvia* was named for the blackcap by Scopoli in 1769, and the common consent of present systematists refers the Dartford warbler to it, also. The English vernacular name "Dartford warbler" is now extended to the whole species: vernacular names do not, of course, follow the priority rules that apply to the Linnaean names.

The discussion of these 3 species will have illuminated some practices in scientific naming (see also p. 62). For the birds that follow I discuss such matters in less detail.

4 Red grouse, named *Tetrao Scoticus* Latham 1787. As *Lagopus scoticus* accepted as full species by the British Ornithologists' Union as recently as 1952. Now by most systematists demoted to 1 of the 16 races of the willow grouse *Lagopus lagopus* (Linnaeus 1758). Linnaeus's name goes in parenthesis here as he named it *Tetrao lagopus*, i.e. in another genus. The full scientific name of the red grouse thus becomes *Lagopus lagopus scoticus* (Latham 1787). Most ornithologists' deprecate vernacular names for races that remove any part of the vernacular name of the full species, so in logic the English name of the red grouse should be "red willow grouse". This is so unhistorical (and therefore ridiculous) that an exception is happily made here, and with "red grouse" we continue to celebrate the idea (if no longer quite the scientific reality) of having our own full-species National Bird.[1]

At one time it seems highly likely that the Irish red grouse *Lagopus lagopus hibernicus* (Kleinschmidt 1919) was a "good" race, in Ireland and the Outer Hebrides. However, the present populations, owing to refreshment and restocking which introduced birds of the main British race, are probably too mixed to be distinguishable under the systematic rules.

5, 6 Dipper. *Cinclus cinclus gularis* (Latham 1801) is the British dipper; *C. c. hibernicus* Hartert 1910 the Irish dipper. These are 2 of the 12 good races of a species of Eurasia and N.W. Africa.

7 (British) bullfinch, *Pyrrhula pyrrhula pileata* Macgillivray 1837. One of 10 races in Eurasia and the Azores.

8 Pied wagtail, *Motacilla alba yarrellii* Gould 1837. One of 13 races. Different vernacular names are (as is exceptional) used for the 4 main groups (all distinguishable in the field) of this species' races: the pied wagtail (Britain and Ireland and has rarely bred in western coastal countries of Europe); the white and masked wagtails (S.E. Greenland, Eurasia and Morocco); the mourning wagtails (E. Asia), and the African pied wagtails (Africa).

[1] The National Bird is, in fact, the robin, in so far as such things are official: the robin has the merit of being just about the first bird we hear of in any form of post-Roman literature (pp. 47, 177).

9, 10 Coal tit. *Parus ater britannicus* Sharpe and Dresser 1871 is the British coal tit; *P. a. hibernicus* Ogilvie-Grant 1910 the Irish coal tit. These are 2 of the 18 good races of a widespread Eurasian species.

11 (British) tree creeper, *Certhia familiaris britannica* Ridgway 1882. Named in fact by the American ornithologist Ridgway as [*Certhia*] *brittanica*, but present naming rules allow obvious misspellings in the "original orthography" to be corrected. One of 13 races of a widespread Eurasian species. The brown creeper, *Certhia americana*, with about 10 races in North and Central America, was until recently thought to be of the same species, but behaviour studies (some in captivity) show that these look-alikes should rate full specific status.

12–16 Wren. This widespread species of the northern world, with 35 presently acceptable races, is the only member of its family in the Old World. In America it is known as the winter wren. From the home of the successful American wren family it doubtless colonised the Old World via the Bering Straits (a chain of races inhabits the Aleutian Islands now), spreading west to reach eventually the remotest outlying islands of W. Europe – Britain, Ireland, the Outer Hebrides, St Kilda, Shetland, the Faeroes and even Iceland. This may have happened in the Pleistocene period, the last million years or so. Everywhere it has settled as more or less a resident, and isolated populations have tended to form good races. The indigenous subspecies in our islands are *Troglodytes troglodytes hirtensis* Seebohm 1884, the famous St Kilda wren, first described as a full species, with a present population of about 400 breeding birds on its native smallish and vastly steep archipelago; *T. t. zetlandicus* Hartert 1910, the Shetland wren; **T. t. hebridensis* Meinertzhagen 1924, the Hebridean wren; **T. t. indigenus* Clancey 1937, the British wren (of the mainland of Britain and Ireland); and **T. t. fridariensis* Williamson 1951, the Fair Isle wren, with a population of 90–100 breeding birds on this craggy isle between Orkney and Shetland.

17 (British) great tit, *Parus major newtoni* Prazák 1894. One of 29 or 30 races of a widespread Eurasian and N.W. African species.

18 (British) blue tit, **Parus caeruleus obscurus* Prazák 1894. One of 14 races of a bird of Europe, W. Asia, N. Africa and the Canaries.

19 (Scottish) crested tit, *Parus cristatus scoticus* Prazák 1897. One of 6 races of this European species of evergreen forests; the emblem of the Scottish Ornithologists' Club.

20 (British) willow tit, *Parus montanus kleinschmidti* Hellmayr 1900. One of 16 races of a widespread Eurasian species. It was held by the British Ornithologists' Union until 1952 to be in the species *P. atricapillus*, the black-capped chickadee of N. America, but since that date these two look-alikes have been separated, mainly on behaviour grounds.

21 (British) great spotted woodpecker, *Dendrocopos major anglicus* Hartert 1900. One of 22 races of a widespread species of Eurasia, N.W. Africa and the Canaries.

22 (British) robin, *Erithacus rubecula melophilus* Hartert 1901. One of 8 races of a widespread species of Eurasia, N.W. Africa, the Canaries, Madeira and the Azores.

23 (British) goldfinch, *Carduelis carduelis britannica* Hartert 1903. One of 12 races of a species with the same gross distribution as the robin.

24 (Scottish) crossbill, *Loxia curvirostra scotica* Hartert 1904. One of 20 races of a widespread conifer-forest species of N. America, Eurasia and N.W. Africa. This Scottish race is so big-billed that it has been lately placed as a race of the N.W. Russian and Scandinavian parrot crossbill *L. pytyopsittacus*, also a pine-cone feeder and a very rare vagrant to Britain. But most authorities believe it to be a "red" crossbill (*L. curvirostra*) that has evolved into a rather parrot crossbill-like form in the Caledonian pine forests.

25 (British) lesser spotted woodpecker, *Dendrocopos minor comminutus* Hartert 1907. One of 13 races of a widespread species of Eurasia and N.W. Africa.

26 (British) chaffinch, **Fringilla coelebs gengleri* Kleinschmidt 1909. One of 13 races of a widespread species of Eurasia, N.W. Africa, the Canaries, Madeira and the Azores.

27, 28 Dunnock. Of the 5 races of this bird of Europe and W. Asia 2 are indigenous: *Prunella modularis occidentalis* Hartert 1910, the British dunnock; and *P. m. hebridium* Meinertzhagen 1934, the Hebridean dunnock, of W. Scotland and Ireland.

29 (Irish) jay, *Garrulus glandarius hibernicus* Witherby and Hartert 1911, Ireland and N. Scotland. The rest of the British population is of the

race *G. g. rufitergum* Hartert 1903 whose range extends to Brittany and which is therefore not wholly indigenous to Britain. The species has 34 races, and is widespread throughout the woods of Eurasia.

30 (Hebridean) song thrush, *Turdus philomelos hebridensis* Clarke 1913. One of 4 races of an Eurasian species.

31 (British) black grouse, *Tetrao tetrix britannicus* (Witherby and Lönnberg 1913). One of 5 races of an Eurasian species.

Black grouse (black cock and grey hen); an illustration published in Yarrell's *A History of British Birds* in 1840. The British population is now recognised as racially distinct.

32 (Shetland) starling, *Sturnus vulgaris zetlandicus* Hartert 1918. Shetland and Outer Hebrides. One of 11 races of perhaps the most successful passerine bird, widespread naturally in Eurasia and the Azores, and by introduction in N. America, S. Africa and Australasia.

33 (Scottish) ptarmigan, *Lagopus mutus millaisi* Hartert 1923. One of 22 presently recognised races of a widely spread arctic-alpine species of the northern world. Was recognised as different by the great Scottish ornithologist William Macgillivray in 1837, though the name he gave it cannot be applied to it.

34 (British) redshank, *Tringa totanus britannica* Mathews 1935. One of 4 races of an Eurasian species.

35 (British) long-tailed tit, *Aegithalos caudatus rosaceus* Mathews 1938. Described as a full species by Edward Blyth in 1836 (or 1837) as *Mecistura rosea*; but he had already given this name to the typical race *A. c. caudatus* (Linnaeus 1758) of which it is thus a synonym, and so unavailable for the British population. One of 21 races of a widespread Eurasian species.

36 (Scottish) yellowhammer *Emberiza citrinella caliginosa* Clancey 1940. Scotland, Ireland, Wales and N.W. England. (S.E. English population belongs to the W. Continental race.) One of 3 races of a widespread Eurasian species.

37 (Scottish) linnet, *Acanthis cannabina autochthona* Clancey 1946. One of 6 races of a widespread bird of Eurasia, N.W. Africa, the Canaries and Madeira.

38 (British) red-backed shrike, *Lanius collurio juxtus* Clancey 1951. One of 5 races of a species widespread from Europe to Central Asia.

39 (Western Irish) meadow pipit, *Anthus pratensis theresae* Meinertzhagen 1953. One of 2 races of a purely European species.

The modern view of the process of species formation among birds owes much to one of the greatest systematists working, Professor Ernst Mayr of Harvard University. Over the last decades his work has shown conclusively that bird races evolve their characteristics in geographical isolation, and that species are formed when the amount and quality of differentiation crosses certain thresholds.

Nowadays, 2 populations of obviously closely related birds, descended from a common ancestor, are regarded as of distinct species if they can co-exist in the same breeding-area without competing and interbreeding. In former times biologists tried to define species as populations that could not interbreed. Now that they *do* not naturally and normally interbreed is enough. Good species are distinguished from their closest relatives, if they overlap with them, by using a different spectrum of food, by preferences for different habitats, by differences in migration and other seasonal movement patterns, and by behaviour patterns which prevent them from interbreeding in the wild, even if, as is often the case, they can interbreed (even sometimes freely) in captivity. Such species-pairs are descended from what were once but geographical races of an ancestral species. In the course of history, with continued evolution in isolation, the populations underwent reorganisation and change of their hereditary characters. When their later fortunes and successes permitted them to spread into each other's range these differences proved enough to keep them from interbreeding and competing.

Speciation (species-formation) of this sort stares us in the face upon the continental land-masses; it also happens on islands. Colonists of islands quickly settle down to evolution in isolation. Often an island is colonised at considerable intervals from a continental stock of one species. If the early colonists have had time to evolve distinctly, and with some ecological specialisation, later colonists from the same ancestral stock may invade and settle without hybridisation and competition – and the island ends up with two species, the earlier of the two being an indigenous species.

As we can see from the list, Britain and Ireland have no indigenous full species of bird presently: though they have two borderline cases. The real test of the species status of the red grouse would come if willow grouse from the Continent invaded Britain's or Ireland's grouse moors. They have not. What would happen if they did is uncertain. There will always be a limbo of island forms like our red grouse whose real status as species or races must therefore be decided on common sense. The "lumpers" (I am a lumper) and the "splitters" have to battle the case out, and can often fill half a bird journal with their disputations.

The other borderline case is the Scottish crossbill. This does appear to have a very stable population in the ancient Caledonian pine forests of the central Highlands, descended doubtless from crossbills of the Continent, though now much bigger beaked. As we shall see (p. 180) continental cross-bills still continue to invade our islands periodically in some numbers, and settle to breed for some years in quite large areas. The invaders have less specialist food habits than the Scottish race. One year a Highland colony of the continental race may impinge on the older natives of Rothiemurchus Forest or some other part of the Highlands and put the status of the natives to a test. If they settle down to peaceful co-existence without competition or interbreeding, then the Scottish crossbill will be proved to be worthy of specific rank. If they do not, it will remain only a race, and a race re-organised by a new mingling of hereditary characters.

I have discussed species formation in some detail because Britain and Ireland are in a rather interesting position at the edge of a continent. As we saw (pp. 22–23), England became finally separated from France when the Channel broke through, as recently as about 5000 B.C. Ireland became dis-connected from Wales probably a little earlier. This has of course encouraged the isolation of populations. Of the 39 valid races quite indigenous (as breeders at least) 16 are British–Irish, 6 British (not Irish), 10 Scottish, 2 Scottish–Irish, 3 Irish and 2 English. The score of indigenes is higher than that of any European country of comparable size, though Iceland (about the size of Ireland) has about a dozen, some of which it shares with the Faeroes.

The only country really comparable to Britain–Ireland with a Palearctic (or Old World northern) fauna is Japan. If we take, as best comparison, the four main islands of Japan and their near satellites, including the Seven Islands of Izu, but not the former or more distant Japanese islands of the Kuriles, Ryukyus, Bonins, etc., we find a bird fauna of about the same size, with a list of 425 full species. But the number of indigenous forms is greater – about 55, of which 12 are full species. This probably derives from the longer and greater isolation of Japan, and its greater variety of climatic zones.

Where do the birds of Britain come from? The British and Irish climate is now temperate and constant, bathed as our islands are by the warm west wet winds from the Atlantic and Caribbean Sea (which bring us, as we now are beginning to appreciate, a surprising harvest of American vagrants). Bird geographers like Karel H. Voous, whose excellent *Atlas of European Birds* was published in England in 1960, have gone far in analysing the bird stocks available to colonise most of Europe during and after the Ice Ages – the last million years of alternating freeze and thaw. The situation is so complicated that the movements in Europe and around it, of the ecological zones (with their typical birds) that our fauna comes from, is only beginning to be understood. But it is possible from the study of present (and fossil) distributions to make some sort of educated guess about the origin of most of the British–Irish breeding birds.

COSMOPOLITAN BIRDS

A few of our breeders are almost cosmopolitan, being distributed all over the globe, though some only in a scattered pattern that is obviously an aftermath of earlier, greater success. Our oystercatcher, Sandwich and little terns, barn owl and perhaps also gannet and Manx shearwater are such birds. The gannet has a curious distribution with three populations, in Australia–New Zealand, South Africa, and the North Atlantic which are held by some to be 3 species, by others to be but 1. Some fossils of the past are close and appear to fill in the tropical gaps between. If we treat the northern gannet as a full species, our islands become its world headquarters, for (with the Channel Islands) they have exactly half the 30 known breeding-colonies, and (with the vast St Kilda colony) about three-quarters of the present population of around a quarter of a million breeding birds. We enjoy a big population of that common cosmopolitan, the moorhen; and a comparatively big one (the biggest in Europe) of that now scattered cosmopolitan, the beautiful roseate tern. Some other cosmopolitans have tenuous or occasional breeding groups with us : the Kentish plover *may* still survive as a breeder in south-east England ; the night heron nests in Edinburgh, but with help from the Royal Zoological Society of Scotland ; the black-winged stilt nested successfully at Nottingham Sewage Farm after a freak invasion in

Peregrine; Joseph Wolf's portrait of a now vanishing bird, from John Gould's *The Birds of Great Britain*, published in 1862.

1945 (never before or since as far as is known); the gull-billed tern nested at Abberton in Essex in 1950 and probably also 1949.

The late fate of one of our greatest cosmopolitans, the peregrine, as admirably measured by D. A. Ratcliffe, shows that a fairly stable population of about 650 pairs, in Britain (the figure does not include Ireland) in 1930–39, began a rapid decline in south England in about 1955. The decline spread quite fast through more northerly populations. By 1961, as Ratcliffe summarised it, "two-fifths of the pre-war populations had evidently disappeared and only 82 pairs were known to rear young; in 1962 only half the known territories were occupied and the number of successful nestings had fallen to 68". In 1963 a good sample showed only three-quarters of those in 1962. There was an improvement, though, in 1964 to about the 1962 status. The widespread use of organic (chlorinated hydrocarbon) pesticides was proved to be a factor leading to the death and infertility of the peregrines; and the recovery in 1964 was probably a consequence of reduction in the use of these toxics.

The hydrocarbon deluge has concerned conservationists deeply in the last decade and more, all over the civilised world (in fact, the more civilised peoples have been most prone to use these poisons widespread). It has provedly wrecked huge bird of prey populations already : at the top of the pyramid of life these birds are most prone perhaps of all to accumulate the almost indestructible hydrocarbon toxics from their prey.

Our remaining cosmopolitan, the osprey, has perhaps a better story ; though lately the toxic hydrocarbons have been found in an infertile Scottish clutch of the eggs. To put it mildly, this was serious ; for though the osprey departed from our fauna in 1908, when it last bred at Loch Arkaig in the county of Inverness (it may have bred at Loch Loyne in the same county till 1916) and returned to breed again only in 1954 (or perhaps a year or two before), we still only have 2 (or perhaps sometimes 3) nesting pairs in Scotland, 1 of them in the county of Inverness widely known to the public and guarded night and day by the Royal Society for the Protection of Birds (p. 272). The nests of this and another pair were destroyed by a gale as this book lay in proof in spring 1966.

The osprey (see map) has never provedly bred in Ireland or Wales, and has had but a tenuous hold on nesting-sites in England, though the Anglo-Saxons had a word for it; it has been found as a fossil in Late Ice Age deposits in Essex. In Scotland it had a wide distribution once, though – especially in the Highlands. There is scarcely any doubt that its decline in Scotland, which began early in the nineteenth century, was largely at the hands of sportsman-collectors.

Charles St John's adventures in the west of the county of Sutherland in the summer of 1848 present us with a little example of the wanton destruction of rare birds and their eggs that went on at that time. St John concentrated on ospreys. Near Scourie he shot the hen of a breeding pair and took two eggs. At Rhiconich he took, from a nest, one young bird and an addled egg; he could not shoot the old birds, though he tried hard enough. At another nest near Rhiconich he shot the male, missed the female and took three young birds. He afterwards found that the male at Scourie had mated again; its female had laid an egg which he took.

To top all, St John ended his account of the destruction of what was then possibly the entire osprey population (save a few survivors) of north-west Sutherland by writing : "There are but very few in Britain at any time, their principal headquarters seeming to be in America; and though living in tolerable peace in the Highlands, they do not appear to increase nor to breed in any localities excepting where they find a situation for their nest similar to what I have already described (an islet in a lonely loch). As they in no way interfere with the sportsman or others, it is a great pity that they should ever be destroyed."

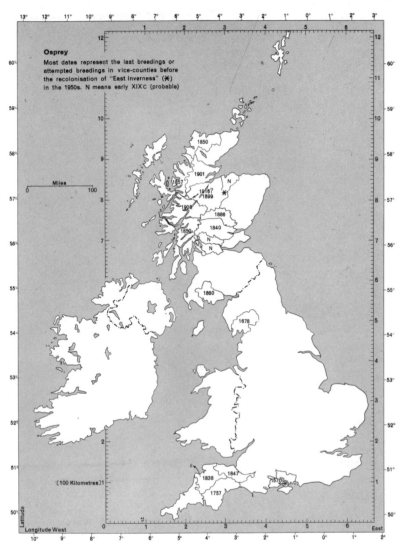

Osprey

Most dates represent the last breedings or attempted breedings in vice-counties before the recolonisation of "East Inverness" (✱) in the 1950s. N means early XIXc (probable)

The ospreys got destroyed, all right, by the likes of St John. Philip Brown and George Waterston have lately filled in all the findable historical details in their R.S.P.B. book (1962) *The Return of the Osprey*. Even when the birds eventually returned to Inverness county after about forty years' absence,

Charles St John collecting a nesting male osprey at Rhiconich in Sutherland in 1848. Drawing by "W.B.S." (unacknowledged by St John) engraved on wood by Richard Thompson.

egg-collectors raided the early broods, showing that the curious wild-life-property-owning spirit that filled thousands of glass cases and drawers with the remains of living things as status symbols (not as scientific research material) did not die out with the nineteenth century.

HOLARCTIC BIRDS

The Holarctic fauna is the accepted name for the community of animals that is distributed over the whole of the northern world south to the border of México, the Sahara, Arabia, the Himalayas and central China. It is clearly distinguishable in its pattern of animal families and orders from the other great faunas of the world – Ethiopian (Africa south of the Sahara), Oriental (the Indian subcontinent and south-east Asia), Australasian and Neotrópical (Central and South America and the West Indies). Over 40 of the non-arctic breeding birds of Europe are also birds of North America and over 30 of these are British–Irish. Our Holarctic breeding birds include 9 ducks, waders like whimbrel and snipe, the common and black guillemots, swallow, sand martin, redpoll, crossbill and wren. Some of them have a rather tenuous footing with us as breeders: thus the black-throated diver, Slavonian grebe, Leach's storm petrel, golden eagle and hen harrier are practically confined to Scotland, and ducks like scaup and goldeneye only breed irregularly. The black tern, with the draining of so much of the English wetland, has been virtually extinct as a breeder for a century. The survival of the whimbrel (headquarters in Shetland), hen harrier (Orkney), golden eagle (Highlands of Scotland, with occasional outposts in Lowlands, England and Northern Ireland) and goshawk (several well-guarded secret nests) is watched most carefully by the R.S.P.B. and other conservationists, as is that of the Slavonian and black-necked grebes.

The North American fauna is scientifically called the Nearctic fauna, our northern Eurasian and North Africa fauna the Palearctic fauna. They are but subfaunas of the Holarctic fauna, for they resemble each other more closely than either resembles any other of the great faunas. Europe has 3 birds which (in the time of geologists) are rather recent Ice Age (or even

Great northern diver; published in Yarrell's *A History of British Birds* in 1842. A fundamentally North American species that has Britain at the edge of its range.

post-Ice Age) invaders from the Nearctic fauna: the great northern diver (which the North Americans call the common loon), Barrow's goldeneye and the herring gull. The first 2 of these do not normally breed nearer to us than Iceland, their main invasion point; but the loon has probably bred in Shetland and winters on our coasts. The herring gull is connected by a chain of races, that goes all around the northern world, with the lesser black-backed gull; in Britain, Ireland and north-west Europe the end-members of the chain overlap, and breed happily on the same cliffs, behaving as full species, which of course they are. Our native herring gull is racially distinguishable from the herring gull of North America, but only just so.

(*Left*) The great spotted woodpecker, and (*right*) the lesser spotted wood-pecker, also formerly known as the barred woodpecker. Both birds are woodcuts from Thomas Bewick's great collection of 1797 onwards. These 2 British birds are typical of our peculiarly Palearctic fauna.

PALEARCTIC BIRDS

Over a third of our native breeding birds are, not unexpectedly, Palearctic in their main distribution and presumable origin. A few, however, are also found through the tropics into other zones of the Old World, and play a part in the Ethiopian, Oriental and sometimes the Australasian faunas as well. The solid bird communities of our woodlands and farmlands are largely from this fauna: among them sparrow hawk, lapwing, woodcock, cuckoo, nightjar, swift, the spotted woodpeckers, skylark, house martin, 6 tits, blackbird, wheatear, stonechat, willow warbler, chiffchaff, goldcrest, nuthatch, tree creeper, yellowhammer, reed bunting, hawfinch, bullfinch, siskin, house and tree sparrows, jackdaw, crow, rook, magpie and jay. Many water birds come from this fauna, too. As breeders, white stork and spoonbill,

The blue tit, another of Thomas Bewick's woodcuts from his 1797 volume. All British and Irish tits are of the Palearctic fauna characteristic of these islands.

white-tailed eagle, great bustard and ruff are all extinct; though there seems some chance that the spoonbill and ruff may re-establish themselves in the now well-protected wetlands of eastern England.

In a real sense Britain and Ireland are at the edge of the zone now occupied by the Palearctic birds; and all edges must be tenuously occupied

Ruff (from John Gould's *Birds of Great Britain*). A Palearctic wader, once breeding regularly here, which could permanently recolonise England if the present wetland reserve programme develops.

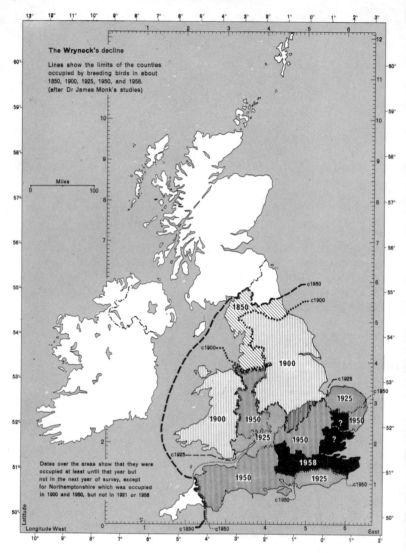

The Wryneck's decline

Lines show the limits of the counties
occupied by breeding birds in about
1850, 1900, 1925, 1950, and 1958.
(after Dr James Monk's studies)

Miles
0   100

Dates over the areas show that they were
occupied at least until that year but
not in the next year of survey, except
for Northamptonshire which was occupied
in 1900 and 1950, but not in 1921 or 1958

Longitude West

Latitude

by some species. Certainly some are withdrawing their range, while others
are moving in, causing (needless to say) concern or excitement to our ever-
increasing band of bird-watchers.

The causes of the withdrawal to the south and decrease in numbers of some of our birds are being very thoroughly investigated by our main field-work organisation, the British Trust for Ornithology. For some time field men have been working on the decrease of the nightjar, which has withdrawn rather far in the last decade, partly as a consequence of the destruction of heathlands and glade woodlands.

Perhaps more serious is the rapid disappearance of that charming summer visitor the wryneck, which used to breed north to the Lake District, and west to Wales, but seems now to be confined to the Thames Valley counties, Suffolk and Essex, with a very scattered distribution in but a score or so of headquarters: in 1958 the B.T.O. reported that "only 65 individuals or pairs were *recorded* in the whole country during the breeding season, 46 of them in Kent, and only 15 pairs were proved to breed". James Monk thinks the summering population is unlikely to have been more than 400 in that year.

Wryneck; an illustration from Yarrell's *A History of British Birds*, published in 1839. A Palearctic species, once a regular summer visitor, now fast declining in the British fauna.

In 1961 J.D. Magee organised a B.T.O.-aided investigation into the diminution of the stonechat, and found a gradual decline of this pretty bird had been going on throughout the present century. The species is withdrawing to the coastal areas under the steady destruction by builders and farmers of inland heaths. Hard winters also can reduce populations severely.

The wryneck is possibly on the way out as a summer visitor to England. So, maybe, is the red-backed shrike. In 1960 D.B. Peakall's B.T.O. investigation showed that this bird, which formerly summered, like the wryneck,

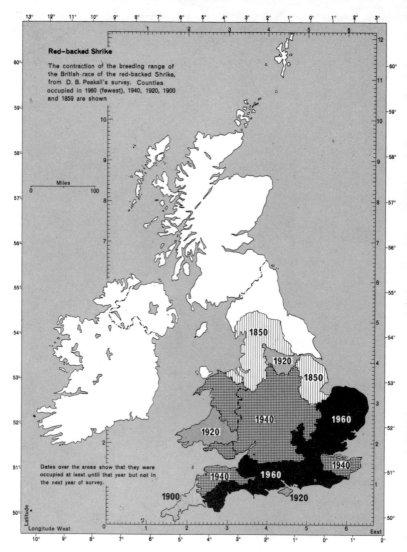

Red-backed Shrike

The contraction of the breeding range of
the British-race of the red-backed Shrike,
from D. B. Peakall's survey. Counties
occupied in 1960 (fewest), 1940, 1920, 1900
and 1859 are shown

Miles
0   100

Dates over the areas show that they were
occupied at least until that year but not in
the next year of survey.

north to the Lakes and west to west Wales had withdrawn entirely to East
Anglia and southern England. A big campaign of investigation at all past
haunts could not raise 200 breeding pairs in all, of which about a third were
in Hampshire. A similar decline has taken place in Europe, whose ornitho-

The red-backed shrike, specially drawn by Robert Gillmor in 1966; another declining Palearctic species, whose British (now, only English) population is racially distinct.

logists believe that a succession of warmer, wetter summers in the present century have led to a reduction in the number of the larger flying insects upon which the butcher-bird mainly preys. Peakall thinks that this may, indeed, be a more important reason than the destruction of its open-land habitat of heath and scrub.

With the Dartford warbler, which I discuss presently, the British race of the red-backed shrike is in global danger of extinction, and has been lately put on the Red File of the Survival Service Commission of the International Union for Conservation of Nature and Natural Resources. This sounds, and is, a mouthful; but it means that our butcher-bird's fate is of international concern. It is true, of course, that in the process of evolution species and races inevitably become extinct. There are about three times as many races as species of birds (or in other words the average number of races per species is about 3). In an issue of the I.U.C.N.'s *Bulletin* (September 1965) Jack Vincent (in charge of the bird Red File) lists 95 full species and 65 valid races of birds that have become globally extinct since 1600. My own list (with Roger Peterson) of full species (October 1964) named 85. Our differences are partly due to different systematic judgments. Probably the number of races that have really become extinct in the period is much higher; the status of many is, rather naturally, less intensively studied than that of full species. It seems likely that since the surge of human agricultural and scenery-changing progress all over the globe since 1600 (before that year we know that birds became extinct in historical times but do not always know what they looked like), several times as many (some think about four times as many) birds became extinct as would have so become in the natural process of evolution *without* any help from man. The British red-backed shrike may be being killed off by wet warm Atlantic summers, and if this is the sole cause it is no fault of ours. But conservation ethics demand that we do not help this process by further habitat destruction. Luckily a significant part of the Hampshire population already lives in some form of Nature Reserve. On the other side of the coin I can offer a recolonisation and a new colonisation of Britain by two Palearctic birds.

The black-tailed godwit, once a member of our wetland breeding bird fauna, met the fate of the spoonbill and ruff. Well over a hundred years ago it had ceased to breed, regularly, in the fenland. Since 1829 there are only scattered records, in certain years, of its nesting in any place in Britain. All the same, though it did not breed much it continued to visit Britain in fair numbers, mainly on passage, though quite often in winter, and sometimes, as a non-breeder, in summer. Thirty years ago its visits began to get more frequent; a pair may have bred in Norfolk in 1934, another pair laid eggs in 1937, and a pair, or pairs bred in Lincolnshire in the early 1940s, as did pairs in northern Scotland. There is some indication that the British nesting population, which has become stabilised in an anonymous area in East Anglia since 1952, may be of the Iceland race, arrested (as it were) in passage; though it would be a cruel and senseless (and without licence, illegal) academic exercise to collect some specimens to prove the point. A better point is that East Anglian and national conservation organisations have continued to buy and administer black-tailed godwit land, under the general idea that a black-tailed godwit crop is worth as much to our civilisation as a few tons of potatoes.

E. R. Parrinder, in a succession of papers, has covered the adventures of our new Palearctic invader with his typical precision. The little ringed plover has been on the list since 1850; but not until 1938, when Tring Reservoirs in Hertfordshire were dry and low, was it found to breed in the kingdom. Its colonisation of England's gravel-pits and similar habitat has been an inexorable process since, for this sand- and gravel-bank lover; it coincided fortunately with the vast development all over England of the gravel industry with the improvement of our national roads and communications. Parrinder's regular surveys (see map) have established a steady spread in both space and population. One pair summered at 1 breeding site in 1938; 3 at 3 in 1944; 29 at 21 in 1950; 74 at 47 in 1956; 157 at 87 in 1962. The precision of these figures is real; bird-watchers *like* little ringed plovers; the birds' gravel-pit habitat is limited and relatively easy to find by anybody who can read a one-inch map; the observer network has been available to anybody who can address envelopes for three decades. The only rub is that anybody who takes on a national status inquiry like Parrinder's has to resign himself to one hour in the field to nine at the desk. It's the weekend, postcard-writing bird-watchers that get the pleasure, the

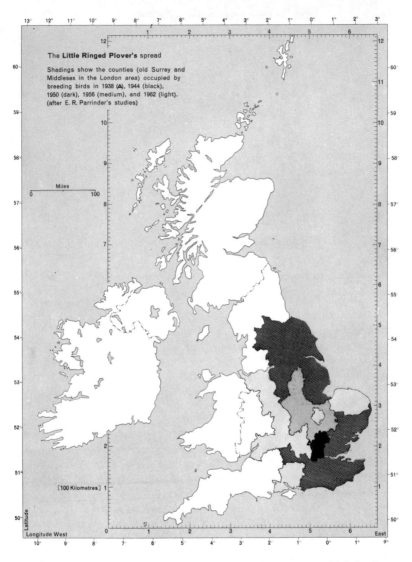

The **Little Ringed Plover's** spread

Shadings show the counties (old Surrey and Middlesex in the London area) occupied by breeding birds in 1938 (△), 1944 (black), 1950 (dark), 1956 (medium), and 1962 (light). (after E. R. Parrinder's studies)

Miles
0   100

[100 Kilometres] 1

Longitude West   East

wretched organiser who gets the . . . blame? Work anyway; which is where, from time to time, we all come in.

ARCTIC AND SUBARCTIC BIRDS

A special group of the Holarctic fauna that we have already discussed lives either in the *taiga*, the northern conifer forests that abut on the true tundra,

Ptarmigan: from an illustration published in Yarrell's *A History of British Birds* in 1840. The most typically arctic-alpine of the British bird species.

or on the tundra itself, the large open areas of the true Arctic that are partly frozen underground permanently. From this group various species of birds have pushed south to colonise Britain, probably at some time in the Ice Ages. Indeed, the remains of quite a few have been found as Ice Age fossils in Britain and Ireland – the red-throated diver (Late), eider (Late), long-tailed duck (Late), grouse (Middle), ptarmigan (Middle), and ringed plover (Early). Besides these, our dotterel, Temminck's stint, dunlin, red-necked phalarope, arctic skua, kittiwake, arctic tern and snow bunting are all probably tundra or arctic coast birds that have pushed south; and from the taigas of western Siberia we probably have the greenshank, redwing and brambling, and seem to have had the hazel grouse in Late Ice Age times.

The diver remains a pretty stable breeder in the Highlands, and breeds still in Donegal. Grouse are well established on the moors, with effective and expensive arrangements to keep them so. Ptarmigan are stable in the Scottish alpine zone. The ringed plover has broken right into the temperate zone round all our coasts and seems to stay there. The eider shows some signs of increasing and pushing south a little; the kittiwake has a big population that has increased, especially in England and Wales during the present century following a decrease during the previous one, which John Coulson, its investigator, considers due to the relaxation of human predation and interference; the arctic skua is stable or slightly increasing in the northern isles and the arctic tern seems stable. Temminck's stint has nested lately in Yorkshire and the Highlands, but only two or three times.

With the slight amelioration of the European climate in the present century the rest seem to be retreating north. The red-necked phalarope, it is true, hangs on in one place in Ireland; but the dotterel is extinct in England now, and confined to alpine tops in the high central mountains of Scotland; the dunlin is withdrawing north; and the snow bunting, always a desultory and unpredictable Highland mountain breeder, is being found nesting less often.

Of the taiga birds, though, the greenshank seems to stay well established in the boggy tracts, usually (but not always) at the edge of Highland woodlands; the redwing appears to be slowly colonising a few woods in northern Scotland, and the brambling, the chaffinch's northern counterpart, has nested in four Highland counties since 1920. Birds can be fossilised in their winter range, of course, and the redwing is a common winter visitor; but it is interesting to note that this Scandinavian taiga-thrush has been recorded fossil from Early Ice Age Somerset, and Late Ice Age Devon, Derbyshire, Clare and Sligo. Robert Hudson thinks that another taiga-bird, the greenish warbler is a possible future colonist of Britain; it has already spread west (as a fair number of taiga species have of late) from Russia to Sweden, and is being recorded in Britain more frequently than ever before.

EUROPEAN BIRDS

About 20 of our indigenes have world ranges purely European, or almost so; among them such typical and common natives as the meadow pipit, song thrush, robin, chaffinch and dunnock; the green woodpecker which continues slowly to push its range north in Scotland; the woodlark which may be gaining range in central England; and the Scottish crested tit which holds on well in Highland pinelands. Of the summer visitors the redstart, blackcap, garden warbler and wood warbler are well distributed; and the nightingale has continued reasonably common for years, breeding mostly east of the Severn–Humber line, and not in Cornwall. Other summer visitors like the marsh warbler are rare, or like spotted crake and icterine warbler exceptional breeders; the handsome pied flycatcher has a curious patchy distribution still being intensively studied by Bruce Campbell. C. A. Norris's classic study of the corncrake (one of the pioneer early B. T. O. investigations) has shown that this summer visitor has stayed common only in the edge-zones of marginal agriculture in the Highlands of Scotland and Ireland, and that nearly everywhere else it has been driven out of the corn- and hay-fields that the poets and medieval writers used to mention so often as the home of its creaky voice. Here new, earlier mowing dates have destroyed the breeding crakes, and about nine-tenths of all our farmers' boys and girls, I guess, are brought up in the English countryside without ever hearing a landrail.

Corncrake; drawing by J. H. Blackburn (Mrs Hugh Blackburn) published in her *Birds from Moidart*, 1895. A peculiarly European bird (its range extends to Iceland) decreasing in Britain and perhaps somewhat in Ireland.

Of the European bird stock Britain still supports 2 great birds of prey whose range is now, alas, but a relic of what it once was. The honey buzzard, beloved of Gilbert White, bred in at least sixteen counties in the nineteenth century. In the first half of the present century it nested in but five and perhaps no more than ten times in all. However, there is now at least one regular breeding-place in England, and birds have tried to nest in Scotland for the first time for many years. The honey buzzard is a conservation bird, as is, perhaps even more so, the surviving relict red kite of Wales.

At one time or another in the nineteenth century the beautiful red kite was reported nesting in all but one county of England and two counties of Wales; in the Isle of Man, most Highland and three Scottish Lowland counties. Persecuted by chicken-farmers, gamekeepers and collectors its population crashed, to the extent that a few pairs survived at the beginning of the present century only in central Wales. Under careful wardening and management the number of pairs has slowly crept up in the last decade from around 6 to around 10. At one time there were considerably more members of the kite preservation committee than there were kites. There have been few signs of spread, though, from the refuge hanging oak-woods of one of the wildest parts of Wales; odd pairs have bred in Devon and Cornwall; but a big and spectacular recovery cannot yet be predicted.

(*Opposite*) Red kite; a painting by Joseph Wolf in John Gould's *The Birds of Great Britain*. Formerly a widespread British breeder, this European bird is now surviving only in Wales under careful protection.

Honey buzzard; drawing by E.A.R. Ennion, 1964, by kind permission of Mr and Mrs Peter Scott. Another European bird, with but a relict foothold in Britain.

MEDITERRANEAN AND CENTRAL ASIAN BIRDS

These are the birds believed to have evolved in the more southerly and dry areas which (except in high mountains) escaped the glaciations of the Ice Ages. Some elements of the present British fauna are thought to have come originally from as far as Tibet, for instance perhaps the twite. All our pigeons, except the latest (the collared dove) may have come from the dry strip from the Mediterranean and south Europe to Turkestan – that is, woodpigeon, stock dove (which has colonised nearly the whole of Ireland since 1875) rock dove (ancestor of the domestic pigeon) and turtle dove. So may the Dalmatian pelican, last breeding with us, from sub-fossil evidence, 2000 years ago at Glastonbury on what is now Sedgemoor, and perhaps also the shelduck; such familiars as the partridge, tree pipit, reed and sedge warblers, the two whitethroats, the spotted flycatcher, mistle thrush, greenfinch, goldfinch and the now successful and (after introductions) near-cosmopolitan starling. From this region, too, doubtless came the little owl, which was from fossil evidence a member of our fauna in Late Ice Age times, only to die out and be restored to our breeding list by deliberate introductions in 1874 and 1889 (it has now conquered virtually all England and Wales and has bred over the Scottish border since 1958).

From the dry hills came ring ouzel, chough and dipper, and perhaps a recent colonist, the black redstart. The black redstart first bred in England in 1845 and 1909 but was not really established there until 1923 when 2 pairs nested; between 1920 and 1939 the pairs were apparently never fewer than 3 or more than 5, but from 1940, aided presently by the ruination of London buildings and the consequent provision of suitable habitat, the British breeding stock, centred at first on the Great Wen, built up to about

Black redstart; an illustration from Yarrell's *A History of British Birds*, 1838. A new colonist from the Mediterranean fauna, established in Britain only since 1923.

35 pairs in 1950, and has now increased considerably and reached Yorkshire. There are other Mediterranean candidates knocking on the British door or already with footholds: Savi's warbler, the moustached warbler (which has bred once), the bee eater (which has bred in two years), the serin, which is still waiting to colonise us just across the Channel after a considerable north-westerly spread in southern Europe. The queer invasions of Pallas's sand grouse from the dry Russian steppes east of the Volga and Caspian are over now; but there were at least 10 between 1848 and 1909, and in the 1880s these birds actually bred in Yorkshire and Moray. Some of the established Mediterranean-type British species are living the life of relicts, now; the stone curlew has a rather unpromising future (outside Nature Reserves) on the downlands and dry moors of south-east England, and Montagu's harrier has rather collapsed as a breeder in what was previously its East Anglian headquarters, though it seems probable that the British nesting population may still be not far short of 100 birds. Perhaps the most important of our Mediterranean species, from the conservation point of view, are the Dartford warbler and the avocet. The Dartford warbler is the second of our indigenous bird races to be in survival danger. C. R. Tubbs thinks that "in the foreseeable future it may become virtually restricted, as a regular breeding species, to the New Forest in Hampshire". In the last century its range extended from Cornwall to Suffolk. Today our sole strictly resident warbler breeds regularly only in Dorset and the New Forest, and sometimes in north Hampshire, and Surrey, where its breeding stock gets wiped out in almost every very hard winter. Its future much depends on the conservation policy in its New Forest headquarters, and on the systems now employed for the small-block burning and piecemeal regeneration of its gorse-heath habitat.

The Dartford warbler, also from Yarrell's *A History of British Birds*, 1838. The British resident stock is racially distinct from, and an outpost of, a primarily Mediterranean population; and rare.

The avocet is the official symbol of the Royal Society for the Protection of Birds, and rightly so. Once this lovely bird was part of our wetland fauna with large colonies in south-east England; but persecution (perhaps even more than marsh draining) extinguished it in the first half of the nineteenth century. Avocets last bred in Norfolk in about 1825, in the north Lincolnshire marshes in about 1837 (they were also still common in the south Lincolnshire–Peterborough fens in about 1831, by John Clare the poet's private notes), in Kent in 1843. Avocets laid eggs in Suffolk in about 1882; but since then the species was believed to be quite lost from our fauna, until a surprising couple of pairs nested in a coastal Wexford marsh in 1938.

The recovery of the avocet – probably from Holland, where the reserves were by then producing good dividends in the way of breeding results – dates from 1944 when new-hatched chicks were observed in Essex. In Norfolk a pair laid a clutch in 1946. In 1947 the colonists concentrated on Suffolk, which has been their British headquarters ever since; 8 or 9 pairs tried to breed at Minsmere but only reared 2 young. In 1948 they reared 13. Thenceforth for some years their sole headquarters became Havergate Island, promptly purchased and ecologically restored to suit the lovely black-and-white waders by the R.S.P.B. At this Suffolk sanctuary, now part of a National Nature Reserve, 17 pairs reared 31 young in 1949. The population built up to 40 pairs, rearing nearly 100 young, in 1952; in the last decade over 60 pairs have bred annually at Havergate and new offshoot breeding-stations have started elsewhere in East Anglia.

THE INDIAN INVADER

On 2 June 1960 an experienced bird-watcher, W. A. Cunningham, saw a strange bird in Stornoway on the Isle of Lewis. It was the most north-westerly collared dove that anybody had seen anywhere. Fifty years before this rather close relation of the turtle dove, and even closer relation of the semi-domestic laughing dove had never been seen north-west of Belgrade in Jugoslavia about 1460 miles away.

The spread of *Streptopelia decaocto* across Europe has been a more remark-able natural explosive spread and colonisation than that of any other land bird. At the fastest period of the spread, the twenty years between 1932 and 1952, the little pigeon colonised a broad strip of Europe 1200 miles long. Sixty miles a year on average was even faster than the spread of the intro-duced European starling and house sparrow over North America.

The collared dove did not reach Asia Minor from its ancestral home (probably in India and places east) until the sixteenth century. By the early years of this century it seems to have achieved a fairly stable outpost in Balkan Europe.

The great spread gathered way after 1912. The doves reached Hungary

Collared dove; specially drawn by Robert Gillmor, 1966. Britain and Ireland's only "Indian" bird, and the most powerful land-bird colonist of Europe in the present century.

in about 1928, Czechoslovakia in 1935, Austria in 1938, Poland in 1940, Germany, Italy and Ruthenia in 1944, Holland in 1947, Denmark and parts of the U.S.S.R. in 1948, Sweden and Switzerland in 1949, France in 1950, England and Belgium in 1952, Finland in 1953, Norway and Luxemburg in 1954, Scotland and Estonia in 1957, Wales and Ireland in 1959.

In the spring of 1952 I saw my first collared dove in Milan. It had arrived in the Upper Po valley only two years before. One of my companions on that trip, Reg May, Lincolnshire postman and brilliant field man, told me a month later that one was cooing its "k'*koo*-kuk" song near his home at Manton.

The official British bird-list committee have evidently "square-bracketed" this 1952 Lincolnshire bird because around that time they believed a dealer had been selling collared doves not very far away. But Reg May and I were sure from its behaviour that it was, more probably than not, a wild immigrant – the first collared dove known to have crossed a fairly wide sea on the great spread. The Norfolk immigrants of 1955 are, however, "official": they nested in north Norfolk that year and have increased ever since.

In 1956 collared doves were seen in Surrey. In 1957 they were seen in Essex, bred in Kent and Scotland, and the Lincolnshire male of 1952, which had been bravely singing away in the seasons since, attracted others, and a female laid an egg before Reg May's eyes. In 1958 birds bred in Northumberland, Hertfordshire and probably Sussex, in 1959 for the first time in Wales and Ireland. Analyst Robert Hudson had found, by 1963, a breeding record for every English county save Rutland; and at the end of 1964 had such records, via the B.T.O. network, from 503 localities, involving nearly 19,000 birds, with a headquarters in eastern Kent.

"After a long period of stagnation", as Ernst Mayr puts it, a land-bird species "suddenly enters upon a phase of aggressive range expansion." He thinks that a genetic alteration of the population at the edge of the old range may give the initial impetus to spread. This may well be so; though a simpler hypothesis to account for the spread could assume that the collared dove was already, by nature, a parasite of the chicken-farming industry.

The collared dove is a panhandler; a grain-eater that lives where cultivated land marches with scrub. It has little fear of man and nests freely in gardens (often in conifers) and feeds with chickens, and raids ripe corn and stackyards; it goes everywhere where there is waste grain. A zoo, where there is plenty of spare corn in the paddocks for an opportunist bird, is a favourite place. In the last six years I have visited over thirty zoos on the continent of Europe. Twenty of them had abundant resident breeding flocks of collared doves, all descended from wild stock that had "discovered" the zoos in very recent years and built up rapidly, sometimes raising 2 young (their normal clutch) three times a year.

Once the collared dove had penetrated up the Danube into the Carpathian Basin about thirty years ago, every further move north-westerly took it into country where the human population was increasingly tolerant of wild birds; even of parasites of cultivation, poultry-rearing and zoos if the bird can be so described. The collared dove was virtually, and in some cases actually protected in most western European countries before its arrival. It has now conquered Britain and Ireland far more quickly and completely than the Romans or the Normans: its next moves are west in France and east in Russia, where it has already reached Kiev.

ANTARCTIC BIRDS

The 4 skuas now living in the world are probably of arctic origin, in the course of evolution. One of them, the arctic skua, is one of the birds which I hold to have colonised Britain straightforwardly from the Arctic. The great skua, though, which is the largest and most gull-like of these parasitic sea birds, which live partly by forcing other sea birds to disgorge their last meal, is one of the few birds of the world which has a "bipolar" distribution. R. M. Lockley and I believe that the bonxie may have originated in the north like the other skuas, but has colonised the Antarctic continent and surrounding subantarctic islands from there.

These southern territories are now the main world headquarters of the species (or superspecies, I had better write, for there are *possibly* 2 species, very closely and lately related). Skuas are probably descended from gulls: only 1 fossil extinct skua species is known – a Late Ice Age (i.e. late in the last million years) bird found in Oregon; but fossil gulls go back nearly 60 million years (p. 17) to the Lower Eocene period. Perhaps the great skua colonised the south when at a more gull-like stage than its present congeners; perhaps it evolved there (where gulls are few) into a gull-niche and more gull-like form than the other skuas. Whatever happened, the possibility that the present breeding-outpost of the bonxie in the North Atlantic is a recent development seems high.

The northern bonxie is only racially distinct from the main groups of the southern birds. It could well have arrived at the end of the Ice Ages, or even more probably after the last glaciation. The outpost is a relatively small one; in historical times it was known to be in simply south Iceland, the Faeroes and Shetland, whence within living memory it has spread to north Iceland, Orkney (1915), the Scottish mainland in Caithness (1949), the Outer Hebrides in Lewis (since 1945 or before) and St Kilda (1963). The southern skuas are great wanderers in the off-season, and cross the Equator in the Pacific. Though none of the South Atlantic races has yet been proved to cross the Equator, a wandering of this magnitude resulting in a colonisation of (say) Iceland or the Faeroes or Shetland, where the climate and richness of sea-bird "prey" resembles that of its nearest southern home on Tristan da Cunha, seems highly possible.

The colonisation of the north by the fulmar may have been earlier. The southern or antarctic fulmar (or silver-grey petrel in the older textbooks) is doubtless the ancestral form of the birds that have become so familiar around all our British and Irish coasts lately. There is even some question as to whether it is a separate species – even if it was put in a different subfamily by a textbook as late as 1931. Probably it should be regarded as a separate species in the same superspecies. Though the antarctic fulmar has a fully high antarctic distribution it ranges extensively in the off-season and has indubitably reached western México across the Equator. The North Pacific race of the present northern fulmar, while certainly classable as of the same species as our North Atlantic breeding birds, has characteristics, particularly those of bill shape, intermediate between those of the antarctic and Atlantic populations. The general consensus of opinion, largely aroused by the careful work of my friend Karel H. Voous, is that the Bering Sea headquarters of the Pacific fulmars was colonised from the Antarctic; and that the Atlantic fulmars are descended from Pacific fulmars that crossed the Polar Basin during the last Ice Ages in one of the interglacial periods when the climate eased for a considerable time. Perhaps the Atlantic birds' ancestors crossed even *before* the Ice Ages, and were cut off into groups, which became the present well-marked races, by them. The only fossil bits of fulmar known (apart from prehistoric material) are material belonging to the modern northern form from Late Ice Age deposits in Pacific California, and the left humerus (or upper arm bone) of a bird found in the coastal cliffs of Chesapeake Bay in Maryland, Atlantic U.S.A. Alexander Wetmore, who examined it, found that "in size and structure it agrees perfectly with

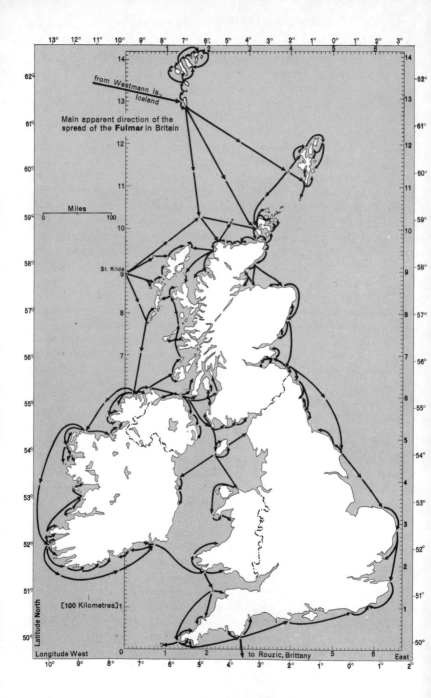

from Westmann Is., Iceland

Main apparent direction of the
spread of the **Fulmar** in Britain

Miles
0   100

St. Kilda

[100 Kilometres]

Latitude North

Longitude West

to Rouzic, Brittany

East

modern *Fulmarus glacialis*; and must be closely allied to that species".
However, there is evidently some doubt about this rather mysterious bone,
for it is not cited in Dr Wetmore's latest list (1956) of North American fossil
birds, which means that he was still not satisfied about the species; and the
age of the deposits in which it was found are also uncertain, for its bed was
not clearly identified, and while most of the fossil beds of the cliffs of Calvert
County are Miocene, some are of the Pleistocene Ice Ages. Whatever its
origin or species, the Chesapeake fulmar does not destroy the pattern of
historical distribution that Dr Voous has established for the presently living
fulmars. Within the present Atlantic fulmar's range the racial status is much
confused, and in my opinion (with the weight of Charles Vaurie's authority
supporting it) warrants the adoption of no separate subspecific names,
though there are plenty of names to choose from! But even if we stick to
Fulmarus glacialis glacialis for the Atlantic lot, the north-westerly birds
breeding in the Canadian arctic are more slender and short-billed and thus
Pacific fulmar-like, than the now big population of the southerly (or boreal,
as opposed to arctic) light-coloured form that has excited ornithologists for
about eight human generations. The story of the boreal fulmar of the Atlantic,
doubtless the most recently evolved population of the species, is worth
telling in some detail.

The extraordinary saga of the fulmar begins truly in a Saga, an ancient
tale of the heroic age of Iceland. A thousand years ago, almost exactly, the
first man we know to have used the word fúlmár – foul maa, or foulgull –
flourished. He was a knavish satirist called Hallfredh, unpopular with
Iceland farmers and other husbands. Hallfredh said of one such farmer (who
had married an old love of his, Kolfinna) that he went to his bed like an
overfed fulmar swimming on the ocean wave.

Fulmars feed, indeed, rather grossly; they have a fierce appetite for
fatty offal, and eat any that they can get in preference to their normal food
of surface shrimps, small fish, swimming molluscs, and even arrow-worms
and jellyfish. Often they will gorge until they can scarcely fly without
vomiting part of their meal. Even before they are fully hatched from the egg
they can produce a musty, oily, waxy secretion from glands in the wall of
their stomach, which serves them well as a defence against most enemies.
Fulmars nest on open cliff-ledges, and both adults and young (young a
fortnight old or more, which are often left unattended) vomit this wax, or a
mixture of it and their last meal, with some accuracy up to a couple of
yards at any kind of intruder. Second barrels, or even third barrels are quite
in order; many a novice bird-ringer, keen to mark his quota for one of the
national migration organisations, has avoided the first moist, musty mouthful
only to walk or climb straight into the second.

In the old days man was the sole important enemy of the Atlantic race of the fulmar. Huge crops of young were taken around 12 August at St Kilda, in the Faeroes and Iceland and sometimes in west Greenland. However, the St Kilda community abandoned our most westerly Scottish islands in 1930, and the Iceland–Faeroe fulmar-men have much reduced their toll of young since fulmars were proved, about thirty years ago, to carry a form of ornithosis very close to, if not the same as psittacosis, which is communicable to humans and once killed over thirty of them in the Faeroes.

There is some evidence that after the serious cropping of young fulmars ceased in these places there were marked increases of the young birds as a consequence. But the great explosion, the huge increase of the light-coloured fulmar of the North Atlantic started long, long before this. Most human cropping in the Faeroes and Iceland was, indeed, a consequence of this spread: there were no fulmars nesting in the Faeroes until 1816 at the earliest, or on the fowling-cliffs of the Westmann Islands in south Iceland until 1753 or a few years before.

It was in the Westmann Islands that the fulmar's spread began. It is the most spectacular and continuous spread of any wild bird known – apart from the colonisations of the starling and sparrow that were started by human introduction. It is even more spectacular than that of the collared dove (p. 110). It has been going on for two centuries, and has not stopped yet.

Outside their big colonies in west Greenland, fulmars of the light phase of our Atlantic race probably once had but 3 colonies, in the North Atlantic. On the isolated dead volcano of Jan Mayen, about 330 miles east of Greenland, a fulmar colony which was probably then old and big was discovered by our great whaling captain and explorer William Scoresby jun., in 1817. In about 1640 the Icelandic historian Jon Gudhmundsson the Learned recorded a colony on Grímsey on the Arctic Circle off Iceland's north coast; and this may also have been an old one. And in 1697 the tutor Martin Martin visited St Kilda and wrote the first scientific account of what is now known as *Fulmarus glacialis*, and its exploitation by the island's fowlers. The St Kilda fowling had been written of since 1549, and that the St Kilda fulmar colony is very old is certain. Archaeological evidence (p. 39) dates the fulmar-fowling back to the Viking Dark Ages of the ninth century; and the use of the Old Norse word fúlmár by the St Kildans in 1697 confirms the age of the fulmar culture there. Probably because of the steady and high cropping by its fowlers until 1911, and a steady but less high cropping until 1929, the St Kilda fulmar population cannot be proved to have contributed colonists to the great spread, until perhaps very lately.

The great spread came from the north; and we are fairly certain of the when and where of its start through the high learning of native Icelanders. One good scholar, Gizur Pétursson, was a parson in the Westmann Islands from 1687 to 1713. He wrote a list of all the breeding birds and studied the fowling closely. The fulmar was not on his list. Then in about 1753 the first really scientific Icelandic naturalist, the lawyer Eggert Ólafsson, visited the Westmanns and found the fulmar nesting. The nearest colony was Grímsey in Iceland's north; and the colonists must have come from there or from Jan Mayen yet farther north. After 1753 the fulmars steadily colonised cliffs all around Iceland's coast; at first great, high ocean-facing promontories, then cliffs up the fjords; then some inland cliffs and lesser cliffs. There are nearly 200 fulmar stations in Iceland now, and when I last visited the Westmann Islands over 20,000 nest-sites were occupied there.

Some time between 1816 and 1839 the fulmars colonised the southernmost island of the Faeroes, 430 miles east of the Westmanns. By 1900 they were nesting on nearly every cliff on nearly every Faeroe island; by 1930 the Faeroese were cropping 80,000 young every year: which means that the population was vast. Like its larger cousins the albatrosses, the fulmar rears but one single young once a year, after a long incubation of seven weeks and an equally long fledging period.

The move on from the Faeroes, to Shetland, was first noticed at Foula (Shetland's westernmost island) in 1878. Since then, nearly every British and Irish headland and rocky island has been colonised. By 1949 I had found (after organising the British Trust for Ornithology's inquiries) 362 breeding colonies, and 198 others which were being newly prospected (probably by young fulmars) and where no egg or young had yet been seen. By 1959 the total of breeding and prospecting colonies was 487 and 222 and some colonies hitherto separate had joined up into a continuous whole. Apart from St Kilda, the Outer Hebrides (Rona, Sula Sgeir) "fell" (i.e. had first proof of breeding) in 1887, Orkney in 1900, Sutherland in 1903, Caithness in 1905, Mayo in 1911, Donegal in 1912, Kerry in 1913, eastern Scotland in 1916, eastern England in 1922, the Inner Hebrides in 1924, the west Lowlands in 1932, the Isle of Man in 1936, Wales in 1940, the West Country in 1944, southern (Channel) England in 1951. Britain is now ringed; and fulmars now also lay eggs in western and northern Norway, and – most southerly station of all, quite recently colonised – on Rouzic off the coast of Brittany.

If we follow the sequence of colonisation, step by shortest step by sea-routes, we find that the colonising or prospecting fulmars have spread over 2300 miles from Grímsey to Sussex in a couple of centuries. And everywhere, the colonies have grown as well as budded: in Britain and Ireland the growth has been at compound interest for years, and there were in 1959 17 stations with between 1000 and 10,000 nests. St Kilda has about 38,000. The increase is still marked, but in the last decades has shown some signs of passing its highest rate. Nevertheless, in the twenty years 1939–59, the number of British colonies, and breeding birds, have more than doubled, and nearly doubled. Every year birds are still found prospecting new places.

There is now good evidence that a young fulmar (which can scarcely be distinguished from an adult after it has flown) spends the first three or four years of its life at sea, without any recourse to land, and the next three or four years occupying ledges in spring and early summer, displaying and courting, without actually laying or fertilising an egg. Among birds, only the great albatrosses and some large birds of prey, as far as I know, have longer periods of adolescence. The function of this long non-breeding youth must be education: simply, a fulmar needs seven years to learn the open ocean and its food-stores and navigation problems before it is fit to rear young successfully.

How could so slow a breeder have increased so fast, have doubled its stock in a major part of its range every twenty years or less? If fulmars reach maturity in their eighth year, and thereafter all females are immortal, lay and safely hatch one fertile egg a year, and are perpetually fertile with an even sex ratio, then the species could only increase at a little over 18 per cent per year. In Britain they increased more quickly than this for many years – which means, of course, that our islands were steadily colonised from the Faeroes or Iceland. Lately there has been some evidence from ringing that British-bred birds may sometimes go back to the Faeroes; and the situation is rather confused. But the general picture is that young fulmars probably do nearly all, or all the colonisation of new places, having tried to return to their birthplace to be driven away by the superior "display-power" of their parents or other entrenched adults; and that, generally still from the north, the young light-coloured fulmars come prospecting southwards to the cliffs of Britain and, finding them crowded with established colonies, pass on, as far as they must go, joining perhaps other young from the crowded British colonies and prospect up the firths, even inland, even (now) on some grassy banks, dunes, hillocks, wooded scarps and (more traditionally) on cliffs of course, but also skerries, flat islets, ruins, a Scottish baronial castle or two (which they must mistake for cliffs).

What emerges from all this is that the period of the fulmars' adolescence must, about 200 years ago, suddenly have become much safer, and stayed so, so that far more new breeders have been produced than were required to balance normal adult losses. The fulmar must be very long-lived, and may attain a human life-span; George Dunnet and Alexander Anderson have already shown that the *average* age at which the adult fulmars, of the rather stable population on Eynhallow in Orkney, die is about twenty-three years.

The best cause to look for is something which has become very much easier for the fulmar in its learning years. Did anything special happen to the fulmar's food supply? From the end of the seventeenth century onwards, the great wooden whaling fleets of Holland and Britain and Germany discovered and exploited the great right whale herds that then almost swarmed in the ice off the east coast of Greenland; and many of them worked within easy operational range of the fulmars of Jan Mayen and Grímsey in north Iceland. The operational range of a fulmar is vast. When sitting on eggs, parents may relieve each other at intervals of up to eleven days, and even when feeding the young, intervals of up to four; and birds 500 or 600 miles to sea may well be active breeders. Now all the whaler skippers commented that when their whales were flensed (blubber-stripped) at ship's side, the fulmars went mad about the fatty food, and arrived in hundreds, sometimes thousands, from every quarter of the surrounding sea and ice.

Always the main whaling season coincided with the fulmars' breeding season; and there was a remarkable succession of good whaling seasons near Iceland in 1739–58 and 1769–1800 just when the fulmar spread began there. The decline of the Greenland whaling did not begin until about 1820, when the right whales got fished progressively out, and have never recovered. But as the decline of whaling began to tell, the rise of trawling took its place. Modern trawling, with ice and steam, was in full action by the 1860s, before the right whaling had its dying spasm in the 1870s. And (this is my friend R. M. Lockley's first idea), the trawling industry, with its steady discharge of fish offal and unwanted scraps, produced another free meal service for fulmars, this time nearer the Faeroes and especially nearer Britain, where the spread got going in 1878. To this day bands of thousands of fulmars hang around the trawlers all through the trawlers' range, from the North Sea and Rockall Bank through Bailey and Iceland fishing-grounds north to more arctic waters; and virtually all the present breeding fulmars are within range. Only lately has the fulmar population become so big that the trawler offal discharged may no longer amount to absolute super-abundance for it; and only lately has the geometric increase of the fulmar – still going on at compound interest – begun to slow up.

The nearest bird we have to an albatross in our North Atlantic waters, the lovely fulmar, is a glider, a wave-slope soarer, nearly a dynamic soarer. It makes distance at sea, like its large cousins, by sailplaning and tacking, with a style that has driven my best sailor and glider-pilot friends into raptures. It scarcely uses its engine when the wind blows (and the rougher the better). It holds its wing more stiffly in gliding and tilting than any other British bird, and to do this has a wider collar-bone, at the breast end, than that of any other bird I know of.

This grey ghost glider of stormy seas is a primitive bird, of ancient design, as fossils teach us. It is a rather unexpected animal to have become, in an odd way, a dependent of man and – through this dependence – the most consistent colonist of any wild bird.

CHAPTER 4

The Migrants

As I write it has just been announced that Sir Landsborough Thomson, a grey eminence of British Ornithology if ever there was one, is retiring from the chairmanship of the Ringing and Migration Committee of the British Trust for Ornithology after twenty-eight years.

Landsborough Thomson, who wrote the standard work on bird migration in 1926, before the B.T.O. was even invented, is (happily for us all) living proof that the global revolution in bird-migration study spans a human lifetime and no more. Thomson and the late Harry Witherby were the first to start banding wild birds with numbered rings, simultaneously in 1909, in Scotland and England respectively. Numbered bands had been used earlier only in Denmark (since 1899), North America, Germany and Hungary. Thomson's and Witherby's drive, enthusiasm, administrative ability and example have caused the ringing, already, of over 3 million wild birds in Britain and Ireland, which share the same national scheme. Only U.S.–Canada (who also share) and Germany have bigger scores, with about 15 million and nearly 4 million respectively. About 35 million birds have been marked the world over by now, and well over a million of them have been recovered. Yet the technique of ringing, in its modern form, is even slightly younger than the art of recording animal sounds (p. 174).

The study of migration in general, and banding in particular, probably occupies most of the millions of man-hours now annually spent on serious ornithology every year, all over the world. Yet 200 years ago, even the best field men, like Gilbert White, were intelligently puzzled over the rival claims of migration and hibernation. A hundred years ago just a few eccentrics of forward-looking mind – Middendorff in Russia, Gätke in Germany, Audubon, Bachman and Baird in North America, had a proper appreciation of the network of bird flyways that entangles our planet, over every square mile of which the shadow of a migrant must probably at some time have fallen. Migration is an old process: among the birds it must be at least 40 million years old, if we can assume (as seems reasonable) that the modern genera of curlews, redshanks and sand grouse that lived already so long ago were as marked migrants as their descendants are now.

Human appreciation of migration is an old process too, doubtless going

Fair Isle; the Bird Observatory in the foreground, the Sheep Craig in the distance. The most interesting and exciting bird-migration station in Europe.

back to the oldest Stone Ages. But the scientific investigation of it, and the present beginnings of its understanding, are of our generation almost, and were no part of the acts and thoughts of all but a tiny handful of our great-great-grandfathers. As we see (p. 227), co-operative ornithology is not much more than a century old. The co-operative investigation of migration (the only key method in the long run) is even younger in Britain and Ireland. Not until 1879 did pioneer Harvie-Brown (p. 229) and his friend John Cordeaux send questionnaires to those peculiarly well-sited observers (as far as flyway-points are concerned), the lighthouse-keepers of remote islands of Shetland, Orkney, Caithness, Ross, Aberdeen and Fife. Not till 1901 did W. Eagle Clarke, at the Eddystone, start a programme of personal visits to wild islands (and even lightships like the Kentish Knock) at migration time, that brought him and other youngish and energetic island-lovers (R. M. Barrington, Norman Kinnear, the Duchess of Bedford) to an early under-standing of the complexities of bird season and movement. Fair Isle – Europe's classic nodal point for migration and its study – was not pioneered until 1905.

Today the Bird Observatory on the Fair Isle is a Mecca for international field men and women, with a quite sophisticated laboratory, and a staff that even plays a vital part in the economy of this glorious Shetland island. Today our veteran pioneers like Thomson can visit different national ringing scheme headquarters and find that what they started must now be food for computers and IBM machines. Survivors (and there are quite a few) of evenings round the fire in the Duchess of Bedford's croft on Fair Isle, or in the manse or factor's house on St Kilda around the First World War can cogitate that the few score like minds of those days (a good proportion of them doubtless round the same fire) have turned into thousands. In 1965, as I work it out, twenty Bird Observatories were manned in Britain and Ireland for full spring and autumn migration watch, and were represented on the Bird Observatories Committee of the B.T.O. as full followers of its long-worked-out systems and disciplines. Each operated watch-routines, several harmless traps (particularly the great funnel traps pioneered by the Germans on Heligoland), special plans of research, correlated their work with the now highly sophisticated meteorological records available, and had

---

Migration Study Map of Britain and Ireland (opposite)
As they operated in and around 1964 or 1965, the principal Bird Observatories, Field Study or Research Stations, Ringing Stations and Migration Watch Points are plotted, as are Lighthouses, from which intermittent observations have been made since pioneer times. Inland there is a rapidly developing system of Daily Bird Count Points (formerly known as Inland Observation Points), Radar-Stations from which birds are monitored, and Field Study Centres from which DBCs are usually made. Note also that at many of the Bird Reserves in Britain and Ireland (map on p. 143) regular migration logs are made. As the inland system is in the process of rapid change by trial and error, and is unlikely to stabilise for some time, the inland plots are confined here almost solely to the Field Study Centres and inland Research and Ringing Stations of some long standing. Some duck-ringing decoys now inactive are omitted. The map will be quite out of date in a few years, so rapidly does the sport and hobby of migration watching develop under the drive and leadership of the British Trust for Ornithology's Ringing and Migration Section.

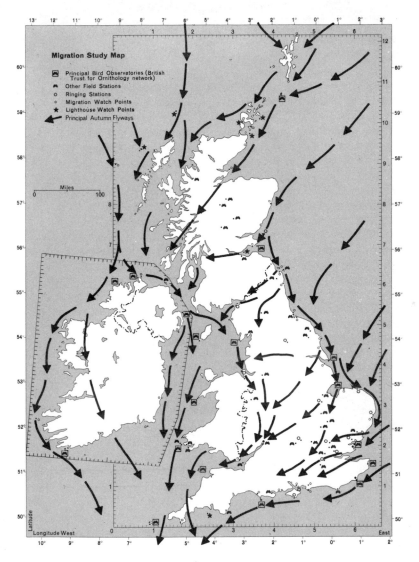

Full locations and grid references of the places are given in Chapter 11, pp. 234–95. The principal coastal and inland autumn flyways presently recognised are shown, largely after Thomson and Simms; they should be read with the reservation that broad-front migrations take place on a large scale and that the arrows, being diagrammatic, only summarise trends and are simplifications of a complex and variable system.

a marvellous time. Only the directors, wardens and a handful of housekeepers, helpers and B. T. O. headquarters staff were paid, and at no princely scale. The visiting workers paid, moreover, board and transport for the privilege and joy of doing their work.

Besides these twenty main Observatories, from Jersey to Malin Head, from Dungeness to the Fair Isle, at least another thirty-three Observatories, field and research stations, some but not all primarily ornithological, carried out routine and useful migration work and ringing. About eleven more units modestly claimed to be not observatories, but simple Ringing Stations, yet one – the duck station at Abberton in Essex – probably ringed more birds than any other. And at thirty-nine other places, nearly all on the coast, Migration Watch Points were manned, in both spring and autumn, by a valiant roster of recorders of visible migration some of them with portable traps for more opportunist, non-programme banding. Throughout this astonishing network, the recovery of a bird at one place, banded on the same passage at another, was the cause of excitement, but not enough for a trunk call – a postcard did!

It is a general belief that an active ornithologist wedded to a self-imposed programme of research, spends if he is lucky one hour in the field to nine in the laboratory or library. It can be understood that the results of a vast seasonal activity of a thousand registered bird-banders and as many helpers, friends, colleagues and supporters cannot all be digested by those who enjoyed it. Through what are now well-organised channels, all ringing data, recorded under a severe discipline and drill, are piped by the wardens and ringing-party leaders to the Tring headquarters of the B. T. O., which took over the *British Birds* ringing scheme from the late Harry Witherby in 1937. Visual data and notes are likewise channelled to the B. T. O. migration staff, headed by Kenneth Williamson and Peter Davies, both with vast experience as ex-Directors of the Fair Isle Observatory, and bolstered by both staff and volunteer analysts. The process of digestion proceeds with punctuality: though it is certain that computers will have to take over to a great extent, as soon as the not heavily financed bird world can afford the use of them. The end products arrive in small-print-detail, and a state of some statistical elegance, on the pages of *Bird Study* and *British Birds*: the modern birdwatcher, who has nourished and grown it as a member of his team, likes to eat meat. Bird-migration papers in the serious journals are twice as terse now, but ten times as detailed as those of a generation back.

Between the wars the "flyway" theory of bird migration streams, developed as much in North America as anywhere else, led to a rather oversimplified idea of the migratory paths of birds. These were presented much as a delta of rather constrained flypaths over the continents and countries, particularly along their coasts. Of course, it is true that such flyways exist,

Fulmar

Peregrine

Lesser black-backed gull

Stonechat

Osprey

Crossbill

A cock capercaillie at Loch an Eilein in the great Cairngorm National Nature Reserve in the Highlands, with two hens—one in a pine, the other the object of his nuptial display. One of the osprey recolonists flies over with a trout. *Donald Watson*

Donald Watson

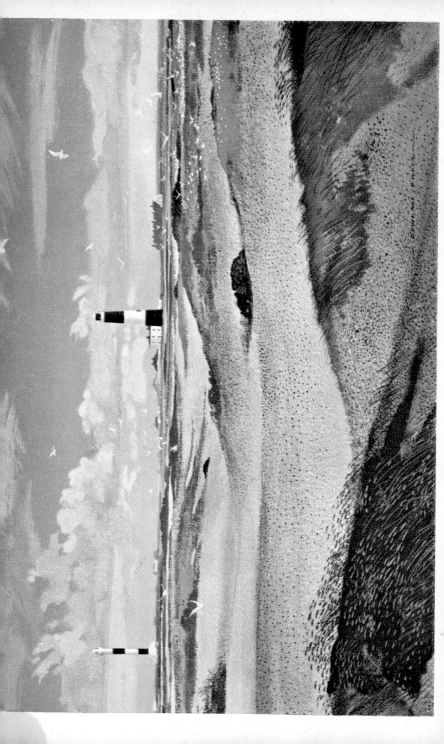

and this is particularly so in North America where the coasts and mountain ranges, and the lowlands and many rivers between them, tend to lie in migration's main north–south direction much more than they do in Europe. But even in Europe a picture of coastal flyways, and mountain-pass through-ways, was offered as a true and full representation of the migratory system until well after the Second World War. Again, the coastal flyways *do* exist, and Fair Isle has the Fair Isle Observatory because it *is* on a flyway, and specially attractive for landfall owing to its isolated position between Shetland and Orkney. But the extent of inland broad-front migration over Europe, and particularly over Britain and Ireland is now known to be very great and very important. What has led to this realisation, most of all, is radar. There were pre-radar bird-watchers who suspected it; but radar has proved it.

The British, who invented radar, were the first to discover, in 1941, that radar could "see" birds. It is not altogether coincidental that David Lack, Director of the Edward Grey Institute at Oxford, who has published migration papers over the last decade deeply analytical and thoughtful, was a radar boffin in the Second World War and rapidly got to work in the 1950s, when high-powered radar became very sophisticated, with colleagues Harper, Tedd, Eastwood and others, on what soon became the monitoring of practically all important bird movements over radii of eighty miles or more. Data began to accrue of the greatest precision, on the speed, density, height, direction and space-distribution generally of the migrant movement as a whole. Soon it was possible to arrive, with the help of controlled visual checks, at identification of the main species involved; and at the same time to collate movements with wind, visibility and other climatic conditions to an extent up to then undreamed of. More lately, workers like Glen Schaefer with their own short-range radar have adapted their tools to follow individual birds across up to eight miles of country, and not merely identify them but extract data on their flight mechanics and physiology hitherto quite unexpected.

The radar breakthrough has *not* become a substitute for conventional migration-watching and banding. On the contrary, it has stimulated a return to the binoculars. I have shown that over a hundred mainly coastal stations were occupied in 1965, by organised groups of migration students: but this was not all. When, in 1962, it was realised that the existing observer-network was so coastally deployed that it would not detect many large inland movements proved by radar, the B.T.O. started to encourage the establishment of a network of Inland Observation Points. Analysis has

The great R.S.P.B. Reserve at Dungeness in Kent, home of the only breeding common gulls in England, is visited yearly by about 170 bird species. *Rowland Hilder*

48. Aug 5   The swift. *Hirundo apus*. seems to be gone.

The stone-curlew, *charadrius ædicnemus*, clamours late in the evening.

Hot summer weather with an high glass, after months of black wet days.

6. The martins, *hirundines agrestes*, begin to congregate on the brash of the may-pole.

Dews large, & white.

Gold finch, *carduelis*, sings still.

Green finch, *Chloris*, chirps.

French & African marrigolds blow.

Winged ants, the male ants, begin to appear.

7. Broad-leaved spurge, *tithymalus platiphyllos* goes into pod. It is a tall, handsome plant.

Lychnidea, *Phlox foliis lineari-lanceolatis, caule elatior, floribus in longam spicam dense spicatis*, begins to flower.

Wheat is beginning to be cut: in many fields it seems to be much blighted.

White maudlin blows.

Yellow-hammer, *emberiza flava*, sings still.

Winged ants forsake their nests.

Laurustines bud for bloom.

(*Above*) A page of one of Gilbert White's diaries, covering 5–7 August 1766. Contrast this admirable but relatively limited record with the sophisticated material (*opposite*) of the British Trust for Ornithology's ringing scheme, with an annual summary return-sheet of birds marked; the recovery data sheet of an individual song thrush; a Hollerith punched slip for mechanical statistical analysis, recording the information from the recovery data sheet above; and one page from a bander's annual detailed return of each and every bird he has marked.

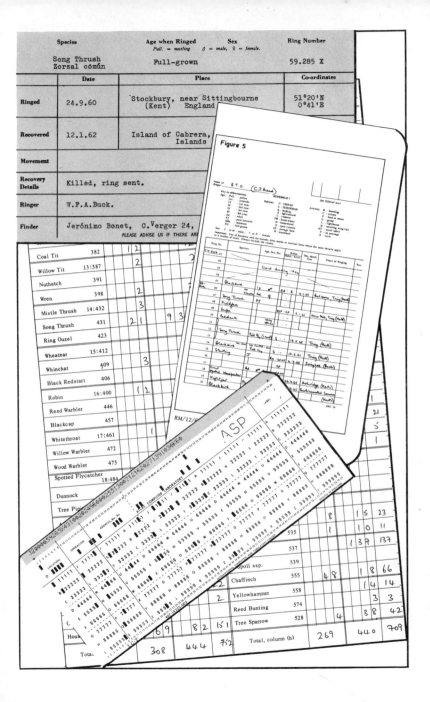

already shown that the system-picture resulting from this timely restoration of the balance of observations bears a far better resemblance to the radar image than the previous caricature based on coastal work. This does not mean that anybody stops coastal work; what it meant in 1965 was that a Daily Bird Count scheme, based on the I.O.P. experience, was started in the spring and is likely to be successful, judging by the early support, and provided the material does not outstrip the analytical resources likely to be available.

All this seems a far cry from Gilbert White's simple log of Arrivals and Departures, so tenderly preserved in the British Museum with the rest of his diary. It is; but it is an evolutionary extension. It is on the family tree. Nevertheless it raises problems. In days not long gone the analysis outstripped the material; now the opposite may be the case. No textbook generalisation of an individual species migratory pattern can any longer be safe. Everybody knew, a generation ago, that a faunal bird book of a country was out of date the day it was published. Today it may be remarkably *false*, however deep the scholarship it was compiled with. A class of analysts will necessarily develop who are not merely migration specialists, or even British or Irish migration specialists, but night-migration or drift-migration or wader-migration specialists. Nobody can even hold in his mind, any more, but the principles and generalisations of others' analysis. No longer the detail. One day not far off a B.T.O. robot computer will be the sole authority on the migration of British and Irish birds; its human slaves content to feed the data in when they have time to fill the forms at the end of their happy holidays, comforted (I hope) that the data-processers they post them to at least, also by way of holiday, have bird-watching fortnights themselves, and press their Achilles heels to the bird-shadowed ground that Ray and White, Montagu and Newton, even later Witherby, once trod with perhaps a simpler idea of what they were doing.

Migration study, complex though it is, still depends – and always will depend – on the observatory and field man, the island-lover, the cape-cliff-haunter, the bunk-sleeper and the sandwich-eater. He can take comfort that his work is now fodder for the solution of deep biological mysteries. With the post-war network of stations and banders and shared information as a background, Kramer, Sauer, and our own G.V.T. Matthews have been able to show us that birds probably navigate as sailors do, by "knowing" the time and by "measuring" the movements of the heavenly bodies – probably also by observing a drift from wave-patterns when out of sight of land. The drift theories will doubtless occupy Williamson, Lack and others for some time before they are thrashed out. That migrational navigation is innate, that is the use of the sun and stars does not have to be learned but is a skill inherited at birth by birds, seems very likely. Without the observer-grid there would be little to base these hypotheses on, far less develop them with.

Four hundred and fifty-five living species of birds have been "acceptably" seen in Britain and Ireland (p. 41). Two hundred and twelve of them are vagrants, and therefore migrants, whose degree of vagrancy has been entirely revised and reassessed by the work of the observatory-grid in the last decade or so. Twenty-five are regular winter visitors, and therefore migrants. Twenty-eight are regular passage visitors, and therefore migrants. Three are non-breeding summer visitors, and therefore migrants. Fifty-four are breeding summer visitors, and therefore migrants. A minority of 133 can be classed as residents, but some of these are partial migrants (that is, a proportion of their population regularly moves), others have marked movements within our islands, and even the most "resident" migrate in hard weather or peculiar circumstances. Birds that do not migrate are *almost* the exceptions that prove the rule that all birds move. It is no surprise this perennial propensity of the birds should be that factor that excites the majority of their devoted followers to pursue them, themselves becoming seasonal migrants to the observation-places, to the cliffs and capes, highlands and islands, sands and strands, refectories and refuges of the globe-spanners.

House martin; an illustration from Yarrell's *A History of British Birds*, 1840. One of the most typical and widespread of our summer visitors.

CHAPTER 5

Bird Protection

The language of bird protection today is complicated, simply because bird-lovers are a powerful minority that can call, when they need to, on what is probably a majority support. Their leaders and political advisers have to wage a careful campaign of tactics and strategy, confrontation and concession, simply because now we are the most heavily industrialised community of Europe. At least this is true of most of England, south Wales and parts of Scotland, which are almost as overcrowded as Bali. The tactics and strategy of the campaign of nature rehabilitation that has been waged in the United Kingdom since the Second World War had to be worked out in a hurried spate of improvisation. If we include National Parks and Areas of Outstanding Natural Beauty, and all reserves and sites of special scientific interest, well over a tenth of England and Wales and close on a thousand separate areas in England, Wales and Scotland are now under some form of administration which demands that nature has special consideration before any change of use and land-exploitation is permitted by our planning authorities. This is fine: but the administrative mind sometimes boggles at the complexities involved.

In Ireland, where population pressures do not yet match those in the rest of the islands, the conservation movement is getting under way with the advantage of less hurry, and with the opportunity of learning from the copious mistakes that have been made during the post-war improvisations of Scotland, Wales and especially England. One thing is certain, throughout: the issues are no longer simple. The bird-lovers' demands have become diverse and complicated. Some want all birds. Some want rare birds. Some want sporting birds. Some want the dear little singing birds but are not so keen on the horrid cuckoos and cruel birds of prey. Some want more birds of prey. Some want birds of special scientific interest. Some still want birds to catch and cage or shoot and stuff, or eggs to encabinet. Some want material that they (and few or none else) can photograph, film or tape-record. Some – perhaps the most enlightened – want good samples, in as pristine a condition as possible, of the ancient, evolving bird *communities* of our island, as living relics whose continued existence is essential to an understanding of what the British–Irish fauna really is, where it came from, and how it evolved. Some hate change and experiment, resist new trends in agriculture, suspect (sometimes with reason) chemical pest control and fertility improvement, and yearn nostalgically for the old days, forgetting that the last full human generation has taken $1\frac{1}{2}$ million acres for housing and industry from an agriculture whose production none the less doubled in its time.

Indeed, our modern problems are a far cry from the earliest ones. The first protectors of birds and conservers of nature, did not, come to that, see what they were doing as the solution of problems. They were kind to birds for love, and as an expression of their philosophical notions of the holiness and beauty of nature as a whole. The first wild-bird-lovers we can detect are the Celtic and Anglo-Saxon saints and scholars, priests and poets, who from the sixth and seventh centuries on, tamed wild animals, made little sanctuaries for them, succoured them, spoke sermons to them, wrote riddles about them, were stirred by their spring voices, felt about them, in many ways, as a child of dawning intelligence feels in its first tottering explorations of field or gardens. Simple though these acts and attitudes were, they are still with us, and still the basis and bedrock of our view of nature. We still conserve nature because nature, like Mount Everest, is there; because someone's got to do it; because nature makes our eyes glisten, and our ears sharp, and our senses smart, and drives us to ransack its secrets, and simplify them in poetic epithets or scientific summaries.

As we have seen (p. 40) throughout the Dark and particularly the Middle Ages the woodland face of Britain began to give way to a farmer's face. Another pressure, partly in the reverse direction, was sport: since the Norman Conquest a widespread system of hunting reserves was developed for the royalty and nobility, whose legacy of place-names comes down to us in the scatter of forests and parks that enliven modern maps. Hunting woodland, falconry and the pursuit of deer (and for a time, boar) occupied significant space and time in the kingdom at least until the Restoration, to be continued in another phase but within much the same rural space by the sporting estates built round the shot-gun, the first instrument that gave men the super-predator's powers of destroying his prey population, and the responsibility of exercising self-limiting ordinances of bag and season if he wanted continued prey to predate. Such self-limiting ordinances had, indeed, been practised since the Dark Ages: we may be pretty certain that the Vikings, who probably founded most of the northern sea-fowling communities and their systems, soon arrived by trial and error at a crop-limit custom in the Hebrides and Orkney and Shetland.

It is interesting to record that only in our nineteenth century did crop-limit custom fail to conserve the balance of the community to any strong extent. Shot-gun man's most important early mistake was the loss of respect for his believed rivals, the animals of prey. Skilful and ruthless enough to assail rival predators to the very last bird and egg, at the turn of the nineteenth–twentieth centuries shot-gun man had depressed to very small populations all but the most tenacious of Britain and Ireland's birds of prey, and succeeded in extinguishing from our breeding list altogether the white-tailed eagle and the osprey. The last stages of the disappearance of these 2 birds were assisted by a particularly eager coterie of collectors, who were prepared to go on until there was nothing left to collect.

Happily the days of St John (p. 92) and other maniacs like Booth and Colquhoun are nearly over, and while there are some very rare species with but a foothold in Britain, whose nesting-grounds are still in danger from and occasionally raided by collectors, a reverse process got well under way in the middle of the current century.

Its arrest by an entirely new factor, the premature large-scale employment of chlorinated hydrocarbons as insect pest destroyers, has put the clock back again, inhibiting (p. 91) what was not long ago believed to be a detectable recovery of the peregrine. Another few years of propaganda, backed with scientific measurement, will be necessary before the birds of prey (most vulnerable of all to hydrocarbons) can be protected fully from the consequences of chemical farming; but there are signs of new sense and late improvements in this sphere, and, on the other side, landowners and keepers are rapidly learning to tolerate, and share nature with, all kinds of birds of prey: hawks, falcons and owls are indeed, now fully protected by law.

The protection laws in Britain have, in the last century, been on the whole ahead of our powers of administration and enforcement. In their modern shape, they have been refined from standards set about a century ago, when there was no real sanctuary and refuge system in our islands to reinforce them. One of the pioneers of bird conservation was the scientific ornithologist and B.O.U. founder Alfred Newton (p. 226) who as much as anybody was responsible for our first really enlightened (though not comprehensive) Bird Protection Act in 1869 (a good bit later than more or less equivalent legislation in Massachusetts, Germany and Holland). It was not only Acts, but action that was needed to put protection on a permanent path. The pioneers of the field conservation of birds in England (apart from the Northumbrian St Cuthbert and the Ilchesters of Abbotsbury in Dorset) were the naturalists of Norfolk, inheritors of an old mantle of curiosity and love of wetlands and countryside that dated back at least to the early seventeenth century (p. 60). By 1888 there were already organised, group-owned and managed bird reserves in East Anglia, with the foundation of the Breydon Society, in a real sense progenitor not only of the Norfolk Naturalists' Trust (first of all such local conservation bodies) but the whole present network of county naturalists' trusts, so nobly assisted, supported and advised by the Society for the Promotion of Nature Reserves.

It is interesting, though not surprising, that local reserve management of the modern type preceded the formation of a national bird protection body. The Society for the Protection of Birds, as it was early called, was virtually founded in 1889 – a full year after the Breydon Society.

Societies like the Royal Society for the Protection of Birds (as it is now entitled) are born in certain climates of opinion, and of certain causes and clashes within those climates. If they are old societies, as the R.S.P.B. now is, the climate in which they operate at present may be quite different from that in which they were born, and the causes for which they stood may have been won, or partly won, and replaced by new, sometimes stronger, descendant causes. No society of the age and standing of the R.S.P.B., that thrives indeed, could have thrived for long on illusion or unreality, and none can thrive without dynamic individuals who become its preachers and politicians and drive it along. It is true to say that the Royal Society for the Protection of Birds had to appear roughly when it did in the last decade of the last century, as to say that the moment and style of its birth owed all to a mere handful of individuals, and in particular to three women.

Most influential and the oldest of bird protection's pioneer women was born Eliza Elder in 1830 and died in 1906. Under her married name of Mrs George Brightwen, she wrote several books about English natural history in the 1890s, in a pleasing and popular style. Eliza Brightwen knew her birds well, and perhaps the most important book she wrote was *Wild Nature Won by Kindness* which was first published in 1890 and went through several editions. I have never been able to discover whether Mrs Brightwen ever belonged to what is now the Royal Society for the Protection of Birds. She certainly does not appear to have joined the famous Fur, Fin and Feather afternoons held at the house of Mrs Edward Phillips in Croydon from early 1889 onwards, nor does she appear to have joined the Manchester Group under the presidency of the Duchess of Portland, which, combined with the Fur, Fin and Feather enthusiasts, formed – in 1891 – the Society for the Protection of Birds. But although Mrs Brightwen may have been administratively inactive, there is no doubt that her books of the 1890s (*Inmates of My House and Garden* and *More about Wild Nature* are the other titles) seriously influenced the opinions of the educated classes of those times about the treatment of wild birds.

Margaretta Louisa Smith, second of the trio of energetic propagandists, was so much influenced by Mrs Brightwen's views, that in later life she used to say that she was inspired by them as a girl of eighteen. Mrs Frank Lemon (as she became) – who died in 1953 in her ninety-third year – may have been a little confused in her reminiscence, for Mrs Brightwen's first book was not published until Margaretta Louisa Smith was thirty. But all who knew the redoubtable Mrs Lemon (and I count myself privileged to have done so)

(*Left*) Margaretta Louisa Lemon, who died in 1953 in her ninety-third year, and (*right*) Winifred, Duchess of Portland, who died in 1954 at the age of ninety-one. Two pioneers of the hard work and builders of the present strong position of the Royal Society for the Protection of Birds. The Duchess of Portland was the Society's President for the astonishing period of sixty-three years.

most certainly believed her oft-repeated boast that in her 'teens she used, when in church, to take a note of the ladies who were wearing plumed hats ("feather bedecked women" she used to call them) and write, upon the following day, to each a letter pointing out the cruelty of a practice which might have meant starvation and death to the orphaned fledglings of un-counted herons and egrets.

The third great lady of bird protection, as many came to call her, was born Winifred Dallas-Yorke, and as the young and beautiful Duchess of Portland became the first President of the Society for the Protection of Birds in 1891. She continued as President for sixty-three years until her death in 1954 at the age of ninety-one. I have never heard of anybody who has been president of anything for longer. I remember well the last Annual General Meeting of the Royal Society for the Protection of Birds, at which the Dowager Duchess of Portland was able to preside. And if her mind, on that occasion, moved among the problems which had excited her in her early pioneer days, such as the plume trade (which had, by then, for some years, been practically legislated out of existence) she made a most masterly speech in which she showed a gracious and simple devotion to the cause of bird protection, and a fine understanding of some of the new problems which it has had (and still has) to face in the post-war years.

The campaign denouncing the wearing of birds' plumage, so enthusiastically taken up by these formidable women, and which led to the official formation of the Society for the Protection of Birds, in 1891, was started, in fact, by Alfred Newton. His original letter of denunciation was published in *The Times* for 28 January 1876, but it took long years and the organised emotions of women to arouse the climate of thinking in which legislation eventually became possible. When the Society began, in 1891, it had a quick success, though perhaps its strong membership of over 5000 by October 1892 owed something to the early minimum subscription, which was two-pence.

In the very first days of the Society the pen of W. H. Hudson was enlisted. I have a pamphlet entitled *Osprey: or Egrets and Aigrettes*, which was first issued in 1891 and for some years was obtainable from the Society's head-quarters in London for a penny or for ninepence a dozen. It is now, needless to say, somewhat of a collector's piece. Many famous naturalists wrote the Society's early pamphlets, including Professor Newton, Mrs Brightwen and Rennell Rodd, whose moving poem, *The Skylarks*, could at one time be obtained for 1s. 3d. a hundred copies. Sir Herbert Maxwell wrote for the Society, as did Sir William H. Flower, Director of the British Museum (Natural History). Some of the men who joined the Society during the first two years of its existence included Lord Lilford, President of the British Ornithologists' Union, Sir Edward Grey, later Lord Grey of Fallodon, J. A. Harvie-Brown, Editor of *The Scottish Naturalist* and a famous authority on the distribution of animal life in Scotland (p. 229) and Dr Bowdler Sharpe, another famous ornithologist. Branches were quickly established in Germany and in Washington, D.C. By 1893 the Society had a sound administrative organisation, with Margaretta Louisa Smith, by then Mrs Frank E. Lemon, as Secretary. W. H. Hudson became Chairman of the Council for a year in 1894. Next year he was succeeded by Montagu Sharpe who remained in office, to the Society's great benefit, until he died in 1942. When the Society became incorporated by Royal Charter in 1904 Mrs Lemon's husband, a distinguished lawyer, took over the Honorary Secretaryship which he conducted until his death in 1935. Mrs Lemon, never much of a scientific ornithologist, but a woman of tremendous drive and a humorous ruthlessness and courage, continued for years as Honorary Secretary of the Publications and Watchers' Committee and preserved her connection with the administrative side of the Society until her death in 1953.

At the turn of the century it became quite clear that the Society was driving into spheres far beyond the narrow, but very vexed matter of the importation of bird plumage. As long ago as 1886, when Sir John Cockburn was Prime Minister of South Australia, a Bird and Arbor Day was celebrated in all the schools of that territory. In 1902 Cockburn suggested, at the Annual General Meeting of the Society, that something of the sort – a Bird and Tree Day – should be established in the United Kingdom, and from this suggestion derive schemes in operation up to this very day – in which the Society offers competitions (regional and national), a club and many facilities for and encouragements to youth. The whole educational activities of the Society really sprang from the Bird and Tree Day scheme. Nowadays they are administered by the hard-working Education Committee, which directs all the Society's copious propaganda activities which embrace, today, our Youth Movement (the Young Ornithologists' Club), their magazine *Bird Life*, ceaseless activity in schools, the design and distribution of posters, wall-charts and leaflets, many courses of lectures and films (the Society has its own film unit) and the Society's main magazine *Birds*. *Birds* (formerly *Bird Notes*) now has a colour cover and a respectable distribution beyond our own membership, competing fairly successfully with commercial magazines on public bookstalls. With its modern, bright layout and keen editorial policy, it compares interestingly with the first issues of a regular bulletin in April 1903, which were headed "Bird Notes and News. A Circular Letter Addressed to Members and Friends of the Royal Society for the Protection of Birds and to all interested in Bird Protection." The early numbers of *Bird Notes*, it must be said, although scrappy, were full of interesting information and effective propaganda, with articles from famous naturalists ranging from W. H. Hudson to Edward Wilson of the Antarctic.

In 1902 a new committee, the Watchers' Committee, began operations under the Chairmanship of E. G. B. Meade-Waldo. It is this committee which now has the duty of managing what can be described as the field half of the Society's activity. The Society is now quite a considerable landowner in its own right, with two dozen reserves totalling about 7000 acres; but besides the chain of sanctuaries which it possesses, and has to staff, it provides the warden management for many others. It also has management agreements with bodies like the West Wales Field Society, which (for instance) looks after the island of Grassholm off the Pembrokeshire coast, a possession of the Society which contains one of the largest gannet colonies in the world. Each year in the season the Society's watchers go to their work from southern England to Uist, the northernmost island of the British Isles.

Before the First World War the agenda of the Society had become full of new problems. On foggy nights hundreds of migrant birds used to fly to their death against the prisms and glass of many of our lighthouses. Many are still killed in this way. The Society learned quickly to alleviate this destruction, first by providing perches for birds below the lights, and subsequently by floodlighting these perches so that the birds could find them. The First World War brought the first really widespread and ghastly corruption of the sea with floating oil, a problem whose solution lies with the managers of international shipping and which would have been solved years ago had more nations followed the line of most European governments, including the British Government. It is worth remembering that Britain passed the Oil in Navigable Waters Act as far back as 1921; and that in 1962 the major oil companies, led by Shell, introduced the "load-on-top" system which makes it virtually impossible for oil tankers using this method to pollute the sea. Three-quarters of all crude oil is now so carried by sea: why is not the rest?

Schoolmasters and schoolmistresses may think that the most important work of the Society today lies in the educational field. Certainly this is a field in which the Society has made great strides, under our past secretaries, the late Robert Preston Donaldson, and the very energetic Philip Brown (now Editor of the *Shooting Times*), and under our present Director, Peter Conder, who has vast experience of our field operations.

To the ordinary bird-watcher our reserve activities appear perhaps most important, for controlled access to our sanctuaries is encouraged and organised, difficult though it sometimes is to accept visitors to some of them in the breeding season without disturbing the birds. The birds come first, but the Society has learnt a lot about permanent hides and watching-boxes since the war, and a visitor to Havergate for instance (our wonderful avocet island on the Suffolk coast) can see all he wants of this great colony of restored British birds without any disturbance to them whatever.

I think that history will judge that the Society's greatest success has been in the improvement of the law. The first comprehensive Wild Bird Protection Bill in this country became an Act in 1880, before the Society existed. It was certainly better than nothing, but had to be modified by a rather rapid series of amending Acts, as the loopholes in it were discovered. Montagu Sharpe and Frank E. Lemon, two barristers who for years formed the backbone of the Society, never felt satisfied that the White List system, brought in with the Act of 1880 and continued with all its amendments, was the right thing, and for years the Society's legal advisers worked on a new bird protection law which would involve the opposite system : that is that all birds should be protected except for game birds in their season, and for other birds which should be specifically named. It was not until after the Second World War that the Government could get around to a Bill on this reverse principle, first promulgated by the Society in the early 1920s. In 1947 the Home Office Wild Birds Advisory Committee was set up to consider and advise the Government on new legislation, and in 1952, as a result of its deliberations, the Government produced a Draft Bill. Times being what they were, however, it found no time to put it through. Fortunately Lady Tweedsmuir, now a Vice-President of the Society, was lucky in a ballot for a Private Members Bill, and with the permission of the Home Office, took over the Government Bill, and aided by the technical advice of the R.S.P.B., guided it through the House of Commons. In the House of Lords she was assisted nobly by her husband, Lord Templewood, and by Lord Hurcomb. The Bill that received Royal Assent on 4 June 1954 bore more than a coincidental resemblance to the drafts, a quarter of a century old, of the Society's barristers, and the Protection of Birds Act, 1954, came into force on 1 December of that year.

Since then the Protection of Birds Act has had its teething troubles, but its impact has already been felt. With new advantages the Society took the initiative in a drive to clean up the remaining illegal egg-collectors and egg-dealers in the country. Some of the denouements in successful court prosecutions disclosed an egg-collectors' ring even more sinister than the Society, in its more pessimistic moments, ever suspected. Although the R.S.P.B.'s magazines and reports have shown that a hard core of quite ruthless egg-collectors quite cold-bloodedly defied the letter and spirit of the Act for some time, this lunatic fringe shows some gratifying signs of disappearing, though some dangerous individuals are known to survive. In so far as egg-collection still has its scientific value, it can be, and is indulged in under licence from the Government. The rest of the hobby seems to be a kind of aggressive kleptomania, coupled with the most naïve schoolboy flaunting of both public opinion and the law. It is certainly true that several of our rarest species have been in grave danger in recent years from egg-collectors, but equally true that the danger may soon be practically removed.

If we make up a profit and loss account of bird protection in the sixty-five years and more since the Society for the Protection of Birds first became active we can say, I am certain, that part of our present riches in Britain of wild, rare birds, is the direct consequence of protection. None of these gains could have been won without a new climate of public opinion, and for that the Society and its writing and broadcasting friends (and there are many of these) is partly responsible. Direct sanctuary management accounts for more gains. Our policy of close co-operation with the Government, and in particular

Bird Reserve Map of Britain and Ireland (opposite)

R. Reserves of the Royal Society for the Protection of Birds; a few are also National Nature Reserves.

N. Other National Nature Reserves which have importance as Bird Reserves; and Wild Bird Sanctuaries of the Government of Northern Ireland.

O. Other Reserves of the Society for the Promotion of Nature Reserves, County

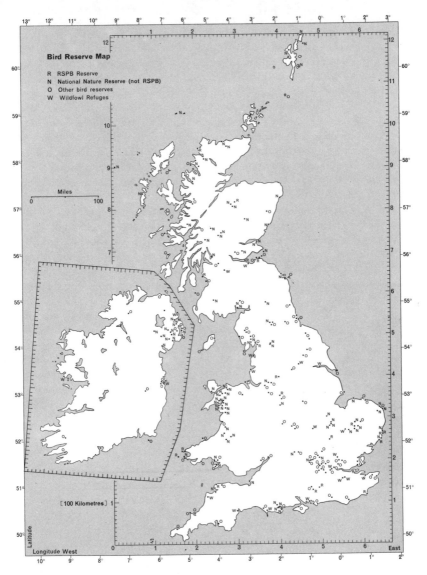

Bird Reserve Map

R RSPB Reserve
N National Nature Reserve (not RSPB)
O Other bird reserves
W Wildfowl Refuges

Miles
0   100

[100 Kilometres]

Latitude
Longitude West

East

Naturalists' Trusts, the National Trust and other private charitable bodies, Local Authorities, Forestry Commission and private landowners which are declared to be Bird Reserves or have importance as such. Some such reserves have been deliberately omitted from the map for security reasons.

W. Wildfowl refuges (national, regional and private).

with the Nature Conservancy, accounts for more. We have still many things to watch carefully, notably the continual erosion of our remaining marshland and wild woodland habitats, the denudation of hedges and cover with the modernisation of agriculture, human population and leisure-pressure on our vast areas of public range-land (which the Society wants to encourage, but can only help by education and propaganda), the administration and enforcement of the current Act, close liaison with aviculturists – the best of whom are as keen as the Society is to see the last of the illegal caging of wild birds; and – perhaps most important lately – research (with the British Trust for Ornithology and many other helpful friends) into the effects of the new chemical poisons with which our agricultural lands have been lately sprayed. That the use of chlorinated hydrocarbons as cereal seed dressings killed very many thousands of birds is indubitable, although since 1961 this use has been restricted. That the poison syndrome has brought some vulnerable species like the peregrine to a danger point is probable. That by good will and hard work this problem will be solved is also probable. I am an optimist; but because I think that the R.S.P.B. way of life will prevail does not mean to say that I believe it can manage without even better public support than it has lately had.

The public support for the R.S.P.B. has lately been good, despite increases of subscription. The membership doubled from a war-time 3500 in 1942 to 7000 in 1953, doubled again to over 14,000 in 1961, and more than doubled again to over 28,000 by the end of 1965. Three doublings in less than a quarter of a century is something: today the R.S.P.B. is probably the largest organisation in the kingdom devoted purely to nature conservation; probably the second largest in Europe, and one of the largest in the world.

Yellowhammer; a woodcut by Thomas Bewick, 1797. As familiar to us now, under this name, as it doubtless was to the eighth-century English under the name of omer, this common bird shares with the vast majority of our avifauna total protection under the Wild Birds Act of 1954.

Crested tit

Bearded tit

Goldeneye

Tawny owl

Kingfisher

Wheatear

Minsmere, perhaps the most important wetland reserve in Britain and Ireland. This Suffolk marsh, a Bird Reserve of the R.S.P.B., is a headquarters of many rare species—marsh harrier and bearded tit among them. *Rowland Hilder*

CHAPTER 6

Bird Gardening

I guess that in every winter now, in every country in Europe, in every state and province in North America, in Japan and some other parts of northern Asia, and in some other countries in the southern hemisphere, hundreds of tons of good and fairly expensive food will be given to the wild birds, on feeding-trays, by broadcast scatter, at the back-door or in what the North Americans call the door-yard.

Richard Fitter's educated guess is that in the terrible winter of 1962–63 the housewives of Britain may have saved the lives of at least a million birds.

Winters like that are mercifully rare in Britain; but we know that about eight times in a century, on average, an island-wide ice-up or white-out puts sources of food outside the foraging range of our resident and winter-visiting land birds; 1962–63 was probably the worst winter of this kind since 1784.

Hard winters with much destruction of birds have been recorded in the literature fairly widely. Some, but not all were accompanied by human famine, which of course was often caused by rain and drought. Famines of the 310s, 360s and 400s we hear of from Roman times; there were others in 446 and 539. The hard winter of 671 is perhaps the earliest we know of in which the destruction of wild birds was recorded by the anonymous Anglo-Saxon chroniclers, though we can guess that it also occurred in the bad famine times of 700 in Ireland, of 791–93 in England (which we know to have been cold), in the 890s, 930–40s, 976, around 1005 (wet), in 1040–44 (wet), 1046 (cold, birds died) and 1069–70 (cold), in 1086–87 (wet) and in 1092–96 (wet). Birds died abnormally on a large scale in the cold years of 1111 and 1115, certainly in the cold famine year of 1124, doubtless in the (mostly cold) famine years of 1143, 1196, 1205, 1217, 1224–25, 1233–34, 1256–58, 1294 and 1315–17, certainly in 1335.

In 1407–08, a cold winter, thrushes and blackbirds and many thousands of smaller birds died of hunger and cold in Britain. More birds died in cold

---

The Farne Islands – looking across Staple Island to the Inner Farne. A sanctuary in the time of St Cuthbert (676 or 677), the Farnes are today a National Trust Reserve. *Richard Eurich*

Redwing: an illustration from Yarrell's *A History of British Birds*, 1838. This winter-visiting thrush from Scandinavia may suffer a population crash in our periodic hard winters.

1462 and 1609. In the eighteenth century bird crashes in cold winters were recorded in 1708, 1716 (many goldfinches died), 1739–40, 1768 (many redwings and other thrushes died), 1776, 1781, 1784 (the coldest year until 1962–63), 1787–90 and 1794–95. Gilbert White's description of the birds in the famous frost of January 1776 is moving. The birds "began to be in a very pitiable and starving condition. Tamed by the season, skylarks settled in the streets of towns because they saw the ground was bare; rooks frequented dunghills close to houses; and crows watched horses as they passed and greedily devoured what dropped from them. . . . The thrushes and black-birds were mostly destroyed; and the partridges by the weather and poachers were so thinned that few remained to breed the following year."

The winters of 1813–14 and 1838 were fatal to many birds, and the terrible cold spell from January to March 1855 (the "Crimean winter") killed not only many residents but also some of the early summer visitors. 1860–61 was another bad winter for the birds, as was that of 1878–79, and that of 1880–81, one of the most intensely cold on record. There was human famine in 1878–81.

The frost from November 1890 to January 1891, lasted continuously for fifty-nine days. In Norfolk the kingfishers, herons and bitterns died of starvation. The mortality among thrushes was very great, and the migratory fieldfares and redwings appeared to have moved out of the country altogether. Even the gulls, which benefit to a certain extent from the deaths of other birds, suffered severely.

In many hard winters in England bad conditions do not extend to the West Country (Devon and Cornwall) and the south of Ireland, and these become a refuge for the very large numbers of the more mobile species. A cold period started in November 1916 that persisted without any important break until April 1917. It was marked by abnormal and persistent snowfalls,

Heron: a woodcut from Thomas Bewick's second volume of 1804. In a very hard winter the resident heron population in these islands is sometimes reduced by half.

followed by drought, which proved the last straw as far as birds were concerned, for fearful conditions then extended to these last western refuges. The report of destruction, written by more sophisticated ornithologists than earlier chroniclers of cold winters, was much more appalling than anything published before. Birds which could scavenge off the bodies of starved smaller birds were not seriously affected; but all native species of finches suffered severely, and there was a heavy mortality of grey wagtails and tree creepers. It was estimated that from 40 to 90 per cent of the great tit population was destroyed, and the long-tailed tit, as sometimes happens in hard winters, was almost exterminated. This species can recover surprisingly quickly from a 90 per cent destruction and after that winter seems to have

Snipe; another illustration from Yarrell's *A History of British Birds*, 1841. In hard winters these waders make long weather-movements; many turn up in gardens.

Fieldfare; a woodcut from Thomas Bewick's 1797 collection. In hard weather this Scandinavian thrush may come to bird-feeders with the more vulnerable redwing.

done so. The bearded tit population of Norfolk was reduced to a few pairs, and there was a marked diminution of that peculiarly British bird (p. 109) the Dartford warbler. All the native thrushes were hard hit but quickly recovered. Stonechats, robins and wrens were seriously – though variably in different regions – decreased. Dunnocks did better than robins. The king-fisher appears to have been exterminated in the upper reaches of the Thames. The larger birds did better, and the herons, where population is often, we now know, halved by a hard winter, seem to have maintained their numbers well: but the stock of coots on one of the Norfolk Broads was reduced to 25 per cent of its previous population.

In 1929 the weather was severe in February and March, and particularly low temperatures were recorded from 11 to 17 February. The thrush family suffered badly, and long-tailed tits were greatly reduced. But most birds, especially the larger ones, were affected seriously only in the extreme parts of England, from which many moved to the refuges of the West Country and Southern Ireland, which remained open. Ronald Lockley, watching the February weather-movement of starlings, redwings, song thrushes, black-birds and others west through the county of Pembroke wrote that "birds were noted dropping into the sea on the very short passage between the mainland and Skomer and on the very small beach were 40 starlings, some song thrushes and a blackbird dead, washed up on the tide-line. On Skok-holm a conservative estimate of the numbers of the chief victims calculated from the remains found was as follows: golden plover 240, lapwing 30, starling and redwing 200 each, and song thrush 100."

The general effect on birds of the severe weather of 1939–40 was far more serious than in 1929, though not so disastrous as 1917, when the cold period was more prolonged. The finches were hard hit, though not all so badly as in 1917. Woodlarks suffered severely, as did grey wagtails. The tits did not

Lapwing; specially drawn by Robert Gillmor, 1966. A resident wader which, despite its mobility, may suffer in the rare general white-outs of Britain and Ireland.

suffer such severe losses as in 1917. The long-tailed tit decreased also very considerably in 1940, and the bearded tit was also reduced. The Dartford warbler was practically exterminated. For the rest, the situation was very much the same as in 1917, except that the kingfisher and the green woodpecker suffered more severely; the heron suffered very severely indeed. Many waders were reduced or driven to make extensive weather-movements.

In the severe winter of 1946–47 bad conditions spread to the West Country and the situation was much the same as in 1940. Nuthatches, which do not always suffer in these hard winters, were hard hit, but the long-tailed tits were not affected quite so generally as in 1940. Once more the bearded tit was practically exterminated in Norfolk, and the Dartford warbler in southern England. As usual kingfishers and green woodpeckers suffered severely: the latter species lives very largely on ants in winter and cannot get at the anthills if the ground is frozen hard. The herons' population was reduced to the lowest level recorded since the number of their occupied nests in Britain was first scientifically measured in 1928. Skylarks and redwings were very badly hit. The 1947 bird crash was investigated specially not only in England, but also in Scotland and Ireland where conditions were similar. The waders were hard hit, especially curlews and lapwings. A large invasion of waxwings from Scandinavia reached Ireland.

There was another hardish winter in 1955–56, covered by several local groups with long-term programmes of population study. It reduced some bird populations, but produced no crash or national survey. But the very severe winter of 1962–63 was covered more intensively by the biggest network of bird-watchers ever deployed in Britain and Ireland, and analysed with more sophisticated methods than had been hitherto employed by M.M. Dobinson and A.J. Richards (in *British Birds* journal for October 1964).

Generally the history of these cataclysms is a terrible one at the time; but the recovery of most species is rather swift, even with slow-breeding birds, and populations may be back to normal in two years. Even the apparently vulnerable species with small populations, and those on the edge of their range, such as the bearded tit and the Dartford warbler, can show extraordinary powers of recovery. This applies particularly to the bearded tit which, unlike the Dartford warbler, is a migrant to some extent and wanders much in weather-changes. Though 1946–47 seems to have wiped out the entire British bearded tit population except for 1 male, England was probably recolonised from Holland in 1948. The Dartford warbler, an indigenous race, *could* be pushed over the threshold of no return more easily. It was not in 1962–63; but it nearly was.

It is too early for the analysts to report fully the recovery *after* 1962–63, with the aid, for the first time, of a large amount of material on modern nest record-cards. But the details of the crash itself are with us in fine detail. Man-given food provedly saved lives. To quote the organisers: "Kingfishers, grey wagtails, goldcrests, stonechats, wrens, barn owls, snipe, long-tailed tits and green woodpeckers, in that order, were apparently the most heavily reduced, but a considerable number of other species had decreased to some extent; almost all those species which in Britain are near the northern limit of their breeding ranges were substantially reduced." Water rails, dabchicks and woodlarks were also hard hit. A few species, though, may even have increased, among them carrion crow, jackdaw, magpie, starling and house sparrow (scavengers or man-associates) and, interestingly, the hardy redpoll.

While the cold spell was still on late in February 1963, I guessed from my own observations, and what checks I could quickly make with others, that it seemed likely that at least half the wild birds living in the country before Christmas 1962 were dead, and allowed myself to be quoted. This seems to have been somewhat of an exaggeration, though the measurements show it probably applied to at least a quarter of our indigenous species, some of which were reduced very much more. It turns out that at least one snow-free oasis persisted in the west Lowlands of Scotland, which attracted many birds, and others got away to the Continent or to west Britain and Ireland before these areas froze up, which they did, but for a shorter time. Lapwings, skylarks and fieldfares, all typical weather-movers, did better than in 1916–17 or 1939–40. I agree with Dobinson and Richards, too, that at feeders, and to an important extent also at sewage-farms and rubbish-tips, man gave the hungry birds of that terrible winter tons of sustenance, and saved vast numbers of them from death.

We have seen (p. 47) that in the middle of the sixth century St Serf of Fife tamed a robin, or so the story goes. To tame a wild robin is to feed one. That in the Dark Ages the country-folk, themselves accustomed to periodic freeze-ups, long rainfalls or droughts and the famines that derived from them, nevertheless shared their food with the door-yard birds seems an axiom. By the Victorian times of over a century ago, when robin redbreast became a principal motif on early Christmas cards, the feeding of the wild birds was doubtless a taken-for-granted social custom, indeed, a ritual. Nearly thirty years ago I analysed many hundreds of answers to a question to the radio public: "Why do you feed the birds?" There were a lot of funny answers, but the only ones that made any sense were common, and can be summarised as "somebody's got to do it". Now, almost everybody does it, who can. It is even big business, with several firms who make up proprietary wild-birds foods making a big, wide trade and spending a lot of money on advertising to promote it. Indeed, the whole business of wild-bird nurture, with not only food but prefabricated nesting accommodation, is Big Time. The human customers and do-it-yourself bird-house builders, the tender tenders of garden and farmyard birds in country, village, suburb or urban area, are legion, and seem to feel their duties pressingly, and so deeply that to them the birds are "their" wild birds, like the family dogs and cats. I do not find this a patronising attitude: on the contrary, it is a very dignified acceptance of a responsibility, and a one-ness with nature, that western and many eastern humans adopt from early childhood, without much senti-mentality, if any at all. People just *do* it.

So here comes an encouragement to the tenders; with an analysis of bird housing and bird feeding, and some notes upon those birds likely to respond to offerings, and sources of the material which should be offered.

Perhaps the pioneer of the modern garden culture of wild birds was the Baron von Berlepsch of Schloss Seebach, a castle and large park in central Germany, who became obsessed, in the 1880s, with the housing and feeding of wild birds in the interest of aesthetics and, as he also thought, insect control. His attitude was far from strictly utilitarian, thus differing from that of the original inventors of nest-boxes and other artificial breeding-sites for wild birds. Nest-boxes must go back in time, of course, at least to the earliest domestication of the rock dove as our domestic pigeon, which seems to have taken place among the Halafian Mesopotamians around 4500 B.C. When the Vikings colonised Iceland a thousand years ago they soon found the eiderdown harvest could be improved by encouraging the nesting popu-lations of eiders to use prefabricated stone shelters. Around the sixteenth century, or perhaps even earlier, the Dutch farmers invented earthenware unglazed pots to hang under the eaves of their barns for the sparrows to nest in: they ate the young ones in pies.

Berlepsch, though – and his many successors – have developed in the last century a new love of bird-boxes and bird-tables, bird-fountains, bird-baths, bird-feeders, grain-hoppers, nut-baskets, tit-bells and the like that are strictly for the birds. The recent discovery that birds may not significantly

Pioneer of wild-bird tending with nest-boxes and feeders, the Baron von Berlepsch of Schloss Seebach, Germany, pouring a fatty food-mixture on to one of his "food-trees" eighty years ago.

control the insect population, and that even if they did to feed them would interfere with this control, does not seem to bother anybody. Everybody feeds the birds, now. In the last three decades, too, the nest-box has come into its own as a scientific instrument for observing and measuring the breeding cycle and ecology of many species of hole-nesting birds.

Let us turn, then, to nest-prefabs and feeders, and the birds that are likely to use them in our islands.

NEST-PREFABS

At one time or another all sorts of materials and objects have been used successfully as nest-prefabs. Many garden bird-lovers I know plant old kettles and tin cans where they are likely to be used by robins. "Boxes" have been made out of natural branch sections, deal boards, compressed hardboard, flowerpots, baskets and baked earthenware.

Effective nest-places have been designed for, and used by, tawny owls and stock doves (H. N. Southern's invention, using 30-inch lengths of 8-inch planking), swallows (wooden trays), house martins (pressed hardboard cups), swifts (long boxes to fit under eaves with an entrance at one end) and tree creepers (strips of bark arranged to resemble a natural crevice).

The main evolution of the man-made nest has been in the direction of the plain deal (cedar is better, though more expensive) box of $\frac{3}{4}$-inch board, 4 inches by 4 inches across and about 6 inches high with sloping tops for standard small birds. The hole: halfpenny (1-inch) size for blue tits and wrens; florin ($1\frac{1}{8}$-inch) size for other tits and nuthatches; half-crown ($1\frac{1}{2}$-inch) for most others, which is not sparrow-proof. The Royal Society for

Dual-purpose nest-box of the Royal Society for the Protection of Birds. The hole-block is being removed to adapt the box to open-nesters, such as the spotted flycatcher.

the Protection of Birds' version has a removable front and can be used, with the front removed, for robin and spotted flycatcher, etc. (see illustration on page 157). Some biggish birds (see detailed list) need more commodious quarters.

Most people put up their boxes between October and December – or clean them out then to prevent the inheritance of parasites by next year's generation. It is always a good idea to do this in the autumn as quite a number of species will use them for roosts, though I have known boxes to be taken over by tits within a week of being nailed up in May.

It is wise to fix boxes, out of reach of cats, on a northerly or easterly exposure to shadow them from high sun. They should hang vertically or with their upper parts tilting slightly forwards as a protection from rain.

FEEDERS

The bird-tenders of today's Britain have spent a million man-hours or more on making tens of thousands of bird-houses; they have sometimes justified this because "little birds are useful insect eaters". They have paid just as much attention, and with as much ingenuity, to contriving feeders, feeder-mixtures, baths and drinking-places. Water is just as important as food in hard weather. My own home has a spring-fed pond that did not freeze in 1962–63, but most of us are not so lucky. Fortunately, a safe electrical device is now available for keeping an outside water-bowl ice-free, which saves the daily labour of putting warm bricks, eight-hour nightlights or old saucepans with hot water under the bowl.

Table scraps are everybody's basis for feeder-meals. The big 1962 apple glut provided a lot of bird food at the right season. Fat, suet, meat bones, cheese rind, *cooked* bacon, nuts, seed, corn, mealworms (not very cheap), bread (brown is best in lean times), halved baked potatoes, oatmeal, halved coconuts (fresh and natural – *not* shredded or dried on any account), are the staples. Shelled peanuts are best served in a basket of $\frac{1}{4}$-inch wire mesh which can be hung from cords.

Some people, who deserve naming, have invented "puddings". Edwin Cohen, the Hampshire ornithologist, makes flat uncooked cakes, floured for easy handling, out of (mixed by ounces) mutton fat (8), coarse oatmeal (12), flour (2 or 3) and water (5). The flour and oatmeal is mixed with liquid fat to form a stiff paste and baked in a shallow pie-dish. H. Mortimer Batten used to make a fat-impregnated bird cake of minced peanuts, cake and bread-crumbs, waste cheese chopped small, a little oatmeal and other ground grains, dried fruits and a little honey. The late Miss E. L. Turner's "maize cake" was based on maize meal (cornflour) mixed in a bowl with chopped nuts, hemp, canary seed and millet seed, stirred with boiling water from a kettle until coherent and consistent, and then tied tightly in a cloth and left

A roofed feeder of the Royal Society for the Protection of Birds. A special grain-hopper can be suspended from the inside of the roof, over the feeding-tray.

to dry; this keeps quite well. Maxwell Knight recommends a simple mix of stale cake and fat with a few dried currants and sultanas. The pudding gives the birds some useful work to do, prevents wasteful scatter and can be put in baskets of ⅝-inch wire netting. Some baskets of spiral wire on the market are *not* recommended – they can catch the feet of tits and injure and even kill them; but one well-designed feeder of this sort is quite safe and approved by the R.S.P.B.

Combined with a good seed-mixture (preferably delivered in a hopper) a pudding should satisfy each and every one of the 50 or so potential table guests that the bird-feeder can attract in Britain. There are now some good wild-bird mixtures on the market and most corn-chandlers will make up their own to customers' requirements. In the seed list, remember all corn grains (particularly wheat, oats – whole or rolled – barley and American "corn" or maize) and sunflower seed, buckwheat and hempseed.

The feeder need not – and some people would even say should not – be a year-round service to the wild birds of our homes. Ideally it should be operated from the first November to the last April frosts plus a little longer for luck, and placed where shy birds can reach it mostly through cover.

When breeding times come, most of the feeder birds and those who do not need wild vegetable food to rear their young, go over to animal food. It is in the November–April period that we can materially affect their survival by feeding them, though many believe that feeding in late summer or early autumn droughts can also save lives.

Ideally, feeders should be roofed. To avoid raids by cats, squirrels and rats they should be suspended (see illustration on p. 159), or erected on smooth poles. Window-ledge or wall feeders should be carefully sited where cats cannot reach or closely watch them.

THE BIRDS OF THE PREFABS AND FEEDERS

These are offered in the systematic order of the *Bird List* of pp. 300–38. Some are by no means garden birds, but all have responded or could respond to the provision of accommodation or food in Britain and Ireland, or have at least come to feeders if only to eat the feeders at the feeders. The word "corn" embraces all cereal grains including American corn or maize. Box dimensions are internal, and as recommended by the British Trust for Ornithology.

Fulmar. Has nested on prefabricated wooden sheltered "ledges" let in to the crumbly cliffs of north Norfolk by the Gresham's School Natural History Society, who like to study these fine birds at their most south-easterly English outpost.

White stork. Nests commonly on traditional cartwheels atop poles in Europe, and if it ever showed any signs of returning to Britain as a breeder would doubtless respond to some such device.

Ducks. Nest-boxes for the several hole-nesting species of ducks have been widely used in Europe by landowners wishing to encourage the waterfowl population, and could be used in Britain for goosander, merganser and introduced mandarin duck. On the Continent such prefabs have been used by smew and goldeneye. Eiders, as we have seen, will nest in (open) stone shelters built for them in Iceland.

Sparrow hawk. Comes to bird gardens – but to raid them for small birds, its natural trade. Its present rigid protection extends to it during this occasional activity.

Osprey. If the ospreys ever recover to reach a population such as that still occupying (despite the effect of toxic chemicals) the shores of Long Island Sound in eastern U.S., cartwheels on posts (see white stork), widely used in New York State and Connecticut, would afford safe nesting-places.

Kestrel. Has used large boxes on the Continent, top-opening with 8-inch hole, and the Southern owl or "chimney" box, see above, which also has an 8-inch opening.

Moorhen. Becomes quite tame in some suburbs and parks and comes to ground scatter, feeds off bread, scraps, potato peelings.

Woodcock. In hard weather, even this shy woodland wader has come to eat a well-known proprietary bird food-mixture.

Snipe. In hard weather will come to bird drinking-bowls in largish gardens.

Black-headed gull. A common feeder bird, especially in London : haunts the window-boxes of several bird-lovers I know in Chelsea and Kensington who save their bacon rind in the winter.

Herring gull. Readily tamed to scraps in winter cities, and in some places now nests on buildings.

Kittiwake. Nests in some estuaries on cliff-like warehouse window-ledges, which have been re-jigged as artificial nest-places for the observation of their breeding habits.

Woodpigeon. In towns where tame comes readily to ground feeding-places, for corn.

Stock dove. Can be persuaded to nest in large boxes at least 8×8 inches with 8-inch top-openings.

Rock dove. Domestic form, the domestic pigeon, has used nest-boxes probably a few thousand years longer than any other bird.

Collared dove. Throughout new range in Britain and Ireland tends to colonise chicken-runs and other places where corn is broadcast. Now comes to standard garden feeders.

Budgerigar. "Escapes" of this most populous (now) of our domestic cage birds stand most chance of recapture at garden feeders, so frequently do they come to them. In Florida, where budgies have become truly feral, they use nest-boxes in gardens.

Barn owl. As rodent eater, has been encouraged by our farmers for centuries. Many old barns have built-in barn owl nest-places in the eaves, with open-front access and spacious boarded box within.

Long-eared owl. Uses duck-type nest-baskets in Holland, and could doubt-less be encouraged to use something of the sort in our islands.

Little owl. In hard weather will sometimes take small birds at garden feeders, or even scrobble birds using nest-boxes to roost in as they venture out. Will use large top-opening nest-boxes as long as inside width is nearly 8 inches.

Little owl, from a late woodcut by Thomas Bewick. This reintroduced species will raid feeders in hard weather, to catch its own food – the other birds at the feeder.

Tawny owl. Will use large top-opening or chimney boxes with 8 inch internal width; H. N. Southern invented the chimney box specially to study them.

Swift. Dr David Lack's important life-history study was helped with special wooden prefabs adapted to the eaves of the University Museum, Oxford. Horizontal nest-boxes, about 18 inches long, 8 inches wide and 5 inches high, with entrances at the end, or *below* towards the outside, could be adapted for church towers, etc. The E.G.I box is described in the B.T.O. *Nestboxes* (Field Guide No. 3), as are many others.

Kingfisher. Nests in longish horizontal burrow in bank; yet has been attracted to prefabs engineered into river-banks from which events in the nest have been filmed for B.B.C.

Hoopoe. Uses longish nest-boxes in Europe, and could be persuaded to in Britain, on the few occasions when the opportunity arises.

Wryneck. A summer visitor, rare and decreasing, but still using boxes in its south-east England range. R.S.P.B. box (hole version) suitable.

Green woodpecker. In some (not all) of the range is a regular table-feeder on nuts and fat; likes mealworms. Will nest in box at least $5 \times 5 \times 15$ inches with $2\frac{1}{2}$-inch hole.

Great spotted woodpecker. Has become a regular feeder-user all over its

British range. Loves fatty stuff and big seeds, almonds, maize cake. Will nest in boxes at least 5 × 5 × 12 inches with 2-inch holes. Started life as a feeder and box-nester only fifty years ago, but has got around to the habit widely in the last twenty years.

Lesser spotted woodpecker. Though very shy, has come to some bird-tables, where it likes nuts and hempseed. Uses nest-boxes on Continent and could take to R.S.P.B. box (hole version) in England.

Skylark. In hard weather will come to seed-mixture on ground.

Sand martin. Has been attracted to nest in experimental boxes of a tunnel type in cliffs and banks.

Swallow. Half-coconut shells, simple wooden trays, or even R.S.P.B. boxes (open front), when suitably placed, have encouraged swallows to build their mud nests on the beams of barns and outhouses.

House martin. A clay or hardboard prefab, which can be attached under eaves and windows has been proved to encourage martins to colonise new buildings. They may use them or build their own mud nests adjoining.

Grey wagtail. Quite often visits feeders in hard weather, though normally mainly insect-eating. Could doubtless use R.S.P.B. box (open front) if placed under bridge, culvert or in some natural nest-site.

Pied wagtail. At feeders as grey wagtail: will eat *soaked* food and house waste. Uses R.S.P.B.-type boxes (open front) on houses, walls, etc., quite often.

Waxwing. Visits Britain irregularly in winter, most abundantly in east Britain, where it feasts on berries and has come to feeders in hard weather.

Wren. Unlikely to come to table-feeder, but in very hard weather will take feeder seeds on *ground*. Nests fairly often in R.S.P.B.-type boxes, most readily in open-front version. T.L.Bartlett finds it will nest in dead leaves poked into likely corners.

Dunnock or *hedge sparrow.* A regular scrap scavenger under feeder *on ground*; why not scatter seeds there specially for it, or place special ground-tray?

Robin. Will nest in tin cans, old kettles, etc., in rambling growth, readily in R.S.P.B.-type boxes (open front) and even in biggish flowerpots wired horizontally to walls, enlarged drainhole outwards. Universal and favourite table-feeder bird; eats nearly everything and likes mealworms very much indeed.

Black redstart. Uses nest-boxes in Europe, and could be persuaded to here.

Redstart. This pretty summer visitor (rather local in distribution) nests well in R.S.P.B.-type boxes (most often in hole version). Has been tamed to worms, dried insects, maize cake, etc., at some summer feeders.

Wheatear. This ground-nesting bird has been persuaded to use special observation tunnel-type nest-prefabs at Dungeness made of bricks sunk in the shingle.

Blackbird; one of Thomas Bewick's most delightful woodcuts (see p. 66) from his 1797 volume. One of our 3 commonest land birds, the blackbird is a regular at all garden bird-tables.

Blackbird. Our commonest garden bird. Regular at winter table-feeders, and feeder meals help in summer drought. Likes dried currants and berries. May nest in R.S.P.B.-type boxes (open front) or on covered trays.

Fieldfare and *Redwing.* In very hard weather these berry-loving winter visitors from Scandinavia may take feeder seeds, scraps and berries on the ground, the redwing more nervously and less readily.

Song thrush. Only regular at feeders in hard weather or (when food provided) summer drought. Prefers to take food *on ground*, like dried currants and berries.

Mistle thrush. Rare at feeders in England; only comes in hard weather and

Pied flycatcher, another woodcut from Thomas Bewick's 1797 collection. A regular hole-nester, this bird freely uses nest-boxes of suitable design (see p. 157).

usually feeds on ground. May be more feeder-adapted in Scotland, where some eat at table.

Blackcap. A minority of these common warblers winter in Britain and will come to the bird-table for crumbs and scraps in hard weather, also *soaked* foods, berries and fruit.

Whitethroat. A common summer visitor which has occasionally been known to use open nest-boxes and come to feeders.

Goldcrest. In wooded areas may sometimes come to the winter table for fatty foods.

Pied flycatcher. Freely uses R.S.P.B.-type nest-boxes (hole version).

Spotted flycatcher. A familiar late arrival that will use R.S.P.B.-type boxes (open front) readily on creeper-covered house walls.

Long-tailed tit. Nests quite differently from the other tits (own domed feathery nest) and does not use boxes; may indeed not belong to the tit family. Usually shows up at feeders only in extreme cold, when will eat fat, crushed and soaked dog biscuits, soaked chicken meal, household waste.

True tits (the genus *Parus*; the 6 following birds). These are *the* great nest-box (R.S.P.B. type, hole version, often roost in them in winter) and feeder-table birds; also (since the early 1920s when the habit began to spread) some are cream-robbers from milk-bottles. Those marked * will take food away and store it. All should eat meat on bone, coconut (*not* dried, which is dangerous to their digestion, but natural); peanut, fat, suet, crumbs, apple and pear, sunflower seeds and maize cake.

The tree creeper: an illustration originally published in Yarrell's *A History of British Birds* in 1839. This bird has been known to nest in special crevice-like boxes.

Marsh tit* also likes small seeds.

Willow tit is a rare box- and feeder-user.

Crested tit* (limited range in Scotland) uses boxes and has visited feeders.

Coal tit*.

Blue tit.

Great tit also likes hempseed.

Nuthatch. Will use R.S.P.B.-type nest-boxes (hole version). A regular feeder bird, specially fond of hazel nuts (its natural autumn food), other nuts, hempseed, sunflower seeds, fruit kernels, maize cake and fat; may take food away and store it.

Tree creeper. Nests normally in a narrow crevice behind tree-bark, which can be successfully imitated by special nest-boxes, although it will nest in R.S.P.B. boxes (hole version). Eats almost entirely animal food through the year and does not come to feeders.

Snow bunting. Has nested in boxes in Iceland and Spitsbergen. Has visited Scottish feeders in winter, and taken proprietary food-mixture.

Yellowhammer. Though an open-field hedge bird, the widespread yellowhammer will come regularly to feeders in adjoining gardens. By nature it is mainly a seed eater, especially in winter; will take hemp, millet, corn, canary seed, maize cake and grit at feeder.

Finches (next 11 birds). Do not use boxes; most like hempseed, millet, canary seed, corn, maize cake and grit at feeders.

Chaffinch. Britain's commonest finch. Basically a weed-seed feeder, is much attracted to canary seed at the bird-table, where always a regular. Its closest relative in our islands is the *brambling*, regular winter visitor to east Britain from Scandinavia, which sometimes visits feeders.

Chaffinch; specially drawn at a bird-table by Robert Gillmor, 1966. Britain and Ireland's commonest finch, the chaffinch will come freely and regularly to feeders.

Canary. Escaped examples of this long-domesticated finch naturally gravitate to the nearest feeder.

Greenfinch. Common. An eater of corn and weed seeds, green shoots and buds. A regular table-feeder, likes hempseed and sunflower seed and is one of few British birds that likes buckwheat.

Siskin. A mainly northern tree-seed finch which is so far almost unknown at feeders in our country.

Goldfinch. A handsome bird now increasing its range. In nature eats small seeds, especially those of thistles, teasels, etc. Occasionally at table-feeders, where it likes hempseed.

Linnet. A commonish bird of scrubby land; a weed-seed eater that hardly ever comes to feeders – but you never know your luck.

Redpoll. Close relation of the linnet. Most commonly known at feeders in Scotland, can cling to nut-baskets and wooden bells like tits. Natural food is seeds, including many tree seeds, especially those of alder and birch. ·

Crossbill. Breeds in the remains of the ancient pine forests of Scotland and (another race) in some scattered evergreen woods in the rest of the kingdom. Though a specialised conifer-seed eater, will come to table-feeders within its range, where it is very fond of sunflower seed.

Bullfinch. A weed-seed, tree-seed and berry eater that sometimes visits feeders, though shy and wary.

Hawfinch. Our biggest native finch, shy and local. Naturally eats large seeds and kernels of all kinds. Visits bird-tables more often than supposed, for quick feeds on big seeds and nuts before darting back to cover.

House sparrow. Nests freely in all hole-type boxes, with holes of half-crown size or greater. Used to be farmed for food in olden days in special earthenware "sparrow·pots". Abundant and regular at feeders, where it eats almost everything, especially hempseed, millet, canary seed, corn, maize cake and grit.

Hawfinch; a woodcut by Thomas Bewick, 1797. A shy bird, but more widespread than generally supposed, our biggest finch may visit feeders quite often.

Tree sparrow. More widespread than most of us suppose. Takes readily to R.S.P.B.-type boxes (hole version) for nesting and roosting. Naturally less omnivorous than its cousin; a seed specialist. Tends to visit bird-tables mainly in hard weather.

Starling. Nests in almost any box at least 12 inches square with 2-inch hole. One of the most abundant and successful of all our birds, especially in winter when there is a huge influx from northern Europe. Omnivorous (about half vegetarian); a small hungry gang can clear a feeder-table in a few minutes.

Jay. This handsome, wary crow will become regular at feeders in big towns and sanctuaries where it is not hunted by gamekeepers. Likes acorns (stores them in holes), big seeds and corn.

Magpie. Remarks as for the jay; but even shyer and warier. Often makes quick raids on table just after dawn or before dusk for corn.

Chough. This rare coastal bird will use artificial covered nest-sites in ruins.

Jackdaw. Will nest in boxes at least $7\frac{1}{2} \times 7\frac{1}{2} \times 17$ inches with 6-inch hole. (If these are used it may discourage them from trying chimneys.) In hard weather comes to bird-table for anything it can get and will chase and rob small birds carrying food away from it.

THE BIRD GARDENER'S EQUIPMENT

The following suppliers are recommended.

Bird-boxes and feeders

(a) Royal Society for the Protection of Birds, The Lodge, Sandy, Beds., can supply a catalogue of their present excellent range including a *dual-purpose nest-box* (illustrated p. 157), roofed *bird-table* (illustrated p. 159) with seed-hopper that can be fixed to window-sill, *scrap-basket* and *nut-basket*. The R.S.P.B. are experimenting scientifically with new types of feeders. Why not ask for membership details when writing?

(b) Dept 12, Birdcraft, Greenrigg Works, Woodford Green, Essex, has a wide, good range of *nest-box* and *bird-feeder* equipment, tested over many years. Write for list.

(c) Clent House Gardens, Clent, Worcs., sell *house martin prefabs* (invented and made by the Swiss) for 12s. 6d. each, post free.

(d) Tomtit Products Ltd, Lockwood Beck, Lingdale, near Saltburn, Yorks., sell *tomtit feeder*, a safe (R.S.P.B. approved) spiral-wire feeder for 5s. each, post free.

(e) Paul Davy, Pendrea House, Gulval, Penzance, Cornwall has a range of tit feeders and feeder-tables. Write for list.

Bird-bath heater

Forrest Transformers Ltd, 349 Haslucks Green Road, Shirley, Solihull, Warwickshire, make a mains-fed heater which can keep the water in any bird drinking-bowl or small bird-bath from freezing in the coldest weather. Present price £2 10s., postage and packing 4s. 0d. Write for leaflet.

Food

Many corn-chandlers make up a wild-bird mixture of their own or to customers' requirements. Of several branded bird foods on the market *Swoop* (from all grocers and pet shops) has twelve ingredients, has been tested by and is recommended and used by the R.S.P.B.

Look is a wild-bird food produced by Armitage Bros, 29–31 Castlegate, Nottingham, which sells in polythene packets for 1s. 9d., and keeps indefinitely. It is a blend of grain and seeds made up to attract all British wild birds and is stocked by Boots the chemists and most pet stores.

Mealworms can be bought from many pet shops or from E. W. Coombs Ltd, Cross Street Works, Chatham, Kent, who are bird-food specialists.

Also bird-food specialists with a wide range of *wild-bird food*, including foods for song birds and other insect eaters, are John E. Haith Ltd, Dept B.N., Park Street, Cleethorpes, Lincs. Write for list.

FURTHER READING

Nestboxes by Edwin Cohen (revised edition which is the last word and has the greatest detail on the subject) is a booklet price 3s. 0d., post free, from the British Trust for Ornithology, Tring, Herts. Why not ask for membership details when ordering?

The Bird Garden by P. H. T. Hartley. A booklet price 1s. 2d., post free, from the R.S.P.B., The Lodge, Sandy, Beds.

Bird Gardening by Maxwell Knight, published in 1954 at 10s. 6d. by Routledge and Kegan Paul Ltd, 68 Carter Lane, London, E.C.4.

Photographing Garden Birds by C. H. S. Tupholme, published in 1962 at 18s. 0d. by Faber and Faber Ltd, 24 Russell Square, London, E.C.4.

Birds at My Door by E. Catherine Clements, 16s. 0d., Faber and Faber Ltd (1963).

Birds in the Garden by Ian Woodward, published in 1963 at 1s. 6d. by Take Home Books Ltd, 4 Fitzroy Square, London, W.1.

The Bird Table Book by Tony Soper, published in 1965 by David and Charles (Publishers) Ltd, and obtainable from R.S.P.B. for 22s. 0d., post free.

CHAPTER 7

Bird Song

The earliest bird-watchers we know of in our islands were inspired to be so, doubtless, by the song of birds, as we shall see. They knew the nightingale as an artist songster, listened to the ominous cuckoo; there came to charm the Seafarer (p. 43) the pother of the gannet, and the happy trill of the whimbrel and the voice of kittiwake and tern, whooper swan and erne.

In the long language of evolution, bird voices are as old as birds, that is to say about 140 million years old. *Archaeopteryx* which lived in Bavaria in the last of the Jurassic times was a very reptilian bird, doubtless descended from small, already feathered representatives of the dinosaurian reptiles. We need have no doubt that it was noisy, and by voice communicated with others of its kind. Probably it guarded a territory in its woodland home: reptiles are territorial (and for that matter, also fishes). It is doubtful, though, whether it sang; that is to say produced an organised, ritualised pattern of special musical sounds peculiar to its kind, with scope for variation (individual variation particularly), sound combination and recombination. It certainly could not have approached the higher avian musicians of today. These, as Charles Hartshorne seems first to have had the courage to suggest in a scientific journal, are proprietors of a primitive form of music, which is "an evolutionary anticipation of human music". They use musical devices which are comparatively elementary, but nevertheless properly musical: they avoid mechanical regularity; they *learn* songs and tunes. Hartshorne correctly recognises, in the song of the more "sophisticated" birds, "the partial detachment from utility, and the playful cultivation of sound production: and the tendency of species with more elaborate and, by our criteria, more 'musical' songs to spend a larger fraction of the minute, day and year singing".

That no serious mainstream scientist and behaviour student would really admit, indeed positively demonstrate, that bird song could be a form of art until 1958, proves the point that poets' intuition may sometimes reach the truth sooner than the searchings of scientists. For years the bird-song analysts had been overwhelmed (and correctly – first things first) with the detection and diagnosis of the biological function of song. They have not quite worked it out yet, and still argue deeply. But the musical, artistic, superstructure is now also conceded. Birds *are*, or some can be, musical poets – as the bird-lovers from Aristophanes to Aristotle, from Pliny the Elder to C. P. Olina, from Aldhelm and Alcuin to Keats and Clare have been trying to tell us all along. It is probable that birds have been musicians for about a third of the geological life of their Class. Rather over half of the birds of today belong to one only of three dozen (or so) orders of their class that are now recognised. This order, the Passeriformes, has a majority suborder, the Passeres or Oscines with just under half the living species and rather over a quarter of the living families in it. The Oscines are the musicians, and the first members of their suborder appear as fossils (as tit-like and starling-style birds) in Upper Eocene formations of rock a little more than 40 million years old. Song birds do not get fossilised so easily as the bigger birds and the water birds; but shrikes, warblers wagtails and weavers go back, as families, over 20 million years and larks, nuthatches and buntings about 10 million; and fossils will have to be collected for many years more before we can be sure that these and other song-bird families did not evolve a good deal earlier.

It is possible that whales, only lately discovered to be animals of remarkable intelligence and a power of sound communication (including the use of sonar) of some complexity, may be musicians. If they are they are doubtless older musicians than man. Man, but a quarter of a million years remote from men-apes, but not much more from ape-men and apes, is the greatest musician, but in the evolutionary sense the youngest. As the greatest of the professionals he must have been the first collector of other animals' music – unless the members of a scant half-dozen song-bird families that shine as mimics (of other birds and other animals) can be so regarded. We know the culture of, and writing about bird song goes back to ancient Egypt, Israel, Greece and Rome; and it is impossible to believe that the earliest Old Stone Age people were oblivious to the spring chorus round their caves and camps.

The human collection of bird song began, of course, with writing and for ages consisted of poetry, whose onomatopoeia was the nearest bird-lovers got to an actual transcription of the songs. Not long after the Renaissance bird voices were rendered into musical notation by Athanasias Kircher (1650) and other musicians (p. 210). This exercise has been continued to the present day by both musicians and scientists; but has largely been supplanted now by disc, tape and by the sound spectrogram image which is a mechanical record of the song, with all its time pattern and sound frequencies, that enables the most deep analyses and comparisons to be made. The point is that ever since bird-watchers have been beyond the stage of admiring the nightingale's complaint with a thorn against her bosom, or debating the presage of the cuckoo's call, or disputing whether the robin's liquid pourings are sweet or sad, they have longed to compare and collect songs. In the

Athanasias Kircher's transnotation of bird voices in 1650. The six lines of music at the top can be readily recognised as the song of the nightingale.

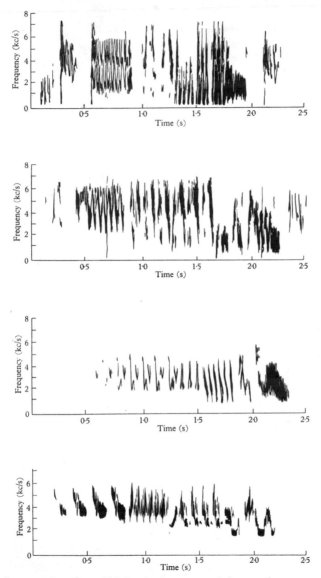

Modern transnotation of bird voice by means of the sound spectrograph. Spectrograms of the chaffinch, published by W.H.Thorpe in 1958 and reproduced with his kind permission: (a) subsong, with chirps and rattles; (b) subsong in transition to full song; (c) full song; (d) full song with *huit* call note in the middle of its second phrase.

early seventeenth century – in 1622 to be exact – Olina of Italy first realised the connection between song and territory, knowing that it was "proper" to the nightingale "at *his* [my italics] first coming to occupy or seize upon one place as its freehold, into which it will not admit any other nightingale but its mate". A century and a half later Gilbert White, who also knew that "during the amorous season such a jealousy prevails amongst the male birds that they can hardly be together in the same hedge or field", began to collect birds' territorial songs, the banners and signatures of their ownership, because he realised that these were attributes the most useful, sometimes, for telling t'other from which. The pilgrims of today, who listen to the leaf warblers in the beech-wood edge of Selborne Common, hear the lineal descendants of the look-alike owners of 3 voices that White finally distinguished; chiffchaff, willow warbler and, "making a sibilous grass-hopper-like noise, now and then, at short intervals, shivering a little with its wings when it sings", the wood warbler.

Nowadays the field man, whether he be on some programme of behaviour study, or co-operating in the British Trust for Ornithology's Common Bird Census, or just enjoying himself in the woods, is a song man. Experienced song students could almost make a territory census blind, fortified as they are by their practice disciplines (though even the best have to re-learn a few songs at a season's start), by the remarkably detailed accounts, interpretation and renderings of song (some unconsciously comical) in the current handbooks and field books, and most of all by Ludwig Koch and all he started. We are still the first generation of bird-recordists. Ludwig Koch made the first known recording of a bird song (of a common Indian shama) on an Edison wax cylinder in Frankfurt-am-Main in 1889. He is still working in England. The revolution though, is a post-Second World War one on the whole; Koch is the greatest pioneer and, accompanying E. M. Nicholson's and his *Songs* . . . , and *More songs of Wild Birds*, published the only British wild-bird records (of 36 species) before that war.

In a fine and useful piece of scholarship Jeffery Boswall has lately listed the history of bird recording and records in Europe[1] and indeed the entire temperate northern Old World or Palearctic Region of which Europe is a part. Quite apart from unpublished disc and tape material in private hands and in those of radio authorities, of Britain and Sweden particularly, a substantial majority of the voices of western European and British birds is now available on published disc. Of special interest to the British and Irish bird-watchers who want to know their bird voices, are the following (latest editions, but in order of first publication):

[1] Well worth consulting; a special supplement to vol. 57 of the journal *British Birds* (1964), published by Witherby, 61–62 Watling Street, London, E.C.4.

Ludwig KOCH (1958). *Songs of British Birds*. HMV 7 EG 8315–16 (two 7-inch × 45 r.p.m.) with booklet; 27 species.

Myles E. W. NORTH and Eric SIMMS (1965). *Witherby's Sound Guide to British Birds*. (Thirteen 7-inch × 45 r.p.m.) with two booklets; 195 species: (mostly Koch and Eric Simms material from B. B. C. archives) from Witherby (see footnote [1]).

John KIRBY (1962). *Listen . . . the Birds*. Sandy, Bedfordshire; the Royal Society for the Protection of Birds EFC 7–9 (three 7-inch × 33 r.p.m.); and (1964) *Minsmere Bird Reserve*. As above, EFC 10–11 (two 7-inch × 33 r.p.m.). R.S.P.B. also issue six 7-inch × 33 r.p.m. recorded on the Continent by Hans TRABER, EFC 1–6. Whole collection is pretty comprehensive.

Lawrence C. SHOVE (1963). *The Country Sings*. One 7-inch × 45 r.p.m., from L. C. S. at Copplestone, Dunsford, Exeter, Devon; 16 species.

Victor C. LEWIS (1964). *A Tapestry of Bird Song*. HMV CLP 1723 (one 12-inch × 33 r.p.m.) with leaflet; 56 species.

Lawrence C. SHOVE (1966). *Shell Nature Records—British Birds Series*. DCL 701–03 (three 7-inch × 33 r.p.m.) from L.C.S. (above) or Discourses Ltd, 16 Frant Road, Tunbridge Wells, Kent (12s. 6d. each including postage). Four more (DCL 704–07) to come.

Skylark; an illustration from Yarrell's *A History of British Birds*, in 1838. The lauricæ or lawerce of the Anglo-Saxons is our laverock or lark, a delight to poets' ears for longer than literature.

CHAPTER 8

Birds in Literature, Music and Art

At the end of this chapter I offer some remarks on musicians (not all British or Irish by any means), who have been inspired by the sounds of our island birds, or at least by the same species on the continent of Europe; and some on our native bird artists; and offer a list of our native heroes who in poetry and prose, literary and scientific, have celebrated, and contributed, something at least a bit special to our knowledge of, or to the expression of our love for, our birds.

It is not possible, really, to divide the men of words into separate literary-cum-artistic and scientific streams until the Renaissance times of 1544, when William Turner's great first bird book was printed. After then, some of them, of course, operated in both streams – for instance White, Edward Jenner, Charles Waterton, John Clare, Edward Lear, d'Arcy Wentworth Thompson, W. H. Hudson, W. Warde Fowler, Abel Chapman, Edmund Selous, H. Eliot Howard and E. W. Hendy. But on the whole these exceptions prove a general rule: however deep a scholar's literary or classical scholarship, through the ages he nearly always fits himself into one school or the other by his approach, if not also by his style. Lord Grey of Fallodon and T. A. Coward were almost exact contemporaries, whose masterpieces have been often and still are reprinted; but there is no doubt that, well though he knew his birds, Edward Grey was a hero of letters; and that, felicitously though he wrote, Thomas Alfred Coward was a man of science, and thus in the strict sense (the sense gets less strict, I find, as life in the twentieth century unfolds) a hero of ornithology.

The "ornithologists" have a chapter to themselves. Here, from the Renaissance on, I write mainly of the men and women of the arts and letters whose work has reflected, at least until lately, most clearly the *attitude* of our evolving civilisation to its wild birds.

To start our poets' tales of birds, with the records of the historians of the saints, we must begin with another Renaissance – the Irish-led Christian culture of the Dark Ages. The bird loving of the early saints is beyond doubt, though the accounts of it come largely from the pens of their historians, and the details may be embroidered by time and biographers' affection. It is easy to believe, with them, though, that Columba or Columkille, who founded

176

the community on Iona in 563, nursed an exhausted migrant crane for three days; that Serf, and Kentigern or Mungo tamed robins in Fife around the same time (p. 47); that Baldred watched the birds of the Bass Rock before he died in 606; that Cuthbert tamed eiders and preached to the crows on the Farnes in about 676. We have *Beowulf* and the Seafarer's poem of (probably) the time of Cuthbert (p. 45), the latter, with its whoopers, gannets, whimbrels, kittiwakes, terns, erne and cuckoo not only a nature-lover's poem from the real, external world, but (p. 43) surely (with the exception of the cuckoo) a field man's record of a Day at the Bass Rock not equalled – as far as I can discover – until John Ray and Philip Skippon logged 6 species on the rock on 19 August 1661, a thousand years later; gannet, cormorant, shag, kittiwake, guillemot and black guillemot.

By the end of the Dark Ages with the Norman Conquest we had a modest recorded identifiable bird list – but much evidence from Irish poems and Anglo-Saxon riddles of birds large and small as part of the familiar tenderness of life. From a tenth-century Irish hermit Kenneth Jackson translates for us this:

> In pleasant summer with its coloured mantle,
> Good tasting savour
> Pignuts, wild marjoram, fresh leeks,
> Green purity.
>
> The songs of the bright red-breasted folk,
> A beloved movement,
> The carol of the thrush, familiar cuckoos
> Above my house.

and here from the *Exeter Book*, of the same or a rather earlier vintage, is Geoffrey Grigson's translation of an Anglo-Saxon riddle:

> Clothes make no sound when I tread ground
> Or dwell in dwellings or disturb the flow.
> Gear and lofty air at times
> Above men's towns will lift me:
> Then brisk breezes bear me far, and then
> My frettings loudly rush and ring
> Above the folk and clearly sing
> When I forth-fare on air and know,
> And feel, no fold or flow.

"The answer to that riddle was a swan, of course," said Grigson to me, "the white bird, the bird of the long neck, the bird that floats and sees its own image in the water, bird of gods and poets and Kings, of myth and legend, madrigal and opera. Not, my dear ornithologist, with your prosy ways and your prosy field-glasses and your prosy statistics, not your kind of bird."

The earliest extant version of the *Nomina Avium* in the Latin to Anglo-Saxon vocabulary of Ælfric the Grammarian, *c.* 998. It is in the Museum Plantin-Moretus, Antwerp; the list was copied, probably in the late eleventh century, in the margin of another work of Ælfric's copied earlier.

Actually, as Grigson knows perfectly well, the only difference in our attitude to swans is that he files them under *ylfete* or *swan*, or *ilke* or *elk*; whereas I file them, poems and all, under *Cygnus*. But when we broadcast together we have a mock lit.-wit – sci.-wit disputation, invariably. The bird was a mute swan, obviously.

Between the Irish and Anglo-Saxon middle poets and great Middle English poets of the thirteenth and fourteenth centuries there is a poetic gap, as far as the birds are concerned. Our knowledge of the avifauna derives mostly from glossarians like Ælfric, bills of monastic fare, inventories, the "Domesday Book", historians like Cuthbert's later biographer (Bede was the earlier) Reginald of Durham and his contemporary Thomas who compiled the *Book of Ely* (oh that he had made a better bird list then from our

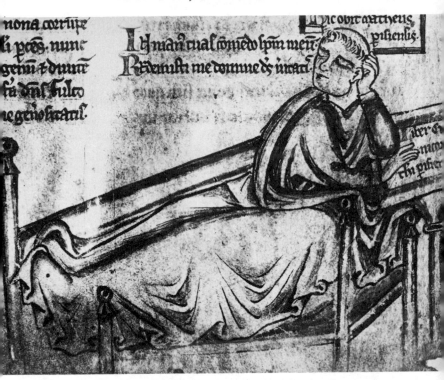

Matthew Paris, the scribe of St Alban's Abbey (1200?–59), who gave us the first English record of the crossbill in 1251.

vast wetland wilderness in those days' fenland!), tract-writers like William FitzStephen, geographers like Gerald di Barri and compilers of learning like Alexander Neckam, Robert Grosseteste, Bartholomew the Englishman and Roger Bacon. The works of these last four were remarkable; but ornithologically almost wholly derivative. But in about 1225, with the French style influencing his plan and plot, John of Guildford gives us a classic dialogue poem, *The Owl and the Nightingale*, with upwards of 18 birds, including crowe, faucun, golfinc, hauec, houle (barn owl that scrichest, tawny owl that yollest), hei-sugge (dunnock), kuke (cuckoo), mose (great? tit), niytingale, pie, pinnuc (chaffinch), rok, throstle (mistle thrush), thrösche (song thrush), wude-wale (green woodpecker), wranne and fowles bothe grete and smale.

"At the turn of [1251], at the season of fruits, certain wonderful birds never before seen in England appeared, particularly in orchards. They were a little bigger than larks and ate the pips of apples and nothing else from the apples. So they robbed the trees of their fruit very grievously. Moreover they had the parts of the beak crossed and with them split the apples as if with pincers or a pocket-knife."

This remarkable piece of ornithological observation, translated from the Latin by the late Canon Raven, is the first known record of an invasion of crossbills in our islands. "Such records, belonging to a different realm from the traditional lore of Neckam and Bartholomew," writes Raven, "remind us that then as now there must have been men who noticed the world around them, without moralising or myth-making." The bird note, which would doubtless have been accepted unchanged by an editor 700 years later, was made by Matthew Paris, chronicler to the monastery of St Albans.

Dafydd ap Gwilym, the Welsh bard of the fourteenth century, wrote of the lark and the thrush as acolytes in the nightingale's church in woods of song in cassocks covered with flowers; and of himself dead for love and carried by a thousand seagulls on a bier of green branches, to the organ chanting of the cuckoo.

Two great bird-bearing collections of poetry come from the England of the fourteenth century: William Langland's *Piers Plowman* (first version 1362); and Geoffrey Chaucer's *Romaunt of the Rose* (*c.* 1369), *Parlement of Foules* (*Briddes*) (1382) and (among many other aviferous poems) *The Canterbury Tales* (*c.* 1386–1391). Langland was the rural, pastoral master of

(*Left*) Geoffrey Chaucer (1340?–1400), poet of the earliest modern English, whose patent delight in birds has warmed our hearts for six centuries. Reproduced from a miniature in Occleve's manuscript. (*Right*) John Lydgate (1370?–1422), from an engraving in the British Museum. His poem *Flour of Curtesye* (*c.* 1401) is the first to express the idea of bird freedom.

Juliana Berners (1388?–1450?), Prioress of Sopwell Nunnery in Hertfordshire, contributed many records of birds in sport to the fifteenth-century
archives. From an engraving in the British Museum.

late Middle English; Chaucer the urban, sophisticated, Frenchified symbol
of the transition from Middle to Modern English. Interestingly, Chaucer's
is the verse in which most often "smale fowles maken melodye, that slepen
al the night with open ye". Langland wrote of domestic birds, and sporting
birds, and ornamental birds and "pest" birds: of doke, dowue (dove) and
gees; of faucuns, sperhauke, egle, fesauntes, patriche and swan; of pokok
and pohen; of crowen, pies and sparwe (sparrow): indeed of the pure (?)
observers' birds (as it were) he finds but few, such as dompynges (dabchicks),

larke and tortle (-dove). But Chaucer knew a score and more of these (p. 54), from alpes (bullfinches) to terins (siskins), from chalaundrès (Frenchified skylarks and not calandra larks, I think) to feldefares. If he took a somewhat emotional view of the cuckoo's habits it is one shared by most of us even in these days of ornithological sophistication.

"Thou modrer", said the merlin to the cuckoo in the birds' parliament on St Valentine's Day:

> Thou modrer of the heysugge [dunnock] on the braunche
> That broghte thee forth, thou rewtheless glotoun! . . .
> Go, lewed [lewd] be thou, whyl the world may dure!

With the dawn of the fifteenth century came the expression of an idea implicit in earlier works, from *The Seafarer* on, but in John Lydgate's *Flour of Curtesye* of about 1401 explicit for the first time I know of: the notion of the freedom of the birds. Lydgate compares the lot of man, imprisoned by his own suffering, by statute, lot and law, with the birds he watches on every tre . . . , alway twayne and twayne.

> Then thought I thus: "alas! what may this be,
> That every foule hath his lyberte
> Frely to chose after his desyre
> Everyche his make thus: fro yere to yere?
> The sely wrenne, the tytemose also,
> The lytel redbreast, have free election
> To flyen yfere and togyther go
> Where as hem lyst, aboute envyron,
> As they of kynde have inclynacion,
> And as Nature, emperesse and gyde,
> Of every thing, lyst to provyde; . . .

The sixteenth century, which brings us the first true ornithologists in William Turner and John Caius (see the next chapter) brings us, of course, more poets: John Skelton, for instance, who so formalised the little birds as characters in a play as to cast them as supporters of a bird funeral in *Lament for Phyllyp Sparowe*; William Dunbar who, around 1503, wrote of spring and bird song in conventional but very robust Scots–English verse; George Gascoigne whose *Philomene*, in a long line of nightingale poems through the age of the English language, is no bird but a wandering literary voice, sorrowful and humanised; Edmund Spenser, who seems to me to have loved birds, and accepted them as part of the literary scene with all their scholars' history and classical lore, but persuades us not that he watched them for himself; Sir Philip Sidney and John Lyly who fancied the nightingale, again, for the human sorrows they believed "her" to express.

In the seventeenth century poets came who were real bird-watchers: the king of them Michael Drayton with his *Owle* (1619) and *Polyolbion* (1623).

John Skelton (1460?–1529), who introduced over 70 kinds of birds into his *Lament for Phyllyp Sparowe*. Reproduced from an engraving in the British Museum.

His poem of the bird songs of a spring morning in Warwickshire is a model of tidy and tender observation. Long days in the field in the Lincolnshire fens give us a fine description of the whooper:

> Here in my vaster pools, as white as snow or milk,
> In water black as Styx, swims the wild swan, the ilke
> of Hollanders so termed, no niggard of his breath,
> (As poets say of swans who only sing in death);
> But, as other birds, is heard his tunes to roat,
> Which like a trumpet comes, from his long arched throat

Good field stuff, was this; and note the apologia for the liberties of other poets.

(*Left*) Michael Drayton (1563–1631), the first of the poets to be a real bird-watcher; a fine field man and poet of the birds of the English countryside. (*Right*) The Swan of Avon (1564–1616). Shakespeare was a scholar of birds, as of every facet of human interest. From the portrait by Martin Droeshout which formed the frontispiece to the First Folio edition of Shakespeare's plays.

In 1871 J. E. Harting gave us a full analysis and working concordance of the birds of Shakespeare, and his judgment on the Swan of Avon is that he was a falconer of practical experience, a field man a cut above the run of poets, and a wide reader of the published natural history of his day. Shakespeare's bird list is in fact of over 50 species, though some are, as usual, indeterminable between close relatives. It is fair to say that Shakespeare provides the ornithologist with a gross and more of quotations, many of them of unprecedented beauty. These are back-up quotations, to the bird-historians. As far as I can discover Shakespeare saw birds well, and remembered them, as he remembered an incredible number of things, with precision. But there is no evidence from his published writings that he ever saw a bird do anything that nobody had written of before.

Nashe, of "cuckoo, jug-jug, pu-we, to-witta-woo" fame, Heywood – "notes from the lark I'll borrow", Donne – "the lyric lark, and the grave whispering dove", Ben Jonson – "oh my fair feathered, my red-breasted birds, come fly with me", are heavenly poets, and bird-lovers, but not discoverers. Why should they have been? They enliven our reading, now.

Enlivening, too, are the seventeenth-century poets. John Taylor, the water poet, was a water-bird-watcher, with a down-to-earth, or at least

(*Left*) John Taylor (1580–1653), the water poet, whose writing is full of thoughtful simplicity in his enjoyment of birds. Reproduced from an engraving in the British Museum. (*Right*) Izaak Walton (1593–1683), a deep nature-lover and nature-analyst, whose *The Compleat Angler* contains much shrewd bird observation. From a painting by Jacob Huysmans, in the National Portrait Gallery.

down-to-table attitude – and an (unconscious) appreciation of bird migration.

> There were rare birds I never saw before,
> The like of them I think to see no more:
> Th'are called wheat-ears, less than lark or sparrow,
> Well roasted, in the mouth they taste like marrow.
> When once 'tis in the teeth it is involv'd,
> Bones, flesh, and all, is lusciously dissolv'd.
> The name of wheat-ears, on them is ycleped
> Because they come when wheat is yearly reaped,
> Six weeks, or thereabouts, they are catch'd there.
> And are well nigh eleven months, God knows where.

Which reminds me of my friend Leo Harrison Matthews's recent dedication of one of his robust natural history books "to bird lovers especially those who love them piping hot, well browned and with plenty of bread sauce".

In 1612 John Webster, normally a fierce user of birds of legend and omen in his formidable plays, perhaps began a new poet's attitude with "we think caged birds sing, when indeed they cry". I can find no earlier example of this logical development of Lydgate's celebration of the freedom of wild birds.

But most of the seventeenth-century writers still ordered the birds as actors; William Browne even allotted them special voice-parts in the spring chorus – "the lofty treble sang the little wren; robin the mean, that best of all loves men; the nightingale the tenor, and the thrush the counter-tenor sweetly in a bush". In *The Compleat Angler* (1653) Izaak Walton was ornithologically a bit better. "But the Nightingale, another of my airy creatures," he wrote, "breathes such sweet loud music out of her little instrumental throat, that it might make mankind to think miracles are not ceased. He that at midnight, when the very labourer sleeps securely, should hear, as I have very often, the clear airs, the sweet descants, the natural rising and falling, the doubling and redoubling of her voice, might well be lifted above earth, and say, 'Lord what music hast thou provided for the saints in heaven, when thou affordest bad men such music on Earth!'"

To Milton (who mentions 16 British birds) as to other seventeenth-century writers and poets nightingales were rather ceremonial chorus members in the back of the rural stage, filling with fresh hope the lover's heart. To George Daniel, a fair poet but clearly no bird-watcher, robins were mere summer chanters: "you have neither wing nor voice", he told them, "in winter". Abraham Cowley's kingfishers were just sad, his robins just pious. Andrew Marvell was better; if his nightingale was sad, and by the current literary conceit inevitably female and thorn-associated, and his stock dove sadder, his thrushes and herons were watched at the nest, and his woodpeckers tenderly observed as they hacked for insects and excavated their nest-holes in great, old oaks. Dryden, on the other hand, was practically bird-blind; his nightingale but a formal choir-queen, his halcyon legendary; his cuckoo conventionally foolish.

Eighteenth-century poetry began firmly in a pastoralist tradition with classical staging. Alexander Pope's world – or at least the world he loved – was the newly developing world of formal garden and park: the new world of the game gun, in which whirring pheasants mounting exulting on triumphant wings were shot in their joy, where doves, woodcocks and lapwings in leaden death aroused the poet's pity. "Oft, as the mounting larks their notes prepare," wrote Pope, "They fall, and leave their little lives in air." Notwithstanding Somerville, the poet of the new field sports, most of the pastoralists brought us much pity and tenderness, and began to build the concept of bird freedom (long before founded, of course, p. 136) into an edifice: for free-wild animals enthused, by their freedom and wildness then as now, not only poets but scientists. Thomas Pennant, though strictly a man of Chapter 10 (p. 62) admired "the elegant and just descriptions of the economy of animals" in the poems of James Thomson, whom he revered and had, as a young man, known. Thomson was, indeed, a bird-lover of the modern kind; so was another pastoralist of the eighteenth

(*Left*) Alexander Pope (1688–1744), from a portrait attributed to William Hoare in the National Portrait Gallery; poet of tenderness among the newly tidied ruralities of mansions and parks. (*Right*) William Cowper (1731–1800), great country poet but not a brilliant bird-knower. Reproduced from the portrait of the poet by George Romney, in the National Portrait Gallery.

century William Shenstone; so, too, Thomas Gray, and William Collins, and the tender Christopher Smart, and Dr Oliver Goldsmith, and the haters of bird-cagers William Cowper and William Blake. Gilbert White, father of field bird-watching and hero of the next essay in this book, was no mean poet but as such quite a different character, a Drydenite and Pope-ite (though he found Pope over-exact) capable of advising his nephew Sam Barker that "a little turn for English poetry is no doubt a pretty accomplishment for a young gentleman", and to add that "the way to excell is to copy only from our best writers". Cowper,.who lived among ruralities in the same limestone strip of middle England as the young Dryden, and later, Clare, was a bird-lover indeed; but his field quality must ever remain a puzzle to those who read his poem *To The Nightingale which the Author heard sing on New Year's Day, 1792*. Burns lovers can make themselves a list of about 37 birds of the Scottish Lowlands and south Highlands from the works of their immortal poet – birds tenderly described as environmental sprites and sometimes more sinister characters in his hot-blooded short life. Burns could never hear "the loud solitary whistle of the curlew on a summer noon, or the wild mixing cadence of a troop of grey [? golden] plovers in an autumn morning, without feeling an elevation of soul like the enthusiasm of devotion or poetry".

The poets and prose-writers, since the writings of White, were really

(Left) John Clare (1793–1864), from the portrait by W. Hilton in the National Portrait Gallery. Clare is the paragon of ornithological skill and observational virtue among our nature poets. *(Right)* James Grahame (1765–1811), the poet-ornithologist of Scotland, whose poems are full of acute observation on bird song. Reproduced from an engraving in the British Museum.

beginning to know their birds – and the literature of them, in the early nineteenth century. As he rode the ruralities of England, Cobbett logged and pondered on the pretty birds; Rogers and Bloomfield wrote with pity and love; James Grahame, pitying, too, and tender, and a bit schoolmarmish, wrote a long series *The Birds of Scotland* in 1806 and the *British Georgics* in 1809 which were prescribed reading (Sunday reading doubtless in enlightened homes) for several generations of Georgian and Victorian children. They are full of acute observations on the different songs of closely related birds.

Four masters, born in the 1770s, were prophets and chroniclers of nature *par excellence*, and of birds more than in passing. The least famous of them, Noel Thomas Carrington, grocer's son, sailor and school-teacher was (with the aid of his Devon friends Dr Andrew Tucker and Tucker's sons Robert and Charles, real ornithologists) a pioneer Dartmoor poet and bird-historian. The "greats" were, of course, Wordsworth (39 British birds in his works), Scott (46) and Coleridge (15).

Wordsworth's birds were deeply analysed by the ornithologist William H. Wintringham in 1892. I suppose that with the possible exception of the artist Thomas Bewick he was the greatest rough-country and fell walker of all the bird-lovers, true ornithologists excepted. Come to that he was a true ornithologist, and a conservationist too, prophet as he turned out to be of

(*Left*) William Wordsworth (1770–1850), the poet of our present conservation conscience – and a fine field man – from the portrait by Benjamin
Robert Haydon in the National Portrait Gallery. (*Right*) Sir Walter Scott
(1771–1832), whose works mention no less than 46 British birds; from the
portrait by fellow-naturalist Sir Edwin Landseer in the National Portrait
Gallery.

the Lake District National Park, which, he said in 1810, ought to be a sort
of national property. To Wordsworth "the least motion which [birds]
made . . . seemed a thrill of pleasure". To him small birds warbled "to their
paramours"; he had not found the aggressive secret uncovered earlier by
White, but with earlier poets had *part* of the truth, there. To Wordsworth the
thrush was undaunted, and constant in love; the blackbird timid; the
fieldfare pensive; the stonechat restless; the robin brisk and pious and tame –
"the whole house is robin's cage"; the nightingale sweet and of a fiery
heart (and he recorded it absent from the Lakes, but heard it in Richmond
and knew enough of it to disbelieve that it sang better on the Continent);
the dunnock a little prattler; the blue tit a giddy sprite; the wren darkling
and self-contented; the swallow fleet; the greenfinch like the dawning leaves;
the linnet a singer in chorus; the jay affrighted; the magpie a chatterer;
ravens blithe and croakers of death; the crow lonely; the rook cawing; the
lark of the dawn, vigorous, buoyant, joyous but singularly carelessly ranged
aloft – he puts it in the sky, in clouds above, his head in sunbeams or a
bowery cloud, in mid-air, on sun-gilt wing high poised, yet no higher than
the pitch of "the inglorious football"; the woodlark soft; the swift by tender
cares opprest; the nightjar solitary; the kingfisher flitting; the cuckoo blithe,
a wandering voice, babbling, darling of the spring, a mystery, blessed; the
barn owl screeching, vagrant; the tawny owl shouting, hooting, silent; the

(*Left*) Samuel Taylor Coleridge (1772–1834), from the portrait by Peter van Dyke in the National Portrait Gallery, a fine field man, always seeing his birds through a poet's binoculars. (*Right*) Percy Bysshe Shelley (1792–1822), painted at the age of twenty-seven by Amelia Curran, from the original in the National Portrait Gallery. Poet of but few birds, Shelley had a keen ear for their music.

golden eagle lord, flame-eyed; the white-tailed eagle lone and wailing; peregrines in clamorous agitation; the kite sailing; the buzzard shrill; the cormorant heavy; the heron silent; swans like sinless snakes, fair, mute, pure, bright, fitted to embrace, winding, glorying, unwearied; snipe darting; sandpiper glancing; gulls sportive, white and from afar. Wordsworth was not too prodigal with his adjectives and epithets; he was precise. Yet English being the language it has become, and birds being the beings they are, the epithets have accrued. In "established" English poetry as a whole, Chambers found that no less than 178 epithets had been applied, not forty years after Wordsworth's death, to the nightingale alone by some one or another.

Sir Walter Scott scored 46 detectable British birds in his works – less watched and loved, more formalised than Wordsworth's. Coleridge, who has but 15, was far better in the field; a nightingale poem of his restores the joyful element in the song of "the merry nightingale that crowds, and hurries, and precipitates with fast thick warble his [note his] delicious notes". "A melancholy bird?" asks S.T.C.; and answers: "O idle thought, in nature there is nothing melancholy; but some night-wandering man, . . ." His field images are through poet's binoculars, as his winter robin singing "betwixt the tufts of snow on the bare branch of mossy appletree, while the nigh thatch smokes in the sun-thaw; . . ."

Like Coleridge, Shelley (with 13) and Keats (18) were poets of few birds; but bird-watcher, bird-listener poets, though Shelley's azure halcyons – "thinning one bright bunch of amber berries, with quick long beaks" – are queer birds, as is his nightingale "climbing in circles the windless sky". Shelley's *To a Skylark*, though, has all the bird-lover's eternal questions, researchers' questions and all. "Hail to thee, blithe spirit! Bird thou never wert. That from Heaven, or near it, Pourest thy full heart In profuse strains of unpremeditated art." And then he goes on to prove that the masters of unpremeditated art are indeed the birds, and that the human probings of the mysteries of their art are models of all human research and philosophy. "Teach us, Sprite or Bird, What sweet thoughts are thine", he asks, and says "I have never heard Praise of love or wine that panted forth a rapture so divine."

The nightingale, inspiration of the poets from Aldhelm of Malmesbury (*c.* 685) to Keats. One of the illustrations originally published in Yarrell's *A History of British Birds*, 1838.

Keats's *Ode to a Nightingale* is doubtless the paragon of all bird poems in modern English. Its eight, great stanzas have been lately analysed with both scholar's and ornithologist's understanding by Miss Janet Spens and T. P. Harrison. The poem was inspired by a bird occupying a territory in the garden of the poet's biographer Charles Armitage Brown, in Hampstead in the spring of 1819. Keats sat under a plum tree and listened to it for hours. Prescribed reading as the ode is in the schools, scholars doubtless learn from scholars' notes three stanzas yearning for escape, four in escape, the last, as the bird flies, a return to reality. The whole poem, though, singing "Perhaps the self-same song that found a path Through the sad heart of Ruth, when, sick for home, She stood in tears amid the alien corn; The same that oft-times hath Charm'd magic casements, opening on the foam Of perilous seas, in faery lands forlorn", *is* a nightingale song.

Subtly, the whole masterpiece has nightingale rhythm and cadence. It was built and inspired by a living bird, as the poet listened night and day under the plum tree. It is, to put it mildly, more than a contribution to the understanding of nightingales, in the way that Wagner's *Ring* is more than a contribution to the understanding of the Iron or Dark Ages. As the poet leaves the bird, or the bird flies, "the plaintive anthem fades Past the near meadows, over the still stream, Up the hill-side; and now 'tis buried deep In the next valley-glades: Was it a vision, or a waking dream? Fled is that music: – Do I wake or sleep?"

The nightingale, then, was the instrument of Keats's deepest inspiration, as it has most deeply inspired poets before him back to Aldhelm and Alcuin, and after him, notably Meredith. It inspired, too, Keats's near-twin, three or four springs later, in the heath and woods of Helpston in the Soke of Peterborough. John Clare's poetry is not often in the same league as that of the inspired Keats, though Clare rightly says of Keats in general that "as is the case with other inhabitants of great cities he often described nature as she appeared to his fancies and not as he would have described her had he witnessed the things he describes"; this indeed was true of Keats without the plum tree. If Clare was not a Keats, though, he was a major poet lost, miserable and verseless without his plum tree. Of all our major poets he was by far the finest naturalist. He knew no less than 135 species of plants, 40 of which no previous person had recorded in print for his county. He wrote of about 147 wild British birds, 145 from his personal observation, 65 of them first county records. His birds are about three times as many as those of any other poet save Tennyson, and more than twice as many as Tennyson's; and they are real, and living; or they were. Keats, criticising one of Clare's early poems, said that "the description too much prevailed over the sentiment". In fact Clare's descriptions contain such an amazing array of original observations as would promote him to the next chapter did his sentiments not entitle him to rank as a major poet. His self-taught skills as a field naturalist flourished from about 1820 to 1837, when he suffered the first of a succession of bouts of manic depression which confined him to what was then called Northampton General Lunatic Asylum for the last two decades and more of his life.

All Clare's bird work was entirely overlooked by Lord Lilford in his supposedly full account of the Birds of Northamptonshire (and the Soke of Peterborough) a quarter of a century after Clare's death. Besides his geographical information, Clare's life-history and behaviour notes were also quite ignored by scholars until lately. Yet this incredible poet records the last hold-ons of many of the Peterborough and Lincolnshire fen birds whose habitat was being rapidly drained away for agriculture in his time. In 1831, when he made up a bird list, the black-necked grebe was still nesting in fair numbers near Spalding. The bittern inhabited Whittlesey Mere which is (or was) just in Huntingdonshire and was finally drained in 1850. The grey lag goose may still have bred in Deeping Fen in Lincolnshire. The kite (see p. 106) still bred near Helpston. Harriers bred in the local fens; quail were still regular (though rarish) nesters; black-tailed godwits and ruffs (since his time quite extinct) still nested, as did the spotted crake. The wry-neck, now also extinct in the area, was a common breeder in Clare's day.

Clare's poems, prose, notes and letters are full of detailed observation – on the heron's food and powder-down; on the nesting of buzzard, kite, what was probably Montagu's harrier, and kestrel; on the injury-feigning and dust-bathing of the partridge; on the display-flight of the lapwing; on

Partridge, from Yarrell's *A History of British Birds*, 1840. Symbol of some anti-Establishment thinking by the Establishment's poet Tennyson (1809–92) – no mean ornithologist, despite some *lapsus calami*.

the food and late breeding of the woodpigeon; on the feeding methods of green and great spotted woodpeckers; on the intruder-display of the wryneck. His nest-habitats of the skylark, when collected, might be a modern *Handbook* entry, as might his accounts of the domestic habits of the crow family. Among all the little passerines he birds-nested for watching (not egging) and found clutch sizes for most and building times for some. Particularly did he love long-tailed tits, thrushes, nightingales, robins, willow warblers, spotted flycatchers, goldfinches and "little trotty wagtail".

Needless to say I have a special affection for Clare, for he is my own county's till-lately-unsung Gilbert White; and a better poet than the curate of Faringdon if not quite so transcendental a naturalist.

Apart from Clare, our bird-list champion poet is Tennyson, who scored about 60. Despite the worthy championship of Watkin Watkins, a member of our British Ornithologists' Union who made a deepish ornithological analysis of the Establishment Poet's works in 1903, the great man does not really shine as a bird man. It is true, as critics from Charles Kingsley on-ward have upheld, that Tennyson exalted in the "handling of everyday sights and sounds of nature". He was brought up – unlike Browning and others of his vintage – in England; in the shire of Lincoln at Somersby under the wolds, and long explored the (then) marshes and coast near Mable-thorpe. Later in life he enjoyed the forests of Essex, the weald and downs of Kent, the Cotswolds and the heaths of Surrey and Hampshire.

Tennyson's ornithology is, in fact, a curious mixture of the naïve and the sophisticated. The naïve includes "what does little birdie say in her nest at peep of day? . . ." a baby song long talked of as tender but to some now ineffably jejeune : a galaxy of over-simple love images over the song of birds : the classic obfuscation of the process of moult "In the spring a fuller crimson comes upon the robin's breast"; a linnet sad because "her brood is stol'n away"; a bee-hunting swallow; and curiously ineffective conceits as " 'f all the world were falcons, what of that?"

Although Tennyson never obtained the depths of field perception reached by Clare some of his poetic images of birds are vivid and clever: "The starling claps his tiny castanets" is a good rendering of the bird's "own" chuckling song; there is good psychological intuition behind "the pretty gaping bills in the home-nest Piping for bread – the daily want supplied – The daily pleasure to supply it". Tennyson's *The Throstle* poem is a good bit of onomatopoeia, though Clare's song thrush verse, and that of their con-temporary William Macgillivray are better; and "the music of the moon Sleeps in the plain eggs of the nightingale" is a fine concept indeed. Well aware of the process of migration, Tennyson wrote of night migrants "that change Their season in the night and wail their way From cloud to cloud", and of lighthouse victims: "As the beacon-blaze allures The bird of passage, till he madly strikes Against it, and beats out his weary life." He knew the eye-colour of the eagle owl; the silence of wood-edge singing birds in the shadow of a sparrow hawk, the drumming of the snipe; and with "The ptarmigan that whitens ere his hour Woos his own end", may have known that cock ptarmigan, white still when the hens, already subfusc, have repaired to the breeding-hill, are then the "expendables" that attract predation away from the future potential of the season. One section of the bird-loving Establishment earned his scorn:

"How pleasant to know Mr Lear"; portrait by W. N. Marstrand of a fine scientific ornithologist and excellent artist, but by most remembered with affection as a comic, tender poet (1812–88).

> These old pheasant-lords,
> These partridge-breeders of a thousand years,
> Who had mildewed in their thousands doing nothing
> Since Egbert.

though, I very much doubt whether Egbert, King of the West Saxons from 802 to 839, had any pheasants to lord over (see p. 36).

The Victorian bird-watchers and bird poets were legion. Dear Edward Lear – brilliant artist and fine systematic ornithologist – is remembered best for his child-verse and limericks in which kind bird-people, and people-birds, tread tender pages of immortal comic and sentimental Carroll-like art. The big poets like Browning put the birds in clever nut-shell pigeon-holes,

Margaret Emily Shore (1819–39) – a portrait painted shortly before the untimely death of one who might have become the first female genius of British ornithology.

like "the wise thrush; he sings twice over Lest you should think he never could recapture The first fine careless rapture"; Browning's river pushes "Its gentle way through straggling rushes, Where the glossy king-fisher Flutters when noon-heats are near, Glad the shelving banks to shun, Red and streaming in the sun"; and his contemporary F. W. Faber's niche poem for the same bird seems as good . . . "Yon tall stone beneath the alder stem Seems a meet throne for a gay crowned thing That wears so well its tawny diadem". Poet of Cherwell and Nene, Faber cast many habitat images of birds in his rather conventional but bird-percipient verse.

"Wildly tender" was the robin's song to Emily Brontë's ears, and com-forting its winter song to Christina Rossetti's; sinister was the charnel carrion crow of the murderer's gibbet to Eliza Cook. But the most remarkable woman bird-lover of Victorian letters was without doubt Margaret Emily Shore, who died in 1839 of tuberculosis, not twenty years of age, having kept notes since the age of eight and a journal since the age of eleven. Her youthful poems had some merit, but were few – the best of them a paean to the willow warbler; but on her considerable ornithological merit I carry her, and her 73 or so observed birds, to Chapter 10.

John Ruskin, most free-minded of critics, artists, architects, planners and poets was born in the same year as Emily Shore but did not begin to disturb the world of ornithology until his lectures in London in 1869 and Oxford in 1873. To us today the extracts from *The Queen of the Air*, *The Eagle's Nest* and *Love's Meinie* must largely be classified as the curiosa of a highly un-usual and original mind that obeyed few philosophical rules. His remarks on the science of ornithology were such that for a couple of human genera-tions the party line of the Bird Establishment held that the less said about his ornithological knowledge, the better, "always supposing his remarks are serious". More liberal and recent analyses have had more sympathy for the wild man of bird words; David Lack lately quotes with some affection Ruskin's pronouncements on the four articles of the natural history of a British bird, current in pro. circles a century ago.

First, the name and estate of the gentleman whose gamekeeper shot the last that was seen in England.

Secondly, two or three stories of doubtful origin, printed in every book on the subject of birds for the past fifty years.

Thirdly, an account of the feathers, from the comb to the rump, with enumeration of the colours which are never more to be seen on the living bird by English eye; and,

Lastly, a discussion of the reasons why none of the twelve names which former naturalists have given to the birds are of any further use, and why the present author has given it a thirteenth, which is to be universally, and to the end of time, accepted.

These remarks were certainly serious: and not altogether unfair. Ruskin had every contradiction in his make-up. Anti-scientific and anti-vivisectionist, he endowed bodies to be devoted to the union of science and art. Super-stitious enough to find all owls' cries prophetic of woe to himself, he was rational enough to ally himself with the Victorian movements for progress, planning, popular art, and the betterment of the working classes. He loved birds and deeply thought about, if he did not very deeply study, all kinds from robins to swallows, from owls to dabchicks. This piece from his Greek myths study *The Queen of the Air* (1869) sums his ornithology up fairly, I think.

We will take the bird first. It is little more than a drift of the air brought into form by plumes; the air is in all its quills, it breathes through its whole

(*Left*) John Ruskin (1819–1900), from whose verbose entanglements some valuable examples of ornithological insight can be sorted – with care. Reproduced from the portrait by George Richmond. (*Right*) George Meredith (1828–1909), from the portrait by George Frederick Watts in the National Portrait Gallery; a mainstream poet with new and felicitous thoughts on old poets' birds.

frame and flesh, and glows with air in its flying, like a blown flame: it rests upon the air, subdues it, surpasses it, outruns it; – *is* the air, conscious of itself, conquering itself, ruling itself.

Also, into the throat of the bird is given the voice of the air. All that in the wind itself is weak, wild, useless in sweetness, is knit together in its song. As we may imagine the wild form of the cloud closed into the perfect form of the bird's wings, so the wild voice of the cloud into its ordered and commanded voice; unwearied, rippling through the clear heaven in its gladness, interpreting all intense passion through the soft spring nights, bursting into acclaim and rapture of choir at day-break, or lisping and twittering among the boughs and hedges through heat of day, like little winds that only make the cowslip bells shake, and ruffle the petals of the wild rose.

Now was the first paragraph of this essay of Ruskin's based on poet's intuition or a scholar's knowledge of the intricacies of the vast and complex inner pneumatic systems of birds, by which they oxygenate their blood as they breathe both in and out? Late researches have shown the frame of flesh of birds more airy than anybody knew in Ruskin's time. Was Ruskin's an inspired guess (saving the respiratory pun) or a breath of poet's wind? Were birds, to him, just love's meinie, man's sprites and nature's puppets? Ruskin's forthrightness in the free association of unassociables, in the comparison of incomparables, in the application of inapplicables laid the foundation for an almost classic Late Victorian gulf between literature and science. Even when I was a boy, bird-watchers and butterfly-collectors were looked down on with Ruskinian scorn by over-educated teachers and scholars on the English literature side who subconsciously still deemed animals as beings capable only of being understood through literary mysteries, which they were at as many pains to construct as Ruskin was.

Ruskin's heirs still natter in the night, but the main stream of later Victorian bird poetry passed the prattle by, on the whole. Matthew Arnold's contributions indeed are of the traditional, pre-Ruskinian fancifulness, with a sad nightingale "still nourishing in thy bewilder'd brain That wild, unquench'd, deep-sunken, old-world pain". Robins were still birds of love in the poems of Coventry Patmore and Sydney Dobell. George Meredith in his *Lark Ascending, The Thrush in February, Love in the Valley* and *Night of Frost in May*, gets nearer to nature with a glorious combination of the romantic classicism of Keats and the bird-sensitive onomatopoeia of Clare. This, true of his May nightingale, is truer even of his skylark:

> He rises and begins to round,
> He drops the silver chain of sound,
> Of many links without a break,
> In chirrup, whistle, slur and shake,
> All intervolved and spreading wide,
> Like water dimples down a tide
> Where ripple ripple overcurls
> And eddy into eddy whirls; . . .

William Henry Hudson, who died in 1922 at the age of eighty, is renowned as a modern prophet of nature, whose writings (and estate) helped (and indeed still help) the cause of the protection of birds on its way. This may seem a somewhat pale description of Hudson's strong influence on thought. He started writing quite scientifically, sending material to the *Proceedings of the Zoological Society of London* before he was thirty. But "though he would never be reckoned among the ranks of the scientific ornithologists," wrote his *Ibis* obituarian, "his work as an interpreter of nature and as a master of the finest type of English prose will endure for many a long year". Both "sides" have done their best to prolong the gulf between great writing and science, it is true. Hudson himself did his bit. These are some things lovers of older, better writers who were truly in both camps cannot quite forgive him for: for instance his exchange with Gilbert White, whom he disinterred in imagination from his modest Selborne grave for a conversation in which Hudson did all the talking, and White had to listen to a pompous dissertation on the discoveries and opinions of the "moderns". Hudson was no more modern than White, and in his writings did not scruple to prevaricate, which White never knowingly did. The St Kilda wren, Hudson reported,

William Henry Hudson (1841–1922), from a portrait by Frank Brooks, reproduced by kind permission of the Royal Society for the Protection of Birds. Prophet, if not a great prognostician, of bird protection.

was extinct, when it was not; it suited his message of human cruelty to nature to say that it was so; and he said that it was so.

Hudson will be forgiven, of course, by the lovers of his novels, in which the "I" has a different personality from the ever-present personal pronouns of his factual essays (about one to every five lines). Intensely egocentric, ambitious and anti-scholarly in his English years, muddled about evolution as so many of his purple-passage-proselytes continue to be, Hudson could never attain the vision of earth ascribed to him by his more sycophantic biographers. He was nature's dramatist, not analyst. His numerous friends and disciples record him as moving quickly from charm to moodiness, from

The St Kilda wren perched upon the skull of the last great auk, from an early R.S.P.B. pamphlet of Hudson's. Both, he said, were extinct. His message was pithily contrived and presented, even if only half true.

silence to garrulity, from "salty prejudice" to "chivalrous courtesy". He was enthusiastic constantly, morbid often, curiously kinky in some of his novel images (e.g. *Marta Riquelme* and *Rima*). None of his closest friends ever suggests that he read widely, or knew much of what others knew of what he wrote about. His friend Morley Roberts indeed reports that he shunned textbooks and bibliographies. He had a sort of Franciscan concept of nature as a whole, yet was intellectually lost in a world of marvellous new ecological discoveries by contemporaries he did not know of (or perhaps want to know of). Back to nature, he preached; yet never did he preach that knowledge is the key to nature. Hudson was a good reporter of the troubled place of nature in a rapidly industrialising, urbanising world; an indifferent logician and diagnostician of ills; a hopeless prescriber; and intolerably ignorant. Yet the work of this perhaps most anthologised of English nature writers lives on, as a sort of anthology indeed; a series of small visions of natural events in vivid detail and faultless prose, an unedited and uneditable, unrelated and unrelatable mosaic of Glimpses of Nature.

Though John Richard Jefferies was born later than Hudson, his spell was cast and he was spent (he died at only thirty-eight) before Hudson published his first English nature book. This, as a matter of fact, *was* a textbook –

Hudson's *British Birds* of 1895. It was neither accurate nor comprehensive, despite the assistance (in part) of the able taxonomist Frank Beddard, and some fine early illustrations by Archibald Thorburn and George Lodge. It is quite clear to me from the internal evidence of this book that Hudson, at the time he wrote it, knew less than 100 British birds from personal observation. Jefferies, at the same time, knew at least 120, from the evidence of such of his novels, essays and illustrated newspaper articles as have been published in book form.

As an observer, Jefferies was as close to nature as John Clare, knowing rather more flowers and rather fewer birds than the earlier ransacker of field life. He wrote without Hudson's skill, and at the same time without Hudson's morbidity, and with a Wiltshire farmer's son's true feeling for the soil and those who lived on and by it. To English and rural folk Hudson acted as, and doubtless seemed to think like, a man from Mars. Jefferies was of the rural folk. As a schoolboy I found his enthusiasm incredibly inspiring, especially *Wild Life in a Southern County* (1879), *The Life of the Fields* (1884), the posthumous *Field and Hedgerow* (1889) and the novel *Bevis* (1882). Lately (1948) S. J. Looker has edited some scattered and even unpublished material into *Chronicles of the Hedges* which includes some gold, notably a fine and scholarly essay on the nightingale written when Jefferies was sick to death.

Jefferies memorabilia are not like Hudson's. He comparatively seldom turns up in anthologies, though a "Bird's Nest" passage from *Field and Hedgerow*, and "The Hovering of the Kestrel" and "Birds climbing the air" from *The Life of the Fields* have a sure future as anthology material. From this last collection two essays on game, sport and conservation (like the flight articles, first published in the *St James's Gazette* of 1883) show a deep grasp of such data as there were and a remarkable anticipation of present issues and thinking: they were certainly ahead of the ideas of the conservation societies of that time and, in the assembly of the facts backing their conclusions, superior in scholarship to Hudson's rather later excursions – with some special selection of data and some special pleading – into the same field. Notwithstanding Hudson's apparently unassailable literary reputation I cannot like him very much. But despite the Victorian essay-heads of Jefferies – The Pageant of Summer; Meadow Thoughts; Clematis Lane; In the Fields; The Meadow Gateway; The Midsummer Hum; etc., which would send me straight over to the *Daily Mirror* (or *British Birds*) if I met them in the 1960s, I like Jefferies's long, pouring paragraphs of clear and clean-watched ruralities very much indeed. Better these than Hudson's cheerless vision of Earth, direct ancestor of the Romps with Dame Nature which, garnished with cultivated ignorance, are still occasionally to be found, expressed in a Suitable Tone of Voice, in the Top People's Paper and (bless it) now and then in that liberal phenomenon that does not seem to bother who its customers are, as long as they get a good read.

Jefferies, much more a human realist than Hudson, was a defender of legitimate blood sports and himself a keen shooter, poacher-sympathiser and man of the blustery fall and winter days with retrievers and pointers. One of the greatest nature writers of all time, the Border sportsman and wildfowler Abel Chapman, epitomised the benign combination of naturalist and sportsman, like many after him. Chapman made redoubtable contributions to the plain ornithological logging of Cheviotland – as also did his contemporary the sportsman-poet Robert Service of the west Lowlands. Chapman sought the atmosphere of the hunter's battle of wits as much as the achievement, and his classics – like *The Borders and Beyond* – inspired a manly tradition of wildfowling that doubtless drafted the evolutionary path that has brought the present Wildfowlers' Association of Great Britain and Ireland to its presently respected role as the leader and exemplar of legitimacy and discipline in shooting, and an active and forward-looking conservation organisation in its own right.

Other Late Victorian and Edwardian poets like William Sharp (Fiona MacLeod) tenderly delved into history to remind us that the bird lore and bird love of the ancients, from Greeks to Irish saints, was a reality and no idle bookish tradition, and here they were robustly abetted by such scholars as d'Arcy Wentworth Thompson and John Henry Gurney jun., all persuaders and remembrancers for us that birds are not just birds but animals with a history. To others, of course, the birds remained as fascinating literary symbols, as the favourite bird of the English writers was to Oscar Wilde in his story *The Nightingale and the Rose*.

We move into the present century with the tenderness and pity of A. C. Benson, celebrating in pithy, tidy moving verse the busy life of the dipper, the battues at pheasant-shooting time, the prey's feathers drifting over the heather after a falcon's strike. Pioneer of the elder-statesman-syndrome of British bird-loving was Edward Grey of Fallodon, of whom an anonymous *Ibis* obituarist sagely said "a bird to him was an illustration in that book of nature which he so deeply reverenced and so ardently desired to read". Grey wrote like a dream: his *Charm of Birds* is a minor classic of dedication to the pursuit of the most observable and lovable of all wild animals; and if he was ever the prototype of the amateur enthusiast, who could never decide whether birds were pictures, or flowers in some garden, or – wild, tame or captive – some kind of personal property (*his birds*), nevertheless Grey's influence on the transition of ornithology from a happy hobby to a serious pursuit was such that the most important and prolific organisation for scientific field ornithology in western Europe now bears his name. From Grey's time on, the Establishment has run in favour of birds, and St James's

Viscount Grey of Fallodon (1862–1933), photographed in his Northumbrian home by Seton Gordon – with a robin perched upon his head, just as one is said to have perched on St Serf 1300 years earlier.

Park has echoed to the tread of cohorts of Cabinet Ministers with binoculars in their despatch-boxes, admirals with bird-log charts in their briefs, field-marshals with Bell & Howells in their suitcases on their way to the army's greens and heaths south of the Thames to watch manœuvres and perhaps get in an hour or two in the near-by hide, on their hobby (please forgive another pun).

Of the poets of our time (that is, born in 1865 or since) I celebrate none living, but several who lived to a ripe old age and loved birds dearly: W. B. Yeats with all his Celtic love and lore of animal imagery, and deep, economical Irish dramatic capacity for scene setting, and passion for swans and geese and curlews : all Yeats's birds live. So do W. H. Davies's ; his little birds were birds of war and fights and territories as well as of love. So do those of tender, admirable Walter de la Mare, whose poet's eye saw robins, wrens,

The Bird Reserve (in effect) of St James's Park dates from the founding of the waterfowl collection on Charles II's restoration in 1660. *S. R. Badmin*

W.H. Davies (1871–1940), drawn by his friend Augustus John. A keen observer of the beauties of the English countryside, Davies had a fine understanding of bird behaviour.

linnets, tits, martins, rooks and owls so simply that a superficial scanner can confuse them with elfin characters from fairyland only to find, on close reading, that their characters are natural, not nursery notions and that de la Mare had a better, and more total, recall of the "jizz" of a wild bird even than Hudson who invented the word.

De la Mare's stream of bird poetry was deeper than that of most of the other moderns, with the exception of the verse of the short glory of Edward Thomas. Mary Webb's bird images, despite her own depth of emotional feeling for ruralities, were in my view no more than fuel for the St James's Park bird-charm school (Stanley Baldwin was a great Webb fan). The felicitous bird pictures of Robert Lynd were likewise; indeed his best bits in

The famous Abbotsbury Swannery in Dorset dates from the fourteenth century, and is still the sole *social* breeding-place in England of a herd of mute swans. *R.B. Talbot Kelly*

Solomon in All His Glory concern the ducks of the Inner London Parks. H. J. Massingham's copious prose, full of nostalgia for some idealised country image and not without Hudsonian tamperings (with history and fact) showed an inability to face deep rural and ecological realities, and yet a capacity for minute observation and golden enjoyment, often slightly betrayed by an (unconscious?) identification of most of the wild and garden beasts, birds and plants he observed as *his*. Like many fine writers of late, he was a master of birds as Club Talk. The consequent "I must tell you about *my* robin", bars the ornithologist's way to his Brook Street or Pall Mall Club bar, too often for this bird-watcher's liking when he is thirsty. But this is an unfair intolerance of mine, perhaps : if it wasn't for the charm birds have for the Establishment, and the ability as nature *aficionados* of our ruling classes of all parties, we would never have got a decent Wild Birds Protection Act or launched the Nature Conservancy and the National Parks Commission – just in time, perhaps, to save nature's bacon in the most heavily industrialised country in the world. If we can acclaim Grey, Mary Webb, Lynd, E. V. Lucas, Alfred Noyes, Massingham, J. C. Squire and other modern prose and poetry prophets of nature for this, then they are heroes, of natural history and conservation. Scientific biologists (who read poetry as often as any class of scholars except English literature's own servants) recognise these writers' dream of nature as not always what nature is. But they do not know what nature is, either ; they are only trying to find out ; and they are just as fond of Club Talk as anybody else.

In my view the major English bird poet of our century was Edward Thomas. He wrote, as a poet, only for about the first year of the First World War, and was killed in France in 1917, not forty years of age. Earlier he had been a copious writer of literary criticism and belles-lettres ; he was Richard Jefferies's first (and most) important biographer, and a friend of Hudson's.

It was Robert Frost who encouraged his poetry and unloosed a short spate of superlative nature images from a near-genius, who had the observational powers of Clare (whose work he deeply read and loved), and a disciplined economy of style almost without parallel. Nobody, perhaps, but Thomas would have thought of "The swift with wings and tail as sharp and narrow As if the bow had flown off with the arrow". Like J. C. Squire, Thomas saw past rural slow permanence and history in present birds : "When these old woods were young The thrushes' ancestors As sweetly sung In the old years". Birds as artists Thomas saw : the sedge warblers as "small brown birds Wisely reiterating endlessly what no man learnt yet, in or out of school" ; damsons dropping from the bough "Because the starling shakes it, whistling what Once swallows sang" ; a pied wagtail "twittering Happily and sweetly as if the sun itself Extracted the song As the hand makes sparks from the fur of a cat."

Philip Edward Thomas (1878–1917), from a drawing by E.H.Thomas. He understood birds as symbols of rural history and continuity more deeply than any other poet I know of.

In a slow train shortly stuck in Adlestrop Station Thomas listened through the window.

> And for that minute a blackbird sang,
> Close by, and round him, mistier,
> Farther and farther, all the birds
> Of Oxfordshire and Gloucestershire.

Farther and farther all the birds of the English counties sing for the English, and the Welsh birds for the Welsh, come to that. They sing farther in the sense that there are ever more to hear them sing – and not just more people, of course, but more bird people per people.

This is a process without a single origin that has evolved by cause breeding consequence, and consequence new cause – by a sort of feed-back system. "To what historical process do you ascribe the rise of ornithology?" an examination question might ask. My guess is that nowadays an English literature examinee is just as likely to quote the scientific revolution at the Renaissance (Turner, Ray, . . .) as the succession of nature poets from the Dark Ages on ; and a scientific examinee might well consider first the poets, if he knew well the history of his own language.

(*Left*) John Heywood (1497?–1580?), dramatist and musician, the first to note and transcribe accurately the successive changes in the cuckoo's song as the season advances. (*Right*) Orlando Gibbons (1583–1625), whose madrigals demonstrated his keen ear for the confused music of the birds and his ability to translate their natural rhythms into beautiful melodies for the very different human voice.

We have considered the poets, then. In the next chapters we list the men of birds, and then study those other artists, the scientists, the ransackers, the researchers. Before we move to meet these, a note on the musicians of birds; and the painters of birds.

Music knows as few frontiers as the birds, and it is idle to seek a peculiarly British stream of bird-minded composers. The western European bird fauna has been the common inspiration of composers whose work has been at once understood in every country it reached, at least since the sixteenth century. The poets' bird dialogues became bird part songs that have lived down to us at latest from 1529, when Clement Jannequin of France wrote his 4-voice *Chant des Oiseaux*. The English composer John Heywood's analysis of the cuckoo's voice arrived, only a little over-simply, at the conclusion that the male sings in a minor third on arrival, then in a major third, then in a fourth, and later in a fifth, after which its voice breaks without attaining a minor sixth.

It is, of course, not surprising that the composers should have their repertory of favourite music birds. England's Giles Farnaby may have written songs about woodcock and other sporting birds; but the musicians'

(Left) George Frederick Handel (1685–1759), whose glorious music was enlivened by carefully noted bird song to provide pastoral backgrounds for many of his arias; from the portrait by Thomas Hudson in the National Portrait Gallery. *(Right)* Sir Henry Rowley Bishop (1786–1855), one of the many fine nineteenth-century composers with a quick and attentive ear for the music of birds.

seventeenth-century sport was mainly with the avian *prima donnas*, if I may so describe male birds. In 1604, for instance, Thomas Bateson set Philip Sidney's fine nightingale sonnet to equally fine music; Johann Staden composed a charming cuckoo-nightingale song dialogue; Johan Kerll wrote his cuckoo cappriccio; Bernardo Pasquini wrote the famous cuckoo piece that inspired Respighi years later; at the very end of the century in 1700 Alessandro Scarlatti wrote his immortal nightingale cantata. Earlier in the century madrigals like Orlando Gibbons's *Silver Swan* and Thomas Vautor's *Sweet Suffolk Owl* had shown that some musicians were perhaps catching the natural rhythms and jizz of birds, their style and character, more quickly and accurately, and with less tradition-enforced formalisation than the poets.

With the eighteenth century seriously contrived and tenderly composed bird voices rippled and flowed from the harpsichords of François Couperin (nightingales, warblers, canaries, linnets) and Jean-Philippe Rameau (some with charming humour – listen to his *La Poule*): and in Johann Sebastian Bach's *St Matthew Passion* a bird voice became, perhaps for the first time in music, a symbol of intense drama as, through the Evangelist, the cock crew towards the end of Peter's denial of Jesus. George Frederick

Handel took more notice of the country birds than Bach: "pretty warbling quires" are found not only in *Acis and Galatea*; doves, cuckoos and nightingales provide pastoral motifs commonly through his operas and masques. Louis Daquin and Thomas Arne and Mathias van den Gheyn loved cuckoos; Leopold Mozart integrated them, and quails and many of the birds imitable on Italian hunters' decoy whistles – as well as the instruments of the orchestra – into the famous and jolly *Toy Symphony* often attributed to Joseph Haydn: Haydn's own tenderness for birds shows as humorously in his *Poule* symphony (no. 83), and more seriously in *The Creation* and other works. Wolfgang Amadeus Mozart loved birds, too, but wrote little around them – just a song or two: he was his own bird.

Late-eighteenth- and nineteenth-century music-makers brought a happy sophistication to the treatment of birds, and some spirit of research investigation into the music of their fellow-artists. The nightingale-fanciers included Jan Ryba, Alexander Nikolevich Alabiev whose famous soprano song was lifted by Gioachinno Rossini for the Singing Lesson scene in *The Barber of Seville*; also Franz Schubert, Charles Gounod, Johannes Brahms, Camille Saint-Saëns, Piotr Tchaikovskii and Nicholas Rimskii-Korsakov. Lark-fanciers included Henry Bishop, Schubert, Karl Otto Nicolai, Stanislav Moniuszko; dove-lovers Felix Mendelssohn, Robert Schumann, Gounod, Antonin Dvorák, André Messager; swallow-followers Ambroise Thomas, Gounod, Bedrick Smetana, Brahms, Dvorák; cuckoo-echoers William Gardiner, Joseph Gungl, Saint-Saëns. Majestic swans flow in the music of Saint-Saëns, Tchaikovskii, Edvard Grieg. In the *Pastoral Symphony* Ludwig van Beethoven brought birds into his most rural of musical scenes with reality and some humour. But Richard Wagner, who makes a bird voice the hub of the sole humorous passage in the whole incredible gamut of *The Ring*, must be the most inventive and sensitive bird composer of the century. His wood bird of *The Ring* and the forest murmurs of *Siegfried*, and the joyous warbler of *Götterdammerung*, and the reconstituted bird cast of *Siegfried Idyll* are musically no known birds, though a resemblance deserves investigation between the song of the wood bird and that of a tropical American solitaire that Wagner could never have heard of, let alone heard. Wagner seems to have been the only great composer consciously to have listened to the bird song (of Bavaria), and to have used the inspiration he got to invent his own superbirds for the supermen and superwomen of his superdramas.

In the present century the same birds, in new guise, inspire again. Frederick Delius found new things to say about nightingale and cuckoo. In the *Lemminkainen* suite Jan Sibelius's swan of Tuonela mysteriously flies with the deep rhythm of buzzing mute swan primaries pounding the heaviest living flyer through the air. Enrique Granados wrote, in Spain, the loveliest

Ralph Vaughan Williams (1872–1958), who in the wilds of rural Wales captured the lark in a musical *tour de force*. Reproduced from the drawing by Juliet Pannett.

nightingale piece of all – *la Maja y el Ruiseñor*; Vaughan Williams in Wales the loveliest lark piece ever – *The Lark Ascending*. Like the others above, Maurice Ravel wrote bird pieces moving and original before the First World War, and more after, when Ottorino Respighi found new orchestrations for the bird-lover composers of the past like Gallot, Rameau and Pasquini and added his own bird interpretations of nightingales – in one case (as early as 1924) fitting part of an early phonograph record of the great bird music into an orchestral piece *The Pines of Rome*. Beautifully, Peter Warlock made Yeats's *Curlew* poem into a song. Musicological ornithologists find new bird imagery in many of the works of Igor Stravinsky (not only *The Firebird*), and see a deep understanding of the composer-animals in what Benjamin Britten has written (e.g. *Winter Words*, *The Little Sweep*) and even deeper possibilities in what he yet may write.

History alone will show which of our present generation of British bird painters are the great ones; my own guess is that at least four are among masters whose place will be for ever secure in the history of bird art, ranking with not much more than a dozen predecessors.

First of our mainstream bird artists is doubtless the fat, cheerful, kindly and humble figure of George Edwards who, after considerable travel in

(*Left*) George Edwards (1694–1773), Britain's first mainstream orGnithological artist and a fine scientist too. Reproduced from an engraving in the British Museum. (*Right*) John Gould (1804–81), Audubon's English rival, though perhaps more through his skill as impresario, designer and team manager than as an artist in his own right. From an engraving in the British Museum.

western Europe and North America, settled in 1733 as Librarian to the Royal College of Physicians, and wrote and illustrated a fine *History of Birds* and later *Gleanings of Natural History*. Though a good scholar and Fellow of the Royal Society he excelled most as an artist, engraver and hand-colourer of plates, and pioneer in the tradition of fine nature illustrations. For their time, also true-to-life were the bird illustrations of the other eighteenth-century "great" – Eleazar Albin (or Weiss), though he is famous mainly for his insect pictures.

With Thomas Bewick (p. 65) we change centuries, in company with Edward Donovan and George Graves whose hand-coloured plates showed some intelligent efforts to break away from the delineation of stuffed birds. Of the purely nineteenth-century artists Prideaux John Selby, also a fair editor and scholar, was the first to conceive an *Illustrations of British Ornithology* in the same league as Audubon's *Birds of America*, with 218 life-size plates. It came out in parts in 1821–34 and was quite overshadowed by the greater American work. Nevertheless, Selby had very considerable merit, undeservedly neglected, perhaps because of the impact of the younger and greater artist and impresario John Gould.

A complete set of the works of John Gould probably weighs over half a ton. Between 1830 and 1880 this remarkable scientist and artist was responsible for no less than eighteen great folio works, some in seven volumes; and over 300 little works, notes, papers and scientific memoirs. At the height of his

(*Left*) Joseph Wolf (1820–99), the greatest member of John Gould's team. From a photograph taken in 1892 and reproduced in A. H. Palmer's *The Life of Joseph Wolf, Animal Painter* (1895). (*Right*) Allen W. Seaby (1867–1953), a bird artist of neglected talent, famous for his first-rate illustrations to F. B. B. Kirkman's *British Bird Book*; from a drawing by Cyril Pearce.

fame over 1000 people, institutions and libraries subscribed to one or more of his folios: altogether he produced 2999 different folio pictures, reproduced by lithography and coloured by hand; reproduced and hand-coloured in the case of his more popular works such as the *Birds of Great Britain* as many as five hundred times.

Gould's father became a gardener at Windsor Castle when he was four-teen; and young John put his passion for birds to some practical use by stuffing skins for the Eton boys. When he was twenty-three he was summoned from an under-gardener's job at Windsor to act as curator of birds and chief taxidermist to the newly formed Zoological Society of London at the London Zoo. The first giraffe ever to come to England was stuffed by Gould for George IV.

Gould never "did" the bulk of his 2999 great plates on his own, and as an artist was inferior to most of his own team which included his wife, Edward Lear, W. Hart, H. C. Richter and Joseph Wolf. Gould was really a designer and impresario; shrewd, rough and hard – his own agent, salesman, publicity man, accountant and general manager. Though not always entirely scrupulous he kept his team of artists and lithographers together for years. As a field man he was not great: soon after the young Prussian-born Joseph Wolf joined him in 1848 the farmer's son from Germany became the one who usually identified the species and found the nests on their trips together.

Lear's contributions to the Gould file were early (notably in the *Birds of Europe*), few, rather formal, though fine. But the drawings for the finest of them all, the birds of prey in the *Birds of Great Britain* were by Wolf, who has a right to be thought the best animal painter of the nineteenth century with the possible exception of John James Audubon. Wolf, indeed, became a popular artist in his own right, hung on the line of the Royal Academy in his first year in England, praised unreservedly by Edwin Landseer (now equally restored to critics' favour).

Few nineteenth-century bird artists shine outside Gould's ample shadow. Benjamin Fawcett did some good illustrations for F. O. Morris's popular *History of British Birds* for which he gets little credit, even in bibliographies, and Edward Neale is another Victorian British bird artist of talent without enough honour. Between Gould's *Birds of Great Britain* (last plates 1873) and about 1900 scarcely any important work on ornithology (scientific journals included) was issued in Britain without a coloured plate by the very competent if slightly academic artist John Gerrard Keulemans. In 1892 a thirty-four-year-old animal artist of greater competence (in my opinion) and field experience came to England from Denmark: Henrik Grönvold's best work, perhaps, is to be seen in the late H. Eliot Howard's great *The British Warblers* of 1907–14.

Of the British bird artists of living memory the greatest is certainly the Scot Archibald Thorburn who with his techniques of tempera and flake-white made pictures admirably suited to the more sophisticated reproductive processes of the twentieth century. Most famous, perhaps, are his illustrations for Lord Lilford's *Coloured Figures of the Birds of the British Islands*, doubtless the most widely reproduced bird pictures of all time, since they still persist in modern editions of T. A. Coward's *Birds of the British Isles* (since 1920) and other publications of Messrs Warnes. Thorburn's faultless technique and the field knowledge which brought his birds so much to life have lately found new favour; and an original Thorburn is a collector's piece. I own my best liking not for his Lilford plates, painted to order, but for his free, field-wise, environment-sensitive pictures in his later folios.

Thorburn had a near-twin in George Edward Lodge who died but a decade ago, working to the end, and to whom fame really came at the end of his life, with his magnificent illustrations to David Bannerman's *Birds of the British Isles* (1953–63). Lodge could always paint birds of prey better than Thorburn, or indeed anybody; but for long he lay under Thorburn's shadow, though never eclipsed – with other fine artists of somewhat forgotten talent like John Guille Millais, great wildfowl and mammal artist and fourth son of that redoubtable President of the Royal Academy Sir John Millais; and Allen W. Seaby whose contributions to F. B. B. Kirkman's underrated *British Bird Book* of 1910–13 were excellent indeed.

CHAPTER 9

A List of Bird-Watchers

This selection will doubtless be disputed, as all such inevitably are for their errors of omission and commission. The names are a gross and more of those not now living who have made some mark on the chronicles, the poetry, the literary prose and the scientific investigation of our islands' birds that is, in my opinion, original and unlikely to be ignored by future historians and analysts. Since Renaissance times a distinction can be made between those who wrote of birds primarily as masters of literature or history, and those who wrote of them primarily as masters of science. Certain great ones were both. By my rating (doubtless disputable) those who were primarily scientific get one asterisk *; those who were both get two **; not all are mentioned in the texts of Chapters 8 and 10.

VIc.
St Serf
St Kentigern (Mungo) 518?–603
St Columba (Columkille) 521–97

VIIc.
St Cuthbert 637?–87
The writer of *Beowulf* ? fl. *c*. 664
The Seafarer ? fl. *c*. 685–705
St Aldhelm *c*. 640–709
St Guthlac 663?–714

VIIIc.
Bede 673?–735
The writers of the *Husband's Message* and the *Fortunes* (or *Fates*) *of Men* and some riddles in the *Exeter Book*.
Alcuin 735–804

IXc.
King Ælfred (Alfred) the Great 849–901

Xc.
Irish poems
Ælfric the Grammarian *c*. 955–*c*. 1020

XIc.
Contributors to "Domesday Book" *c*. 1086

XIIc.
Reginald of Durham ?–1173
Thomas of Ely ?–*c*. 1174
William FitzStephen ?–*c*.1190

XII–XIIIc.
Gerald di Barri (Cambrensis) 1146?–1223

Alexander Neckam (Nequam)
1157–1217
Robert Grosseteste 1175–1253

XIIIc.

John of Guildford fl. *c.* 1225
Bartholomew the Englishman
(Bartholomaeus Anglicus) fl.
c. 1231
Matthew Paris 1200?–59
Roger Bacon 1214?–92

XIVc.

Dafydd ap Gwilym
William Langland 1330?–1400?
Geoffrey Chaucer 1340?–1400

XVc.

John Lydgate 1370–1452
Juliana Berners 1388?–1450?
Sir Thomas Clanvowe fl. 1389–
1404
Sir Richard Holland fl. 1453
John Russell fl. *c.* 1460
William Botoner (Worcester)
1415–82?

XVIc.

John Skelton 1460?–1529
William Dunbar 1465?–1530?
Hector Boece (Boethius) 1465–
1536
*William Turner *c.* 1500–68
*John Caius 1510–73
Henry Howard, Earl of Surrey
1516–47
George Gascoigne 1523?–77

XVI–XVIIc.

William Camden 1551–1623
Edmund Spenser 1552?–99
Sir Philip Sidney 1554–86
John Lyly 1554?–1606

*Nicholas Carter fl. *c.* 1600
Alexander Hume 1560?–1609
Francis Bacon, Baron Verulam
and Viscount St Albans 1561–
1626
Michael Drayton 1563–1631
Christopher Marlowe 1564–93
William Shakespeare 1564–1616
Thomas Nashe 1567–1601
Thomas Weelks fl. *c.* 1602
Thomas Heywood 1570?–1650
John Donne 1573–1631
Ben Jonson 1573?–1637
Richard Barnfield 1574–1627

XVIIc.

John Taylor 1580–1653
John Webster 1580?–1625
Phineas Fletcher 1582–1650
William Drummond 1585–1649
John Mundy *c.* 1586–1630
William Browne 1591–1643?
Robert Herrick 1591–1674
Francis Quarles 1592–1644
George Herbert 1593–1633
Izaak Walton 1593–1683
Thomas Carew 1595?–1639?
*Sir Thomas Browne 1605–82
Edmund Waller 1606–87
John Milton 1608–74
Robert Wild 1609–79
Samuel Butler 1612–80
Richard Crashaw 1613?–49
*Christopher Merrett 1614–95
George Daniel 1616–57
Abraham Cowley 1618–67

XVII–XVIIIc.

John Evelyn 1620–1706
Andrew Marvell 1621–78
Matthew Stevenson fl. 1654–85
*John Ray 1627–1705

John Dryden 1631–1700
*Francis Willughby 1635–72
Sir Robert Sibbald 1641–1722
John Oldham 1653–83
*William Derham 1657–1735
Joseph Addison 1672–1719
Nicholas Rowe 1674–1718
William Somerville 1675–1742
*Martin Martin fl. 1697–1719
John Gay 1685–1732

XVIIIc.

Alexander Pope 1688–1744
*George Edwards 1694–1773
James Thomson 1700–48
John Dyer 1700?–58
*Eleazar Albin fl. 1713–59
Lawrence Sterne 1713–68
William Shenstone 1714–63
Richard Jago 1715–81
Thomas Gray 1716–71
**Gilbert White 1720–93
William Collins 1721–59
Mark Akenside 1721–70
Christopher Smart 1722–71
Thomas Warton 1726–90
*Thomas Pennant 1726–98
*Daines Barrington 1727–1800
Oliver Goldsmith 1728–74
John Cunningham 1729–73
William Cowper 1731–1800

XVIII–XIXc.

James Beattie 1735–1803
*John Latham 1740–1837
Anna Letitia Barbauld 1743–1825
Michael Bruce 1746–67
John Logan 1748–88
**Edward Jenner 1749–1828
*George Montagu 1751–1815
George Crabbe 1754–1832

John Bidlake 1755–1814
William Blake 1757–1827
Robert Burns 1759–96
William Cobbett 1762–1835
Joanna Baillie 1762–1851
James Hurdis 1763–1801
Samuel Rogers 1763–1855
Mary Lamb 1764–1847
James Grahame 1765–1811
Robert Bloomfield 1766–1823
James Hogg 1770–1835
William Wordsworth 1770–1850
Sir Walter Scott 1771–1832
John Montgomery 1771–1854
Samuel Taylor Coleridge 1772–1834
Robert Southey 1774–1843
Charles Lamb 1775–1834
Ricard Mant 1776–1848
Noel Thomas Carrington 1777–1830
*Robert Mudie 1777–1842
William Hazlitt 1778–1830
Thomas Moore 1779–1852

XIXc.

**Charles Waterton 1782–1865
Washington Irving 1783–1859
Allan Cunningham 1784–1842
*William Yarrell 1784–1856
**John James LaForest Audubon 1785–1851
Bryan Waller Procter (Barry Cornwall) 1787–1874
Percy Bysshe Shelley 1792–1822
John Keble 1792–1866
**(Mrs) Felicia Dorothea Hemans 1793–1835
John Clare 1793–1864
John Keats 1795–1821
Thomas Carlyle 1795–1881
Hartley Coleridge 1796–1849

*William Macgillivray 1796–1852

Thomas Hood 1799–1845

Mary Howitt 1799–1888

William Barnes 1801–86

Robert Chambers 1802–71

William Kidd 1803–67

George Borrow 1803–81

*William Thompson 1805–62

Elizabeth Barrett Browning 1806–61

*John Hancock 1806–90

R. C. Trench 1807–86

Charles St John 1809–56

Alfred Lord Tennyson 1809–92

William Makepeace Thackeray 1811–63

**Edward Lear 1812–88

Robert Browning 1812–99

Frederick William Faber 1814–63

*Thomas Edward 1814–86

Emily Brontë 1818–48

Eliza Cook 1818–89

Margaret Emily Shore 1819–39

Charles Kingsley 1819–75

John Ruskin 1819–1900

Jean Ingelow 1820–97

Matthew Arnold 1822–88

Coventry Patmore 1823–96

Sydney Dobell 1824–74

J. G. Wood 1827–89

Dante Gabriel Rossetti 1828–82

XIX–XXc.

George Meredith 1828–1909

**D'Arcy Wentworth Thompson 1829–1902

*Alfred Newton 1829–1907

*Philip Lutley Sclater 1829–1913

Alexander Smith 1830–67

Christina Rossetti 1830–94

*Alexander Goodman More 1830–95

Thomas Edward Brown 1830–97

John R. Wise 1831–90

*Henry Seebohm 1832–95

James Thomson (II) 1834–82

William Morris 1834–96

*Howard Saunders 1835–1907

Algernon Charles Swinburne 1837–1907

*Henry Eeles Dresser 1838–1915

Thomas Hardy 1840–1928

*Richard John Ussher 1841–1913

**William Henry Hudson 1841–1922

*James Edmund Harting 1841–1928

*John Alexander Harvie-Brown 1844–1916

Robert Seymour Bridges 1844–1930

H. J. Elwes 1846–1922

*Richard Bowdler Sharpe 1847–1909

**William Warde Fowler 1847–1921

John Richard Jefferies 1848–87

*John Henry Gurney jun. 1848–1922

*Richard Lydekker 1849–1915

**Abel Chapman 1851–1929

*William Eagle Clarke 1853–1938

William Sharp ("Fiona MacLeod") 1855–1905

J. C. Tregarthen 1855–1933

*Arthur Humble Evans 1855–1943

John Arthington Walpole-Bond (1878–1958), type of the latter-day enthusiast; scholar, egg-collector, and of vast field skill and energy. From a photograph.

Oscar O'Flahertie Wills Wilde 1856–1900
*Hugh Alexander Macpherson 1858–1901
*Ernst Johann Otto Hartert 1859–1933
**Edmund Selous *c.* 1860–*c.* 1933
Arthur Christopher Benson 1862–1925
*Richard Kearton 1862–1928
Edward Grey, Viscount Grey of Fallodon 1862–1933
*William Robert Ogilvie-Grant 1863–1924
William Butler Yeats 1865–1939
Francis Charles Robert Jourdain 1865–1940
*Thomas Alfred Coward 1867–1933
*Charles Oldham 1868–1942
Michael Fairless 1869–1901
J. M. Synge 1871–1909
W. H. Davies 1871–1940
*Edward Adrian Wilson 1872–1912
**Henry Eliot Howard 1873–1940
*Harry Forbes Witherby 1873–1943

**Ernest William Hendy 1873–1950

XXc.
Walter de la Mare 1873–1956
*Leonora Jeffrey Rintoul 1875–1953
*Oliver G. Pike 1877–1963
Philip Edward Thomas 1878–1917
*John Arthington Walpole-Bond 1878–1958
*Evelyn Vida Baxter 1879–1959
Mary Gladys Webb 1881–1927
*Edgar P. Chance 1881–1955
*Sir Norman Boyd Kinnear 1882–1957
*Arnold Whitworth Boyd 1885–1959
*Wilfrid Backhouse Alexander 1885–1965
*Bernard William Tucker 1901–1950

Wilfred Backhouse Alexander (1885–1965), first Director of the Edward Grey Institute of Field Ornithology, systematist, field expert *par excellence*, and unparalleled scholar of the literature of ornithology. From a photograph.

CHAPTER 10

The Ornithologists

In Chapter 2 (pp. 43–81) we have studied the rise of the British Bird List, particularly to the Linnaean year of 1758, and the time of Gilbert White and his predecessors as scientific fathers of ornithology, and some of his friends and successors like Pennant, Barrington, Latham and Montagu. After Montagu, the first British scientific ornithologist to have been wholly brought up in the Linnaean epoch was the eccentric squire and traveller Charles Waterton, who contributed more to the science of the Americas than to our islands, though he kept an inquiring-spirited diary all his life.

William Yarrell, of the purely nineteenth-century ornithologists, was a paragon of amateur virtue who came late in life to serious ornithology, which he embraced at the age of forty. He set the style of the modern systematic textbook when his *A History of British Birds* began to come out in 1837; with Alfred Newton and Howard Saunders's help this fine, definitive avifauna continued until well into the present century and many a present ornithologist, myself included, has been brought up on some version of it. In 1837, too, another *History of British Birds* began to emerge in print from the Conservator of the Museum of the Edinburgh College of Surgeons, one William Macgillivray (friend, and in our islands guide and scientific mentor to John James Audubon), shortly to become Professor of Natural History at Aberdeen University.[1] Macgillivray had probably the most original mind of any Early Victorian ornithologist, irritable, enthusiastic, chip-on-the-shoulder, ruthlessly accurate, impatient, scholarly, practical, poetic, kind and generous to those with the same sort of courage. The Establishment (mainly of England) did not like, or at least did not want to understand him. He understood it quite well, and did not like it, either. History, which repeats itself interminably, as it corrects mistakes in fame or

[1] A Chair which today is occupied by another distinguished ornithologist, V. C. Wynne-Edwards, President of our British Ornithologists' Union as I write.

Slimbridge, with the world's greatest living wildfowl collection, is also a refuge for wintering geese and ducks; here a rare red-breasted goose flies with whitefronts (also from Russia) and a pair of mallards. *Peter Scott*

Charles Waterton (1782–1865), eccentric squire and traveller, diarist, and inquiring spirit, an early British ornithologist of the Linnaean epoch; from the painting in the National Portrait Gallery.

favour, has put Macgillivray back in the swim a century late. He badly needs a new biographer, though many of his papers were accidentally burned in Australia long ago.

A lesser scientist, but typical of the stream of Victorian amateur ornithological endeavour, was John Hancock, tradesman (saddler and ironmonger) of Newcastle-upon-Tyne, who made himself into a brilliant taxidermist, formed a vast collection now the basis for the great museum at Barras Bridge in Newcastle that bears his name, was a fairly competent artist, a reluctant though useful writer on the birds of the Tyne province, and a keen falconer. Contemporary with Hancock was another provincial hero – Thomas Edward, an Englishman who spent nearly all his life in Banff as a humble shoemaker, but discovered 20 new species of British crustaceans, knew nearly every plant in the counties of Aberdeen and Banff, and in the 1850s published *A List of the Birds of Banffshire, accompanied with Anecdotes*. In northern England and Scotland most particularly, a tradition of self-education and serious scientific endeavour among working-class naturalists, supported by local natural history societies and museums, dates from Early Victorian days, and Edward is one of the finer products of this movement.

The oldest official Bird Observatory in Britain, the Pembrokeshire sanctuary of Skokholm has fine sea birds, and lies in the country of the red-billed chough. *C. F. Tunnicliffe*

(*Left*) John Hancock (1806–90), taxidermist, local faunist, museum innovator, and a keen falconer; a portrait reproduced from *The Zoologist* of 1890. (*Right*) Alfred Newton (1829–1907), founder of the British Ornithologists' Union, Professor of Zoology at Cambridge, traveller, pioneer conservationist, and the greatest ornithological scholar of his time. From a photograph.

Margaret Emily Shore, in her short life (p. 197) represents another product of the Early Victorian progressive climate. The daughter of an unconventional parson who earned his living teaching and tutoring, she was brought up in an atmosphere of scholarship in a household in which an inquiring view of nature (and indeed everything) was encouraged. By the age of eighteen she had learned over 70 of the birds of England's southern counties on her own, with the aid of the books of the day; she was well aware of the geographical variation of the songs of chaffinches at the age of fifteen. Her thoughtful diary, with its notes on bird song and behaviour, with fine original material on red-backed shrike, nightingale, skylark, redstart, goldcrest and other birds, shows that if she had ever reached maturity and enlarged her obvious capacity for scholarship as well as observation she might have anticipated the behaviour-stream of ornithology by over half a century, and reached perhaps the calibre of Mrs Margaret Morse Nice, today's doyenne of bird-behaviour studies.

In those streets of Cambridge which lie between Magdalene College and the University Museum a tall, bent figure with two sticks and a tall stove-pipe hat, with white hair and white whiskers, was often to be seen in the early years of the present century. This was Alfred Newton, the University Professor of Zoology, and one of the last of the Great Figures at the end of the age of great figures. There is nobody like Newton today, in ornithology. There are many, without doubt, with his ability, there is none with his individuality or his character. After his death in 1907 Dr Guillemard wrote:

"Newton must be accounted an extinct type, as extinct as the great auk and dodo of which he loved so much to write."

Newton was a great Tory, and a great opponent of any sort of violent change. This extended to his personal habits, his clothes were old-fashioned, his manners were old-fashioned (he was for instance, meticulously courteous), his speech was old-fashioned. He called matches Vesuvians years after they had ceased going off like volcanos. But he was also a progressive, for such are all true scientists. In his youth, when human ignorance and greed could extinguish his favourite bird, the great auk, and many other species too, he was searching for knowledge, travelling to Spitsbergen, Lapland, Iceland and North America; in his prime he was teaching his knowledge, founding the British Ornithologists' Union, becoming an early Darwinist and conservationist, writing his *Dictionary of Birds* and other great works; in his old age he saw zoology an established and senior science in his University, and encouraged younger men with wisdom and humour. Newton was the type specimen of the academic scholar, who brought the hobby-pursuit of bird-watching finally, and with respect, into the fold of biological science. When the B.O.U. did a broadcast on the centenary of its own foundation by a group of eleven "gentlemen attached to the study of ornithology", it appropriately met in the very place of the foundation meetings – Alfred Newton's old room in Magdalene College, Cambridge. Very little seemed to have changed.

Philip Lutley Sclater, born in the same year as Newton and first editor of the B.O.U.'s *Ibis*, was a great scholar, too, and ornithologist-originator of what amounts to the present classification and naming of the zones now occupied by the principal faunas on the face of the globe. His assistance to British ornithology was mainly administrative and taxonomic; he was a good committee-man, and made a lasting mark.

Of the vintage of the 1830s four British ornithologists are outstanding. The Irish naturalist Alexander Goodman More made fine faunal surveys in south England and Ireland, and is particularly distinguished for having pioneered (1865 in *Ibis*) the modern techniques of collecting immediate distributional information by a planned correspondence network. Henry Seebohm, a Sheffield steel man, was one of the greatest of academic amateurs, a tireless collector who presented 16,000 specimens to the Natural History Museum, a robust arctic traveller, expert on the thrushes, geographer and monographer. His *History of British Birds* of 1883–85 is a classic repository of much original field observation and ideas before his time. Howard Saunders was another – merchant-banker, active traveller and bird-watcher on the Continent, gull and tern expert, first administrator of the British Ornithologists' Club and famous editor (with Newton) of the perennial Yarrell. The third was Henry Eeles Dresser, zoologist, bee-eater and roller

Richard John Ussher (1841–1913) exploring Shandon Cave, near Dungarvan, Co. Waterford. A fine avian palaeontologist and Ireland's great bird faunist. From the *Transactions of the Royal Irish Academy*.

expert, of another (timber and metal) business family, world traveller and author of the pioneer and highly scientific *History of the Birds of Europe*, who left 12,000 skins to the Manchester Museum.

In the 1840s more giants were born, among them perhaps the greatest of Irish ornithologists, Richard John Ussher of Co. Waterford. His *Birds of Ireland* with Robert Warren in 1900 was a culmination of years of hard work by a big, quiet, blue-eyed, red-bearded figure that was seen, at one time or another, in nearly every wood, on nearly every lough, hill and cliff in Ireland. Unlike most of his fellow-ornithologists, Ussher was a fine archaeologist and cave-explorer, and we owe our relatively deep knowledge of the fossil past of Ireland's birds largely to him.

Of Hudson, also of the 'forties, I have already written; a near-twin of his, James Edmund Harting, was almost his antithesis as a scholar. Harting and John Henry Gurney jun., also born in the 1840s, realised better than most that the British birds had a history and set themselves to search documents back through medieval times to the Dark Ages before them. Like many Victorians they had a firm belief in the values of history; I possess many of Harting's own annotated books and delight to delve into the acute scholar's shorthand and pithy criticisms of one who was perhaps the best natural history editor *The Field* has had, and a distinguished editor of other journals and acute and knowledgeable librarian. Harting's books embraced a useful *Handbook of British Birds*, works on extinct British animals, falconry, county avifaunas, the birds of Shakespeare and many other subjects, including bibliographies. Gurney, son of a namesake who was an original member of the B.O.U., was a prolific Norfolk ornithologist with as tireless a passion for history as Harting's. His most famous work – and my own favourite bird book – is his classic *The Gannet, a Bird with a History* of 1913. This broke new ground in being the first deep monograph ever to have been written on one species of living wild bird, and contained the demonstration

(*Left*) Henry Seebohm (1832–95), monographer, geographical faunist, traveller and redoubtable collector; from *The Ornithologist*, 1896. (*Right*) John Henry Gurney jun. (1848–1922), pioneer species monographer, bibliophile, antiquarian and historian.

that it was even possible to make an educated guess of its world population. Gurney's last work – the *Early Annals of Ornithology* – is a useful quarry of esoteric information from medieval times.

I have always felt much affection and respect for Gurney, and for another great character of his vintage, John Alexander Harvie-Brown of the county of Stirling, once a pupil of Alfred Newton's at Cambridge. Harvie-Brown's scholarship was not always absolutely meticulous; but he had a huge library and (until it was accidentally burned) bird collection. Of independent means, he travelled abroad in northern Europe; but spent most of his life organising, and contributing more than anybody else to the writing of, monographs of the vertebrate natural history of the major faunal regions that he and his colleagues had split Scotland into. The "Harvie-Brown Faunas" were virtually complete on his death, a monument to the skill and energy of a band of close friends, and a dedicated sportsman-yachtsman-historian-organiser. Of all bird-historians, Harvie-Brown earliest pioneered the present-style B.T.O. population surveys when, using the technique of A.G. More (p. 227) he circularised fellow-landowners for lists of their rookeries and fulmar colonies and the numbers of nests therein. His capercaillie survey of 1879 was a monographic classic, though not global as was Gurney's *Gannet*. He was a pioneer of the technique of rounding up migration information from lighthouse-keepers and other isolated observers.

Other striding figures born in the 'forties and 'fifties are Richard Bowdler Sharpe, primarily a global order-bringer to the science of birds but an active encourager of the pursuit of our own islands' fauna; William Warde Fowler, philologist and lexicographer who saw birds with a behaviour student's eye and a scholar's eye, too; Richard Lydekker, anatomist, palaeontologist and many things beside; Abel Chapman and Robert Service (p. 203); Harvie-Brown's friends Arthur Humble Evans and Hugh Alexander Macpherson, formidable island-explorers and, in their own right, even deeper scholars of the literature (Macpherson's *History of Fowling* of 1897 is a forgotten classic). William Eagle Clarke, an Englishman who became the Natural History Keeper of the Royal Scottish Museum, was a thoughtful faunist and fine editor who pioneered, with others, the study and collation of observed migration around our shores and foresaw in *practice* the modern network of more permanent bird observatories, ringing stations and watch points. We pride ourselves today if we watch migration at Cape Wrath, or Ouessant in France, or on the Fair Isle, the Eddystone, the Flannans, the Kentish Knock or St Kilda. Eagle Clarke knew them all before nearly all the present *habitués* of such remarkable places were born.

In the last hundred years the flow of ornithology has been rather delta-like, in that separate but allied streams can be detected. This of course happens to all sciences that become sophisticated and attract a mass following. Indeed, but one of the present streams is less than a century old – the science of bird-voice recording. The global pioneer of this, Ludwig Koch, was born in 1881, made his first bird recording on an Edison wax cylinder in 1891, came to England in 1936 and virtually founded the B.B.C.'s present fine collection of recorded natural sound, and is still happily working in the field as I write. The other streams were all pioneered by men and women born over a century ago. Of course, all streams belong to a system, and however they may proliferate, the central system, with its servants, goes on. Behaviour and migration studies of today may encourage field workers to forget that behind ornithology's progress stands, for all time, the museum and the library and their servants; that is to say, collections of material and facts. Because Edmund Selous (born *c*. 1860) pioneered behaviour studies, Richard Kearton (born 1862) bird photography and Francis Charles Robert Jourdain (born 1865) the present disciplines of field identification does not mean to say that the heroes of older continuing streams are any less heroic. Ernst Johann Otto Hartert (born 1859), the great museum man of the early days of the Rothschild Museum at Tring, brought new and necessary order and system to our arrangements of British birds, and to the concepts of species and race. William Robert Ogilvie-Grant (born 1863) was another valuable servant of order, as was Norman Boyd Kinnear (born 1882) – a great field man as well as museum man.

Among the scores of devoted developers of local recording, precise geographic work without which bird-watching cannot be ornithology, I have room to mention very few – Ernest William Hendy of the West Country (born 1873) who was a poet of birds and a scientist too; and a captive of enthusiasm comparable with the great George Montagu: John

(*Left*) Ernst Johann Otto Hartert (1859–1933), systematist, museum man, and deep faunist of the birds of Europe. (*Right*) Arnold Whitworth Boyd (1885–1959), local naturalist, skilful field man; type of a growing stream of disciplined county and parish fauna analysts and writers.

Arthington Walpole-Bond (born 1878), historian of Welsh and Sussex birds and a magical field finder of every inconspicuous little passerine that ever squeaked a confusing call-note or hid its nest where none but Walpole-Bond could come across it. In this category are two unforgettable heroines, regarded with respect and affection by the many living who knew and admired them: Leonora Jeffrey Rintoul (born 1875) and Evelyn Vida Baxter (born 1879) who for over forty years worked together on the annual records of the birds of Scotland, which they ranged into the tidiest meticulous order, and from which they made a succession of two great textbooks; the second of which, *The Birds of Scotland* of 1953, is still the standard work.

Edmund Selous (born *c.* 1860) is one of the least understood of British ornithologists, largely because of the confused arrangement of a great deal of the material in his books. Yet he was the undoubted pioneer of behaviour studies in our islands. Very much a lone wolf, Selous did not belong to clubs, or publish very much work in scientific journals. I can find no obituary of him in any British bird magazine. But behind the apparent chaos of observation mixed with conclusion in his work lurk gems of discovery about the displays and drives of the sea birds of Shetland, and waders and other birds of the wild northern places that attracted his inquiring, emotional mind. The latest generation of ethologists is happily mining the nuggets from Selous, and finding that things it believed it discovered were known to Selous in their great-grandfather's time. If Edward Adrian Wilson (born 1872), who died with Scott in the Antarctic in 1912 had lived he, with his academic discipline, and field experience on the famous grouse survey of the early years of this century, might have become one of the greatest of ethologists; his last study of emperor penguins showed highly advanced thought. Of Wilson's generation (born 1873) was Henry Eliot Howard, a Midlands steelmaster who early devoted his spare time to the close observation of the behaviour of birds. His classics are *The British Warblers* (1907–15) and *Territory in Bird Life* (1920). Howard wrote later works distinguished by their felicity of expression and their excursions into philosophical depths hard for the reader to penetrate. Like many great amateurs of near-genius calibre he was capricious in his reading and citation of other ethologists, whose analysis has shown that many of the concepts he presented were not as original as was believed when they were first published. Nevertheless, *Territory in Bird Life* is a milestone book, and has built a framework. It identified with clarity and deep understanding a process of birds' lives which is universal and fundamental: every textbook of birds now has a *Territory* heading – put there by Eliot Howard.

Today bird ethology in our islands is organised in great detail, and with new disciplines, at Oxford and Cambridge and many other universities: yet amateurs inspired by the Howardian tradition still usefully vie with the Ph.D. contestants. It is unlikely, though, that present circumstances will allow ornithology another Chance. Praying forgiveness for yet another pun, I cannot leave the behaviour stream without more than a nod at Edgar P. Chance (born 1881), perhaps the last British oologist who put an obsessive urge to collect eggs to excellent purpose. In a nutshell, Chance's great discovery was the minute details of the reproductive life of the cuckoo. His self-designed behaviour experiments, involving egg-translocations, and the early use of the movie camera (aided by the late Oliver G. Pike) were marvels of logical thought. He finally proved that the female cuckoo (his birds were mostly meadow-pipit cuckoos) lays twelve or more eggs in a season; finds host-nests at the right stages to offer a regular laying sequence; and lays directly into the nest. The last edition of his *The Truth about the Cuckoo* was published in 1940.

Oliver G. Pike (born 1877), Chance's talented photographer, was one of the pioneers of bird photography in the world. No proper photographs of wild birds were taken anywhere until the 1890s. The first British bird photographer of fame was Richard Kearton (born 1862) who was at work in places as remote as St Kilda before the century was out. Oswin A. J. Lee (born 1869) and Pike soon followed along the trails to the remote valleys and the northern isles; in the early days environment was captured as happily as close-ups. After a period between the wars, when few bird photographers could drag themselves to photograph anything other than nesting birds from hides (which they collected as others collected skins or ticked-off species on their life tally), the hobby is now broad and big time; with rewards for the top cinematographers on television and – more importantly – a scientific purpose. Both colour film and tape now record birds for comparative analysis. Ethological units have cameras (sometimes sound cameras) as a matter of course. Rare birds, or the rare displays of common birds, can be collected for analysis without killing; and what can be analysed from film and voice record is *different* from, and *complementary* to, the dead skin. For the first time bird behaviour can be collected, stored, analysed and compared in a library, at scientific leisure. Already, with the aid of film and tape, new revisions of the scientific arrangement of the wildfowl have been made, based on comparative behaviour. Photography as a method of collection is benign. It is not *totally* benign, for over-keen photographers have earned a bad reputation for disturbing breeding birds, and even destroying their habitat, in some places. But it is a most splendid instrument of our hobby and science, when properly used.

In Chapter 2 (pp. 67–68) I have shown that many of the works of the later bird heroes cited here are within the normal reading of most present bird-watchers. At the risk of some slight reiteration, I cannot end this chapter without some celebration of the pioneers of the most important stream of bird-watching of the last hundred years. It is just a century since the oldest deviser of the modern disciplines of field identification was born. Harry Forbes Witherby (born 1873) and Francis Charles Robert Jourdain (born 1865) formed a formidable partnership with Bernard William Tucker (born 1901) and Norman Frederic Ticehurst who is still active and as far as I can detect the only living member of our Union elected in the nineteenth century. These were the heroes of field system whose work culminated in the great *Handbook of British Birds* of 1938–41, still a standard for us. Closely associated with them was a group of Cheshire field men: Thomas Alfred Coward (born 1867), Charles Oldham (born 1868) and Arnold Whitworth Boyd (born 1885). My own field days go back long enough to have been shared, now and then, here and there, with all the Absent Ibises of this list. I shall never forget being examined by Harry Witherby about a little auk and a great skua I had, as a schoolboy, claimed to have seen on a west London reservoir. These men were the headmasters and the examiners of a new and necessary teaching system, and all the patent integrity and rigorous record scrutiny of today's bird journals and reports stems from them. The interesting thing is that nobody resents, any more, the probing of the Tucker-trained editor.

CHAPTER 11

A Bird-Watcher's Guide to the Birds' Provinces

I offer here a detailed guide to the bird geography of Britain and Ireland, with an indication of all major accessible Bird Reserves, Wildfowl Refuges, Migration Watch Points, Bird Observatories, Zoos with birds, Museums with bird material, etc. known to me in 1965, and bibliography of the latest regional published works (which of course nearly all contain bibliographies of previous published works). Readers will find a pioneer geographical guide, R.S.R. Fitter's *Collins guide to bird watching* very useful (I have found it a source of much information in compiling this chapter), and my *Shell nature-lovers' atlas* contains fuller details of nature reserves and field stations, with national parks, areas of outstanding natural beauty, national forest parks, State forests, etc., with the appropriate national grid references. Readers are *implored* to consult the appropriate body *beforehand* before attempting to visit any reserve or other place not obviously public.

This guide lists also the major bird-watching societies, and natural history societies with bird interests or sections, operating in the vice-counties, counties, provinces and other areas, to the best of my present information. Most of them publish at least annual printed reports, and many of them periodical journals. The addresses of their secretaries are not so stable as can be given in what is (I hope) a non-ephemeral book, but most county libraries and museums are well aware of them, and many are listed in the current *Scientific and learned societies of Britain* (London, Allen and Unwin). I have given the addresses of the county trusts in the *Shell nature-lovers' atlas*.

In Britain and Ireland, by common consent, ornithologists mainly follow two geographical disciplines in the recording of their data – the vice-county system and the national grid. The vice-county system was devised by H. C. Watson in his *Topographical botany* published in 1873–74, and splits Engla,nd Wales and Scotland into 112 vice-counties of approximately equal area and ecological importance based on the political county boundaries of that time, with his own divisions of the larger ones and certain readjustments (described in the notes that follow). An Irish vice-county system followed in 1901 (p. 286). As county boundaries have changed since then, a large-scale map of the Watsonian provinces and vice-counties is much desired, particularly as biological records *must* be arranged on a pattern that is stable though the years. The grid system is recent, and can be very precise, as the present one-inch maps in Great Britain, and half-inch maps in Ireland, enable any record to be plotted correct to about a hundred yards, and any general distributions to be mapped by blocking in grid units, of which the squares of side 10 kilometres and 5 kilometres are favourites. The 5-kilometre-side square has the advantage of having an area that is almost exactly 10 square miles (9·6526, in fact). Coarse distributions on small scales are still best shown by blocking in vice-counties, as in my *Bird recognition*.

The National Grid and the Irish National Grid (see maps on endpapers) are imposed on all maps produced by the Ordnance Survey from Chessington (Greater London) and Dublin. The grids are kilometric, and each square of side 100 kilometres is identified in Ireland by a single letter and in England, Scotland and Wales by two letters.

The small-scale maps (i.e. 1/625,000 or ten miles to the inch; 1/253,440 or four miles to the inch – the quarter-inch series; 1/126,720 or two miles to the inch – the half-inch series) are gridded within the lettered squares normally at 10-kilometre intervals, the grid-lines being numbered by larger single figures at the margins. The travelling naturalist will find several useful maps in the twin-sheet ten-mile U.K. series – not only a fine Route Planning map (with National Parks, larger National Nature Reserves, etc. thereon) but also beautiful Geological, Land Classification, Land Utilisation, Types of Farming, Vegetation (Grasslands), Rainfall, etc. sets. The quarter-inch is perhaps the most useful scale for a motor or train journey.

Larger scale maps include the one-inch series (1/63,360) and the two-and-a-half-inch series (1/25,000). The first of these is *essential* to the general naturalist, and the second important to his local studies as its detail embraces even field boundaries. These maps are normally gridded at 1-kilometre intervals, the grid-lines being numbered by large double figures at the margins. The small figures that precede some of these belong to the 100-kilometre grid-line and are replaced in this book by the letter code.

Instructions on finding a four-figure national grid reference are given on every sheet of O.S. small-scale maps, and on finding a six-figure reference on every larger scale O.S. sheet. In this book four-figure references are given. Those using the one-inch series can read them straight off, remembering that in a four-figure reference the first two represent the easting, the last two the northing. As an example, the Wildfowl Refuge at Pitsford Reservoir in Northamptonshire is represented by SP 7771–7970. This means that it lies in 100-kilometre square SP, and within that square between the 1-kilometre squares whose south-west corners are at (easting) 77 (northing) 71; and at (easting) 79 (northing) 70. Easting, of course, is read off the bottom margin of the map; northing off the sides. Those using larger scales must usually find the second figures of the easting and northing by estimating tenths from the 10-kilometre grid-lines, or measuring them with a transparent roamer of the proper scale (most map shops sell them).

In Ireland (pp. 286–95) I have used some two-figure references, to 10-kilometre-side squares.

GREAT BRITAIN

The following organisations cover England, Wales and Scotland (in several cases also Ireland) and are devoted at least partly to birds as scientific, or conservation organisations, or as owners or administrators of Reserves. Some of their publications, apart from Reports, are cited.

Association for the Study of Animal Behaviour: Rothamsted Experimental Station, Harpenden, Herts. (*Animal Behaviour*)

Avicultural Society: Hon. Sec. A.A.Prestwich, Galley's Wood, near Edenbridge, Kent. (*Avicultural Magazine*)

Biological Council: c/o Institute of Biology, which see.

British Ecological Society: Hon. Membership Sec. G.T.Goodman, Department of Botany, University College of Swansea, Singleton Park, Swansea, Glam. (*Journal of Ecology*, *Journal of Animal Ecology*, *Journal of Applied Ecology*)

British Junior Naturalists' Association: Gen. Sec. D.M.Smith, Somerdale, Welton Rd, Brough, Yorks. (*Young Naturalist*)

British Naturalists' Association: Hon. Sec. Mrs W.Burnett, Hawkshead, Tower Hill, Dorking, Surrey. (*Bulletin, Country-Side*)

British Ornithologists' Club: c/o Bird Room, British Museum (Natural History), Cromwell Rd, London, s.w.7. (*Bulletin*)

British Ornithologists' Union: as B.O.C. (B.O.C. limited to B.O.U. members). (*The Ibis*)

British Trust for Ornithology: Beech Grove, Tring, Herts. (*Bird Study*, *Bulletin*)

Council for Nature: 41 Queen's Gate, London, s.w.7. The national body for the co-ordination of all national and local natural history societies over conservation issues. (*Habitat*, *News for Naturalists*)

Fauna Preservation Society: c/o Zoological Society of London, Regent's Park, London, n.w.1. (*Oryx*)

Field Studies Council: 9 Devereux Court, Strand, London, w.c.2. (*Field Studies*)

Forestry Commission: 25 Savile Row, London, w.1. (*Guides* to National Forest Parks and State Forests, technical periodicals, etc.)

Institute of Biology: 41 Queen's Gate, London, s.w.7.

International Council for Bird Preservation (British Section): as B.O.C.

International Wildfowl Research Bureau: as B.O.C.

Linnean Society of London: Burlington House, Piccadilly, London, w.1. (*Journal* and *Proceedings*)

National Trust (for places of historic interest or natural beauty): 42 Queen Anne's Gate, London, s.w.1.

Nature Conservancy (the Government conservation and research organisation): 19 Belgrave Square, London, s.w.1.

Ray Society: as B.O.C.

Royal Naval Bird Watching Society: Hon. Sec. Lieutenant-Commander E.S.W.Maclure, R.N. (rtd.), Melrose, 23 St David's Rd, Southsea, Hants. (*Sea Swallow*)

Royal Society for the Protection of Birds: The Lodge, Sandy, Beds. (*Birds*; lately *Bird Notes*: and *Bird Life*; lately *Junior Bird Recorder*)

School Nature Study Union: 12 Cranes Park Avenue, Surbiton, Surrey. (*School Nature Study*)

Sea-bird Group: Hon. Sec. Dr W.R.P.Bourne, Shrodells Hospital, Vicarage Rd, Watford, Herts. (*Bulletin*)

Selborne Society: 57 Crofton Rd, Ealing, London, w.5. (*Selborne Magazine*)

Society for the Promotion of Nature Reserves: as B.O.C. Co-ordinates the activities of the county Naturalists' Trusts (cited under appropriate regions) and manages a chain of its own reserves.

Wildfowl Trust: Slimbridge, Gloucestershire (*Bulletin*)

Wildfowlers' Association of Great Britain and Ireland: 6 Windsor Building, George St, Liverpool 3.

World Wildlife Fund: 2 Caxton St, London, s.w.1. (raises funds for conservation). (*World Wildlife News*)

Zoological Society of London: Regent's Park, London, n.w.1. (*Proceedings, Transactions* and *Journal of Zoology*)

Other journals with bird material (and see under provinces and counties): *Animal Life, Animals, British Birds, Cage Birds, International Zoo Year Book, Kingfisher, Wild Life News, Wild Life Observer.*

General works on the British and Irish avifauna

This has been, of course, selected, with apologies to the authors of valuable works (especially monographs on individual species) considered too specialised to include. Many of the books are highly illustrated, several in colour. Dates of first editions are given; books known to me to have later editions are marked *. No works published before the First World War are included.

MULLENS, W.H. and SWANN, H. Kirke (1916–17). *A bibliography of British ornithology.* London, Macmillan, 691 pp.

MULLENS, W.H., SWANN, H. Kirke and JOURDAIN, F.C.R. (1919–20). *A geographical bibliography of British ornithology.* London, Witherby, 588 pp.

GURNEY, J.H. (1921). *Early annals of ornithology.* London, Witherby, 240 pp.

*COWARD, T.A. (1920–6). *The birds of the British Isles and their eggs.* London, Warne, 3 vols., lately 400 + 384 + 286 pp.

*WITHERBY, H.F., JOURDAIN, F.C.R., TICEHURST, N.F. and TUCKER, B.W. (1938–41). *The handbook of British birds.* London, Witherby, 5 vols., 326 + 352 + 387 + 461 + 356 pp.

*FISHER, J. (1940). *Watching birds.* Harmondsworth, Penguin Books, 192 pp.

SMITH, S. (1945). *How to study birds.* London, Collins, 192 pp.

*FISHER, J. (1947–55). *Bird recognition.* Harmondsworth, Penguin Books, 3 vols. of 4. Full 4, revised due 1967.

IRWIN, R. (1951). *British bird books.* London, Grafton, 398 pp.

NICHOLSON, E.M. (1951). *Birds and men.* London, Collins *New Naturalist,* 256 pp.

*HOLLOM, P.A.D. (1952). *The popular handbook of British birds.* London, Witherby, 424 pp.

BRITISH ORNITHOLOGISTS' UNION (1952). *Check-list of the birds of Great Britain and Ireland.* London, B.O.U., 106 pp.

*FITTER, R.S.R. and RICHARDSON, R.A. (1952). *The pocket guide to British birds.* London, Collins, 240 pp.

*CAMPBELL, B. (1952). *Bird watching for beginners.* Harmondsworth, Penguin Books, 240 pp.

FISHER, J. (1954). *A history of birds.* London, Hutchinson, 205 pp.

FISHER, J. and LOCKLEY, R.M. (1954). *Sea-birds.* London, Collins *New Naturalist,* 320 pp.

FITTER, R.S.R., CHARTERIS, Guy and RICHARDSON, R.A. (1955). *The pocket guide to nests and eggs.* London, Collins, 172 pp.

SCOTT, P. and BOYD, H. (1957). *Wildfowl of the British Isles.* London, Country Life, 64 pp.

NICHOLSON, E.M. (1957). *Britain's nature reserves.* London, Country Life, 175 pp.

NORTH, M.E.W. and SIMMS, E. (1958). *Witherby's sound-guide to British birds.* London, Witherby, 2 vols., 52 + 51 pp., 13 gramophone discs.

HOLLOM, P.A.D. (1960). *The popular handbook of rarer British birds.* London, Witherby, 134 pp.

RICHMOND, K. (1962). *Birds in Britain.* London, Odhams, 160 pp., 2 gramophone discs.

BANNERMAN, D.A. (1953–63). *The birds of the British Isles.* Edinburgh and London, Oliver and Boyd, 12 vols., c. 4200 pp., 385 col. pls.

FITTER, R.S.R. (1963). *Collins guide to bird watching.* London, Collins, 254 pp.

ATKINSON-WILLES, G.L. ed. (1963). *Wildfowl in Great Britain.* London, H.M.S.O., 368 pp.

CAMPBELL, B. (1964). *The Oxford book of birds.* London, Oxford University Press, 207 pp.

Works on general ornithology of interest to the British and Irish bird-watcher

*HOWARD, H. Eliot (1920). *Territory in bird life.* London, John Murray, 308 pp.

*THOMSON, A. Landsborough (1926). *Problems of bird-migration.* London, Witherby, 350 pp.

*ALEXANDER, W.B. (1928). *Birds of the ocean.* New York and London, Putnam, 428 pp.

THOMPSON, d'A.W. (1936). *A glossary of Greek birds.* London, Oxford University Press, 342 pp.

DARLING, F. Fraser (1938). *Bird flocks and the breeding cycle.* Cambridge, University Press, 124 pp.

JORGENSEN, H.I. and BLACKBURNE, C.I. (1941). *Glossarium Europae Avium.* Copenhagen, Munksgaard, 192 pp.

*ARMSTRONG, E.A. (1942). *Bird display: an introduction to the study of bird psychology.* Cambridge, University Press, 381 pp.

*PETERSON, R. [T.], MOUNTFORT, G.R. and HOLLOM, P.A.D. (1954). *A field guide to the birds of Britain and Europe.* London, Collins, 318 pp.

HUTSON, H.P.W. ed. (1956). *The ornithologists' guide.* London, British Ornithologists' Union, 275 pp.

LISTER, M.D. (1956). *The bird watcher's reference book.* London, Phoenix House, 256 pp.

GILLIARD, E.T. (1958). *Living birds of the world.* London, Hamish Hamilton, 400 pp.

ARMSTRONG, E.A. (1958). *The folklore of birds.* London, Collins *New Naturalist*, 272 pp.

VAN TYNE, J. and BERGER, A.J. (1959). *Fundamentals of ornithology.* London, Chapman and Hall, 624 pp.

MACDONALD, J.D. (1959). *Instructions to young ornithologists I. Bird biology.* London, Museum Press, 128 pp.

FITTER, R.S.R. (1959). *The ark in our midst.* London, Collins, 320 pp.

*CAMPBELL, B. (1959). *Bird watching for beginners.* Harmondsworth, Penguin Books, 240 pp.

VOOUS, K.H. (1960). *Atlas of European birds.* London, Nelson, 284 pp.

THORPE, W.H. (1961). *Bird-song.* Cambridge, University Press, 143 pp.

MARSHALL, A.J. ed. (1960–1). *Biology and comparative physiology of birds.* New York and London, Academic Press, 2 vols., 518 + 468 pp.

HOSKING, E. and NEWBERRY, C. (1961). *Bird photography as a hobby* London, Stanley Paul, 95 pp.

GOODWIN, Derek (1961). *Instructions to young ornithologists II. Bird behaviour* London, Museum Press, 123 pp.

AUSTIN, O.L. jun. and SINGER, A. (1962). *Birds of the world.* London, Paul Hamlyn, 317 pp. (first ed. U.S. 1961).

YAPP, W.B. (1962). *Birds and woods.* London, Oxford University Press, 308 pp.

WYNNE-EDWARDS, V.C. (1962). *Animal dispersion in relation to social behaviour.* Edinburgh and London, Oliver and Boyd, 653 pp.

LISTER, M.[D.] (1962). *A bird and its bush*; and *A glossary for bird watchers.* Both London, Phoenix House, 142 and 96 pp.

DORST, J. (1962). *The migrations of birds.* London, Heinemann, 476 pp.

ARMSTRONG, E.A. (1963). *A study of bird song.* London, Oxford University Press, 335 pp.

SPENCER, R. (1963). *Instructions to young ornithologists III. Bird migration.* London, Museum Press, 126 pp.

GILLHAM, M.E. (1963). *Instructions to young ornithologists IV. Sea birds.* London, Museum Press, 144 pp.

HARRISON, C.J.O. (1964). *Instructions to young ornithologists V. Birds' nests and eggs.* London, Museum Press, 130 pp.

WELTY, J.C. (1964). *The life of birds.* London, Constable, 546 pp. (first ed. U.S. 1962).

THOMSON, A. Landsborough *ed.* (1964). *A new dictionary of birds.* London, Nelson for British Ornithologists' Union, 928 pp.

FISHER, J. and PETERSON, R.T. (1964). *The world of birds.* London, Macdonald, 288 pp.

VAURIE, C. (1959–65). *The birds of the Palearctic fauna.* London, Witherby, 2 vols. pp. 762 + 784.

CURRY-LINDAHL, K. (1965). *Europe: a natural history.* London, Hamish Hamilton, 299 pp.

FISHER, J. (1966). *Shell nature-lovers' atlas of England, Wales and Scotland.* London, Ebury Press and Michael Joseph, 80 pp.

CHANNEL ISLES
(vice-county of)

Société jersiaise
Jersey Wildlife Trust
Société guernesiaise

Ornithological Section of S.J. has *Bird Observatory* at St Ouen. S.J. has *Museum.* J.W.T. has *Zoo* with birds Les Augres Manor.

BROCK, H. le M. (1950). *A record of the birds of Guernsey*. Guernsey, S.G., 84 pp.

DOBSON, R. (1952). *Birds of the Channel Islands*. London, Staples, 264 pp.

ENGLAND AND WALES

PROVINCE PENINSULA

Cornwall. Vice-county division A39 Truro–Padstow

Cornwall Bird Watching and Preservation Society
Cornwall Naturalists' Trust

QUICK, H.M. (1948). *Marsh and shore bird-watching on the Cornish coast*. London, Cape, 136 pp.

RYVES, B.H. (1948). *Bird life in Cornwall*. London, Collins, 256 pp.

West Cornwall with Scilly (vice-county 1)

C.B.W.P.S. has *Bird Reserves* at Trethias Island (SW 8573); a private *Bird Reserve* also at Hayle Estuary (SW 5437); at the Lizard (SW 6813) *Migration Watch Point*; *Bird Observatory* at St Agnes, Scilly (SV 8808)

The Lizard. The great Cornish migration watch-point, a typical station in the great network of observation posts that have added so much to our knowledge of migration habits (see map on p. 123).

Quick, H.M. (1964). *Birds of the Scilly Isles*. Truro, Barton, 125 pp.

East Cornwall (vice-county 2)

C.B.W.P.S. has Walmesley *Bird Reserve* near Wadebridge (SW 9974); at Eddystone (SX 3833) *Migration Watch Point*

Devon. Vice-county division along water-parting, approximately SX 3978–5982–Western Canal from SS 9512–ST 0719

Blundell's School Science Society, Tiverton
Devon Bird-watching and Preservation Society
Devon Trust for Nature Conservation

White, W. Walmesley (1931). *Bird Life in Devon*. London, Cape, 256 pp.
Harvey, L.A. and St Leger-Gordon, D. (1962). *Dartmoor*. London, Collins *New Naturalist*, 2nd ed., 273 pp.

South Devon (vice-county 3)

Exeter University Field Club
Torquay Natural History Society

Zoos with birds at Exmouth (SY 0080) and Paignton (SX 8759); National *Wildfowl Refuge* at Exe Estuary (SX 9879); D.B.W.P.S. has *Bird Reserve* at Wembury (SX 5148–5347); *Bird Observatory* at Slapton Ley Field Centre (SX 8244)
Royal Albert Memorial *Museum* at Exeter

Loyd, L.R.W. (1929). *The birds of south-east Devon*. London, Witherby, 176 pp.

North Devon (vice-county 4)

Ilfracombe Field Club
Lundy Field Society

L.F.S. has *Bird Observatory* on Lundy (SS 1445); Regional *Wildfowl Refuge* at Tamar Lake (SS 2911); *Zoo* with birds at Ilfracombe (SS 5246); Royal Society for the Protection of Birds has *Bird Reserve* at Chapel Wood, Spreacombe (SS 4841); National Trust has *Bird Reserve* at Arlington Court (SS 6140); National Nature Reserve at Braunton Burrows (SS 4437–4361) is also a *Bird Reserve*

Allen, N.V. (1940). "Birds of the Ilfracombe district", pp. 8–43 of *The fauna and flora of the I.d. of North Devon*. Exeter, I.F.C., 266 pp.
Perry, R. (1947). *Lundy: isle of puffins*. London, Lindsay Drummond, 2nd ed., 267 pp.
Davis, Peter (1954). *A list of the birds of Lundy*. Exeter, L.F.S., 114 pp.

Gannet's Rock, off the coast of Lundy. Besides being a great breeding-ground for puffins, Lundy is one of the finest stations in the modern Bird Observatory network. (Drawing by John C. A. Dyke.)

Somerset. Approximate vice-county boundary is along River Parrett from ST 2349 through Bridgwater and via River Yeo to Ilchester (ST 5222) and thence along A303 to near Bourton (ST 7530)

Mid-Somerset Naturalists' Society
Somerset Archaeological and Natural History Society
Somerset Trust for Nature Conservation

National Nature Reserve at Bridgwater Bay (both vice-counties, ST 2246–2959) is also a *Bird Reserve*

HENDY, E. W. (1943). *Somerset birds and some other folk.* London, Eyre and Spottiswoode, 165 pp.
LEWIS, S. (1955). *The breeding birds of Somerset and their eggs.* Ilfracombe, Stockwell, 359 pp.

South Somerset (vice-county 5)

HENDY, E. W. (1946). *Wild Exmoor through the year.* London, Cape, revised ed., 320 pp.: (1949) "The birds of west Somerset", *Bird Notes* 23: 241–8

North Somerset (vice-county 6)

Bath Natural History Society
Bristol Naturalists' Society

Bird Observatory on Steep Holm (ST 2260); Potential *Bird Reserve* at Chew Valley Lake (ST 5760); Bird *Zoo* at Rode (ST 8054)

PROVINCE CHANNEL

Wiltshire. Vice-county division Kennet and Avon Canal

Wiltshire Archaeological and Natural History Society
Wiltshire Trust for Nature Conservation

PEIRSON, L.G. (1959). *Wiltshire birds*. Devizes, W.A.N.H.S., 43 pp.

North Wiltshire (vice-county 7)

Marlborough College Natural History Society

Zoo with birds at Leigh (SV 0692)

PEIRSON, L.G. (1940), "Handlist of the birds of the Marlborough district", *M.C.N.H.S. Report* no. 88; 21 pp.

South Wiltshire (vice-county 8)

Salisbury Natural History Society

Zoo with birds at Longleat (ST 8043)

Dorset (vice-county 9)

Dorset Field Ornithology Group
Dorset Natural History and Archaeological Society
Dorset Naturalists' Trust
South Dorset Bird Watching Society

National Nature Reserves at Morden Bog (SY 9091), Arne (SY 9788), Hartland Moor (SY 9485) and Studland Heath (SZ 0184) are *Bird Reserves*: in Poole Harbour area Brownsea Island (SZ 0288), Nature Reserve of National Trust and D.N.T. is also a *Bird Reserve*; D.N.T. has other bird reserves in county: Abbotsbury Swannery (SY 5784) is second oldest *Bird Reserve* in Kingdom (from fourteenth century), also *Migration Watch Point*; Radipole Lake (SY 6779–6780) is a Regional *Wildfowl Refuge*; *Bird Observatory* and *Field Centre* at Portland Bill (SY 6868); *Research Station* of Nature Conservancy at Furzebrook (SY 9383)

BLATHWAYT, F.L. (1946). "A revised list of the birds of Dorset", *Proceedings of D.N.H.A.S.* 67: 95–127

Hampshire and the Isle of Wight

Hampshire and Isle of Wight Naturalists' Trust

COHEN, E. (1963). *The birds of Hampshire and the Isle of Wight*. Edinburgh and London, Oliver and Boyd, 278 pp.

Isle of Wight (vice-county 10)

Isle of Wight Natural History Society

Nature Reserve of National Trust at Town Copse, Newtown (SZ 4290) is a *Bird Reserve*; *Zoo* with birds in Sandown (SZ 5984); *Ringing Station* at St Catherine's Point (SZ 4975)

Hampshire Mainland. Vice-county division A30 and A272, through Winchester

Hampshire Field Club and Archaeological Society
Winchester College Natural History Society

South Hampshire (vice-county 11)

Bournemouth Natural Science Society
Christchurch Harbour Ornithological Group
New Forest Ornithologists' Club

H. I. W. N. T. has eleven Nature Reserves in this vice-county, most of which are *Bird Reserves*. At Sinah Common (SZ 6999) is a *Wildfowl Refuge*; at Tichfield Haven (SU 5302) at Gilkicker Point (SZ 6097) and at Christchurch Harbour and Hengistbury Head (SZ 1791–1790) *Migration Watch Points*

North Hampshire (vice-county 12)

Newbury District Ornithological Club
Selborne Society

Zoo with birds at Weyhill (SU 3146); also private *Zoo* and exotic bird breeding station at Leckford (SU 3737). Gilbert White's immortal Selborne Common and Hanger (SU 7333), Nature Reserve of National Trust, is a *Bird Reserve*. Pigeon Copse, at Liss (SU 7728) is a *Bird Reserve* of the Royal Society for the Protection of Birds

WHITE, G. (1788). *The natural history of Selborne.* A gross of later editions, e.g. London, Cresset Press.

Sussex. Vice-county division is *not* the political one, but approximately Brighton to County Oak via A23–B2036–A272–B2114–A23 through Cuckfield and Crawley

Brighton and Hove Natural History Society
Sussex Naturalists' Trust
Sussex Ornithological Society

At Brighton, the Booth *Museum* of British Birds

DES FORGES, G. and HARBER, D.D. (1963). *A guide to the birds of Sussex.* Edinburgh and London, Oliver and Boyd, 177 pp.

West Sussex (vice-county 13)

Bognor Regis Natural Science Society
Shoreham Ornithological Society
Worthing Natural History Society

S.N.T. has several *Bird Reserves* in this vice-county; S.O.S. has *Bird Reserve* at Shoreham (TQ 2307); Local Nature Reserve at Pagham Harbour (SZ 8796) is also a *Bird Reserve*. A *Zoo* with birds at Devil's Dyke (TQ 2511). At Chichester Gravel Pits (SU 8705, 8703) and Selsey Bill (SZ 8592) *Migration Watch Points*
Museum at Bognor Regis

East Sussex (vice-county 14)

Eastbourne College Natural History Society
Hastings and East Sussex Natural History Society
Tunbridge Wells Natural History and Philosophical Society

Pett Level (TQ 9015) is a potential *Bird Reserve*; and the Mere at Hampden Park (TQ 6102) – Eastbourne College – could be so considered. *Bird Observatory* at Beachy Head (TV 5995)
At Hastings, Municipal *Museum*

PROVINCE THAMES

Kent. Vice-county division is Rivers Medway and Beult nearly to Staplehurst (TQ 7846); thence by Roman road and A229, through Cranbrook (TQ 7736) to Sussex border near Hawkhurst (TQ 7528)

Kent Naturalists' Trust
Kent Ornithological Society
Kent Wildfowlers' Association
Rochester and District Natural History Society

GILLHAM, E.M. and HOMES, R.C. (1950). *The birds of the North Kent Marshes.* London, Collins, 320 pp.
HARRISON, J.M. (1953). *The birds of Kent.* London, Witherby, 2 vols., 510+315 pp.
GILLHAM, E.H. and others (1955). *Report on the breeding birds of the Medway Islands, 3–5 June 1955.* Margate, K.O.S., 21 pp.

East Kent (vice-county 15)

Canterbury and District Bird Watchers' Association
Thanet Field Club

At least 6 of the Nature Reserves of K.N.T. in this vice-county are *Bird Reserves*. At Dungeness (TR 0916) *Bird Reserve* of the Royal Society for the Protection of Birds ; also *Bird Observatory*. At Sandwich Bay (TR 3566) *Bird Reserve* of K.N.T.; also *Bird Observatory*. K.W.A. have *Wildfowl Refuges* at Faversham (TR 0162) and Westbere (TR 1960)

Scott, R.E. (1964). "The natural history of Dungeness, *Bird Notes* 31 : 48–53

West Kent (vice-county 16). Includes Greater London south of Thames west to Deptford, Forest Hill and Beckenham

London Natural History Society
St Paul's Cray Ornithological Society
Tunbridge Wells Natural History and Philosophical Society

National Nature Reserve at Northward Hill, High Halstow (TQ 7876) a *Bird Reserve* of R.S.P.B.; At least 2 of the Nature Reserves of K.N.T. in this vice-county are also *Bird Reserves*. K.W.A. have *Wildfowl Refuges* at Dunton Green (TQ 5156) and Sunbridge (TQ 4955).

Horniman *Museum* and Library, Forest Hill, s.e.23

Harrison, J.M. (1942). *A hand list of the birds of the Sevenoaks or western district of Kent*. London, Witherby, 165 pp.

L.N.H.S. (1964). *The birds of the London area*. London, Rupert Hart-Davis, 2nd ed., 332 pp.

Surrey (vice-county 17). Includes all Greater London south of Thames east to Peckham, Crystal Palace and Croydon, but not Staines area north of Thames now in political Surrey

Holmesdale Natural History Club
London Natural History Society
Surbiton and District Bird Watching Society
Surrey Bird Club
Surrey Naturalists' Trust

Wildfowl Refuge, in effect, at Barn Elms Reservoir (TQ 2277). *Bird Reserve*, in effect, in Richmond Park (TQ 2073) : of S.N.T. Nature Reserves in vice-county at least 2 are primarily *Bird Reserves*: and Royal Society for the Protection of Birds has *Bird Reserve* at Barfold Copse, Haslemere (SU 9232). At Beddington, near Croydon (TQ 2965) is *Ringing Station* of L.N.H.S.; and at Juniper Hall (TQ 1752) *Field Studies Centre* of Field Studies Council. *Zoos* with birds or waterfowl collections are at Battersea Park (TQ 2877), Kew Gardens (TQ 1876), Crystal Palace (TQ 3470) and Chessington (TQ 1762)

Haslemere Educational *Museum*; and *Museum* at Reigate

BUCKNILL, J.A. (1902). "Birds", *Victoria history of the county of Surrey* 1: 202–18

COLLENETTE, C.L. (1937). *A history of Richmond Park with an account of its birds and animals.* London, Sidgwick and Jackson, 164 pp.

FITTER, R.S.R. (1949). *London's birds.* London, Collins, 256 pp.

POUNDS, Hubert E. (1952). *Notes on the birds of Farleigh and district and the North Downs, Surrey.* London, Witherby, 90 pp.

L.N.H.S. (1964). *The birds of the London area,* see vice-county 16

Essex Vice-county division is approximately A121–A122–Chelmer and Blackwater rivers

Essex Bird Watching and Preservation Society
Essex Field Club
Essex Naturalists' Trust

GLEGG, W.E. (1929). *A history of the birds of Essex.* London, Witherby, 342 pp.

South Essex (vice-county 18). Includes Greater London north of Thames and east of River Lea

London Natural History Society
South Essex Natural History Society

Wildfowl Refuge, in effect, at Lea Valley Reservoirs (TL 3703); and City of London Nature Reserve at Epping Forest (TQ 3895–TL 4400), Greater London Nature Reserve at Hainault Forest (TQ 4894), the South Essex Woodlands local authority Nature Reserves of Bull Wood, Belfairs Great Wood, Shipwright's Wood and the Glen (TQ 8392–7887) and Hadleigh Marshes l.a. Nature Reserve (TQ 8185) are *Bird Reserves*; as is a Nature Reserve of E.N.T. *Bird Observatory* at Bradwell-on-Sea (TM 0007); *Field Study Centre* at High Beech (TQ 4097); *Ringing Station* at Romford (TQ 4988)

At Romford, Essex *Museum* of Natural History

L.N.H.S. (1964). *The birds of the London area,* see vice-county 16

North Essex (vice-county 19)

Colchester and District Natural History Society
St Osyth Bird Watching and Protection Society

The National Nature Reserve of Newborough Warren in Anglesey, at a crossroads of bird migration. Flocks shown are of herring gulls (a few great blackbacks) and oystercatchers. *C. F. Tunnicliffe*

Finest of all the Cheshire meres, Rostherne Mere has been a National Nature Reserve since 1961, as an important duck refuge. Population research by Manchester Ornithological Society is done in some comfort from Boyd Observatory on the right. *S. R. Badmin*

Potential *Wildfowl Refuges* at Hamford Water Saltings, around Horsey
Island (TM 2324) and Blackwater Marshes (TL 9812–TM 0415):
2 Nature Reserves of E.N.T. are *Bird Reserves*: Duck *Ringing Station*
at Abberton Reservoir (TL 9818). *Zoos* with birds or exotic waterfowl at
Tewes, Little Sampford (TL 6433), Mole Hall, Widdington (TL 5431),
Stanstead (TL 5126) and Colchester (TL 9925)

Hertfordshire (vice-county 20). Potter's Bar is in vice-county 21

Hertfordshire and Middlesex Trust for Nature Conservation
Hertfordshire Natural History Society and Field Club
London Natural History Society

National Nature Reserve at Tring Reservoirs (SP 9213–9012) is a *Bird
Reserve*. At Rye Meads (TL 3810) a *Ringing Station*. In Tring (SP 9211)
headquarters of the *British Trust for Ornithology* at Beech Grove, and
Rothschild *Museum*, of British Museum (Natural History), at Tring Park

HAYWARD, H.H.S. (1947). "The birds of the Tring Reservoirs", *Records
of Bucks*. 15: 51–62
SAGE, B.L. (1959). *A history of the birds of Hertfordshire*. London, Barrie and
Rockliff, 245 pp.
L.N.H.S. (1964). *The birds of the London area*, see vice-county 16

Middlesex (vice-county 21). Survives only geographically; embraces all Old
Middlesex including Staines area (now Surrey), Potter's Bar (now
Hertfordshire) and Greater London west of River Lea and north of
Thames, including City

Hertfordshire and Middlesex Trust for Nature Conservation
London Natural History Society

Local Nature Reserve at Ruislip Reservoir (TQ 0889) is a *Bird Reserve*; as
are Inner London Parks (Hyde Park Corner TQ 2879). Lea Valley
(TQ 3488–3797) and West London (TQ 0473, 0573, 0769) Reservoirs
are *Wildfowl Refuges* in effect. *Zoos* with birds, or exotic waterfowl
collections at London Zoo (TQ 2883), Tower of London (TQ 3380),
St James's Park (TQ 2979) and Osterley Park (TQ 1478). At 19 Belgrave
Square, s.w.1. (TQ 2879) headquarters of the *Nature Conservancy*; in
Cromwell Rd, s.w.7. (TQ 2679) the British *Museum* (Natural History)

L.N.H.S. (1964). *The birds of the London area*, see vice-county 16

A Reserve now, and Bird Observatory, the Calf of Man has attracted sea-
bird-watchers and migration students for four centuries. *Richard Eurich*

Berkshire (vice-county 22)

Berkshire, Buckinghamshire and Oxfordshire Naturalists' Trust
Middle Thames Natural History Society
Newbury District Field Club
Newbury District Ornithological Club
Oxford Ornithological Society
Radley College Natural History Society
Reading and District Natural History Society
Reading Ornithological Club

Ham Island Nature Reserve (SU 9975) of M.T.N.H.S. and Forest Nature Reserve (SU 9374) of High Standing Hill are *Bird Reserves*, as are some Nature Reserves of B.B.O.N.T. and parts of Windsor Great Park

Museum at Reading

ALEXANDER, W.B. (1952). *An annotated list of the birds of Berkshire*. Oxford, Oxford University Press, 42 pp.

FRASER, A.C. (1954). *The birds of the Middle Thames*. Slough, M.T.N.H.S.

Oxfordshire (vice-county 23)

Banbury Ornithological Society
Berkshire, Buckinghamshire and Oxfordshire Naturalists' Trust
Oxford Ornithological Society
Reading Ornithological Club

The National Nature Reserve at Wychwood (SP 3316), the great gardens and park at Blenheim (SP 4416) and the chain of Nature Reserves along the finest Chiltern escarpment from Chinnor to Watlington Hills (SV 7699–7093 B.B.O.N.T., Forestry Commission, Nature Conservancy and National Trust) all rate as *Bird Reserves*, as do some other Reserves in the county

At Oxford, University *Museum* (SP 5106), and Edward Grey *Institute of Field Ornithology* (SP 5206)

ALEXANDER, W.B. (1947). *A revised list of the birds of Oxfordshire*. Oxford, Oxford University Press, 36 pp.

PICKLES, M.M. (1960). *The birds of Blenheim Park*. Oxford, Oxford University Press, 15 pp.

Buckinghamshire (vice-county 24)

Berkshire, Buckinghamshire and Oxfordshire Naturalists' Trust
Buckinghamshire Archaeological and Natural History Society

Eton College Natural History Society
London Natural History Society
Middle Thames Natural History Society
Stowe School Natural History Society

Of several Nature Reserves of B.B.O.N.T. in this county at least 3 are
Bird Reserves, as is Dancer's End (SP 9009), Woodland Reserve of
Society for the Promotion of Nature Reserves; Royal Society for the
Protection of Birds has *Bird Reserve* at Church Wood, Hedgerley
(SU 9789). The great Thames-side estate of Cliveden (SU 9185), and
the City of London's Burnham Beeches (SU 9585) also rate as *Bird
Reserves*, in effect. At Boarstall (SP 6215) duck decoy *Ringing Station* of
Wildfowlers' Association of Great Britain and Ireland

Museums at Aylesbury and Eton

BLAND, H.M. (1935). *Birds in an Eton garden*. London, Dent, 127 pp.
PRICE, K. (1947). "The birds of Buckinghamshire", *Records of Bucks*. 15:
20–31
FRASER, A.C. (1954). *The birds of the Middle Thames*. Slough, M.T.N.H.S.
L.N.H.S. (1964). *The birds of the London area*, see vice-county 16

PROVINCE ANGLIA

Suffolk. Vice-county division *not* along political boundary but longitude 1°E

Suffolk Naturalists' Society
Suffolk Naturalists' Trust

PAYN, W.H. (1962). *The birds of Suffolk*. London, Barrie and Rockliff,
238 pp.

East Suffolk (vice-county 25)

Dingle Bird Club
Ipswich District Natural History Society
Lowestoft and North Suffolk Field Naturalists' Club

S.N.T. has a Nature Reserve in this vice-county which is a *Bird Reserve*.
National Nature Reserves at Westleton Heath (TM 4569) and Orford-
ness (TM 4549)–Havergate (TM 4147) are also *Bird Reserves*. Latter
belongs to Royal Society for the Protection of Birds and is Britain's avocet
headquarters. R.S.P.B. also has Minsmere (TM 4667) and North Warren,
Thorpeness (TM 4559) *Bird Reserves*; former is Britain's bearded tit
headquarters and perhaps the kingdom's finest bird sanctuary, also a
Migration Watch Point
At Walberswick (TM 4974) *Ringing Station* of D.B.C.; at Flatford Mill
(TM 0733) *Field Centre* of the Field Studies Council

Avocet feeding at Havergate, Suffolk, great National Nature Reserve, and Reserve of the Royal Society for the Protection of Birds. Painted from a built-in hide by N. Wylie Moore.

West Suffolk (vice-county 26)

S.N.T. has 2 Nature Reserves in this vice-county, both *Bird Reserves*: the National Nature Reserves of Thetford Heath (TL 8579) and Cavenham Heath (TL 7672) are also *Bird Reserves*: R.S.P.B. also has *Bird Reserve* at Horn and Weather Heaths (TL 7877)

CLARKE, W.G. (1925). *In Breckland wilds*. London, Robert Scott (new ed. 1937), 208 pp.

Norfolk. Vice-county division along longitude 1°E

Norfolk and Norwich Naturalists' Society
Norfolk Naturalists' Trust
Ornamental Pheasant Trust

Hickling Broad, Norfolk, a National Nature Reserve in the Broads country, and a Reserve of the Norfolk Naturalists' Trust. From a drawing by Allen W. Seaby.

Blakeney Point, Norfolk: one of the many National Trust and Norfolk Naturalists' Trust Reserves along this part of the coast. From a pastel by N. Wylie Moore.

RIVIÈRE, B.B. (1930). *A history of the birds of Norfolk*. London, Witherby, 296 pp.

East Norfolk (vice-county 27)

Gresham's School Natural History Society

Of the fine array of Nature Reserves in this vice-county, the following selection names *some* of what are *Bird Reserves* in·name or effect. N.N.T. has a number of others, mostly in Broadland. Cley Marshes (TG 0544), N.N.T. and National Trust (where also *Migration Watch Point*); Hickling Broad (TG 4122), National Nature Reserve and N.N.T.; Horsey Mere (TG 4522), N.T.; Winterton Dunes (TG 4920), N.N.R.; and Bure Marshes (TG 3216–3575), N.N.R. and N.N.T. *Zoos* (or rather collections of living exotic birds) at Kelling Pines (TG 0941) and (O.P.T.) Great Witchingham (TG 1118)

Museum at Norwich

RICHARDSON, R.A. (1962). *Check-list of the birds of Cley and neighbouring Norfolk parishes*. Cley Bird Observatory, 36 pp.

ELLIS, E.A. (1965). *The Broads*. London, Collins *New Naturalist*, 401 pp.

West Norfolk (vice-county 28)

Selected from many coast and Breckland Nature Reserves which are also *Bird Reserves* (N.N.T. has several others) are Scolt Head Island (TF 8046), N.N.R., N.N.T. and N.T.; Blakeney Point (TF 9845–TG 0445), N.T. and N.N.T., also *Migration Watch Point*; Weeting Heath (TL 7888),

N.N.R. and N.N.T.; and East Wretham Heath (TL 9188), N.N.T. *Migration Watch Point* at Holme (TF 7044). *Zoos* (or rather collections of exotic wildfowl) at Holkham Hall (TF 8842) and Middleton Towers (TF 6717)

CLARKE, W.G. (1925), see vice-county 26

STEERS, J.A. *ed.* (1960). *Scolt Head Island.* Cambridge, Heffer (new ed.), 270 pp.

Cambridgeshire and Isle of Ely (vice-county 29)

Cambridge Bird Club
Cambridge and Isle of Ely Naturalists' Trust
Cambridge Natural History Society

C.N.T. has several Nature Reserves in this county, of which 3 are *Bird Reserves*; also National Nature Reserve at Chippenham Fen (TL 6469) is partly a *Bird Reserve*, National Trust's Wicken Fen (TL 5570) a Regional *Wildfowl Refuge*. At Madingley (TL 3960), Ornithological *Field Station* of Cambridge University, which also has *Museums* in Cambridge

LACK, D. (1934). *The birds of Cambridgeshire.* Cambridge, C.B.C., 118 pp.

EVANS, A.H. (1938). "Birds", *Victoria history of the county of Cambridge* 1: 224–42

ENNION, E.A.R. (1942). *Adventurer's fen.* London, Methuen (new ed. 1949), 67 pp.

Bedfordshire (vice-county 30)

Bedfordshire and Huntingdonshire Naturalists' Trust
Bedfordshire Natural History Society and Field Club

B.H.N.T. has 3 Nature Reserves in this county which are *Bird Reserves*. Sandy Lodge (TL 1847), headquarters of Royal Society for the Protection of Birds, is also a *Bird Reserve* and *Bird Observatory*. *Zoos* with birds, many free-winged exotics, at Woburn (SP 9632) and Whipsnade (TL 0017) Parks; *Bird Reserve* also within latter
Museum at Luton

KEY, H.A.S. (1947). "The birds of Bedfordshire", *Bedfordshire Naturalist* 1: 36–47

Huntingdonshire (vice-county 31)

Bedfordshire and Huntingdonshire Naturalists' Trust
Huntingdonshire Fauna and Flora Society

B.H.N.T. has 1 Nature Reserve in this county which is a *Bird Reserve*. Also *Bird Reserves* (partly so) are the 3 National Nature Reserves of

Holme Fen (TL 2288), Woodwalton Fen (TL 2284) and Monk's Wood (TL 1980); at last of which is *Experimental Station* of Nature Conservancy

PEAKE, E. (1926). "Birds", *Victoria history of the county of Huntingdon* 1 : 161–87; and (1944). *Birds in a Rectory garden*. St Neot's, privately printed, 28 pp.

Northamptonshire and Soke of Peterborough (vice-county 32)

Banbury Ornithological Society
Corby Natural History and Archaeological Society
Kettering and District Naturalists' Society and Field Club
Northamptonshire Natural History Society and Field Club
Northamptonshire Naturalists' Trust
Oundle School Natural History Society
Peterborough Museum Society
Peterborough Nature Council
Wildfowl Trust

Of several Nature Reserves in county, N.N.T. has *Wildfowl Refuge* at North Pitsford Reservoir (SP 7771–7970). National Nature Reserve at Castor Hanglands (TF 1201) is (partly) a *Bird Reserve*. Borough Fen Decoy (TF 2008) is *Ringing Station* of W.T., which has *Zoo* of exotic waterfowl at Peakirk (TF 1606). *Zoos* also at Lilford, exotic birds (TL 0384) and Wellingborough, some birds (SP 8967)

Museums at Kettering, Northampton and Peterborough

SLATER, H.H. (1902), "Birds", in *The Victoria history of the county of Northampton*. London, Constable, vol. 1 : 111–28
FISHER, J. (1956). "The birds of John Clare", pp. 26–69 of *The first fifty years*. Kettering, K.D.N.S.F.C.

PROVINCE SEVERN

Gloucestershire. Vice-county division along Thames and Severn Canal (disused part traceable on O.S. 1-inch) from junction at SO 7510 to old county boundary at Trewsbury SO 9600

Caradoc and Severn Valley Field Club
Cotteswold Naturalists' Field Club
Gloucestershire Trust for Nature Conservation

MELLERSH, W.L. (1902). *A treatise on the birds of Gloucestershire*. Gloucester and London, 111 pp.

East Gloucestershire (vice-county 33)

North Gloucestershire Naturalists' Society

Of G. T. N. C. Nature Reserves in this vice-county, one is a *Bird Reserve*
At Bourton-on-the-Water (SP 1620) an excellent bird *Zoo*

West Gloucestershire (vice-county 34)

Bristol, Clifton and West of England Zoological Society
Bristol Naturalists' Society
Clifton College Natural History Society
Dursley and District Bird Watching and Preservation Society
Nailsworth Recorders' Club
Wildfowl Trust

At Clifton (ST 5674), the B.C.W.E.Z.S.'s Bristol *Zoo*, with fine bird
collection. At Slimbridge (SO 7204) the W.T.'s headquarters, a bird *Zoo*
with the most comprehensive collection of living swans, ducks and geese
in the world; also effective natural *Bird Reserve*; also decoy *Ringing Station*
and *Bird Observatory*
Museum at Bristol

DAVIS, H.H. (1948). "A revised list of the birds of the Bristol district",
Proceedings B.N.S. 27: 225–67

Monmouth (vice-county 35)

Cardiff Naturalists' Society
Monmouthshire Naturalists' Trust
Newport Naturalists' Society

Of M.N.T. Nature Reserves, in county, one is a *Bird Reserve*, as is (partly)
Forest Nature Reserve of Blackcliff and Wyndcliff (ST 5398 and 5297)
in the Forest of Dean
Museum at Newport

INGRAM, G.E.S., SALMON, H.M. and HUMPHREYS, P.N. (1963). *The
birds of Monmouthshire*. Newport, Newport Museum, 56 pp.

Herefordshire (vice-county 36)

Caradoc and Severn Valley Field Club
Herefordshire and Radnorshire Nature Trust
Herefordshire Ornithological Club
Woolhope Naturalists' Field Club

GILBERT, H.A. and WALKER, C.W. (1954). *Herefordshire birds*. Hereford,
W.N.F.C., 2nd ed., 57 pp.

Worcestershire (vice-county 37)

West Midland Bird Club
West Midlands Trust for Nature Conservation
Worcestershire Naturalists' Club

Two Nature Reserves of W.M.T.N.C. are (partly) *Bird Reserves*. *Zoo*, by virtue of ornamental waterfowl, at Spetchley Park (SO 8953). (Dudley Zoo is in vice-county 39)

HARTHAN, A.J. (1961). "A revised list of Worcestershire birds", *Transactions W.N.C.* 11 : 167–86

Warwickshire (vice-county 38)

Birmingham Natural History Society
Coventry and District Natural History and Scientific Society
Nuneaton Bird Watchers' Club
Rugby School Natural History Society
Warwick Natural History Society
West Midland Bird Club
West Midlands Trust for Nature Conservation

Of W.M.T.N.C. Nature Reserves in county, at least 2 are of interest as *Bird Reserves*. *Bird Reserves* also, in effect, at Tile Hill Wood (SP 2779), Edgbaston Park (SP 0584) and Baginton (SP 3573). *Zoo* with exotic birds in Edgbaston (SP 0485)
Museum in Birmingham

NORRIS, C.A. (1947). *Notes on the birds of Warwickshire*. Birmingham, Cornish, 83 pp.

Staffordshire (vice-county 39). Includes Dudley area of Worcestershire

Burton-on-Trent Natural History and Archaeological Society
North Staffordshire Field Club
North-Western Naturalists' Union
West Midland Bird Club
West Midlands Trust for Nature Conservation

Coombes Valley, Leek (SK 0052) is a *Bird Reserve* of Royal Society for the Protection of Birds and W.M.T.N.C. Other Nature Reserves which in effect are *Bird Reserves* include National Trust's Hawksmoor Wood (SK 0344) and Chartley Moss (SK 0029) a National Nature Reserve (with W.M.T.N.C). Belvide Reservoir (SJ 8610) and Gailey Pool (SJ 9310) are potential *Wildfowl Refuges*. *Zoo* at Dudley (SO 9490) has fine bird collection

SMITH, T. (1930–38). "The birds of Staffordshire", *Transactions N.S.F.C.* 64–72 (appendices) : 287 pp.

LORD, J. and BLAKE, A.R.M. (1962). *The birds of Staffordshire*. Birmingham, W.M.B.C., 39 pp.

EDWARDS, K.C. and others (1962). *The Peak District*. London, Collins *New Naturalist*, 240 pp.

Shropshire (vice-county 40)

Caradoc and Severn Valley Field Club
North-Western Naturalists' Union
Shropshire Conservation Trust
Shropshire Ornithological Society

Ellesmere Meres (around SJ 4233) have good potential as *Bird Reserves* or *Wildfowl Refuges*. At Preston Montfort (SJ 4314), *Field Centre* of the Field Studies Council

RUTTER, E.M., GRIBBLE, F.C. and PEMBERTON, T.W. (1964). *A handlist of the birds of Shropshire*. Ellesmere, S.O.C., 59 pp.

PROVINCE SOUTH WALES

Glamorgan (vice-county 41)

Cardiff Naturalists' Society
Glamorgan County Naturalists' Trust
Gower Ornithological Society
Swansea Scientific and Field Naturalists' Society

Nature Reserves in Gower, which are *Bird Reserves* or partly so, include Whiteford (SS 4496–4394) National Nature Reserve with National Trust and G.C.N.T. (in effect also a *Wildfowl Refuge*); adjoining Llanmadoc Woods (SS 4493), G.C.N.T.; Broad Pool (SS 5191), G.C.N.T.; large parts of the Gower Coast between Worms Head (SS 3887) and Mumbles Head (SS 6387), including the National Nature Reserve of Oxwich (around SS 5087), G.C.N.T.'s cliffs from Port Eynon (SS 4684) to Overton (SS 4584) and several National Trust coastal properties. G.C.N.T. also has some small reserves outside Gower. Lavernock Point (ST 1868) is a *Migration Watch Point*
At Cardiff, the National *Museum* of Wales

INGRAM, G.C.S. and SALMON, H.M. (1936), "Birds of Glamorgan", *Glamorgan County History* 1 : 267–87
JAMES, A.F. and WEBB, J.A. (1944). "The birds of Swansea Borough", *Proceedings S.S.F.N.S.* 2 : 212–21

Brecknock (vice-county 42)

Brecknock County Naturalists' Trust
Brecknock Society

National Nature Reserve at Nant Irfon (SN 8355–8452) is in effect a *Bird Reserve*. B.C.N.T. has another *Bird Reserve* in county. Talybont Reservoir (SO 0917–1020) is a potential *Wildfowl Refuge*
Museum at Brecknock

INGRAM, G.C.S. and SALMON, H.M. (1957). "The birds of Brecknock", *Brycheiniog* 3: 181–259

GRIFFITHS, J. (since 1962). *Breconshire birds*. Circulated by author periodically

Radnor (vice-county 43)

Herefordshire and Radnorshire Nature Trust
Herefordshire Ornithological Club

INGRAM, G.C.S. and SALMON, H.M. (1955). *A hand list of the birds of Radnorshire*. Kington, H.O.C., 42 pp.

Carmarthen (vice-county 44)

West Wales Naturalists' Trust

National Nature Reserve at Allt Rhyd-y-Groes (SN 7449–7747) is a *Bird Reserve*

INGRAM, G.C.S. and SALMON, H.M. (1954). *A hand list of the birds of Carmarthenshire*. Tenby, West Wales Field Society (now W.W.N.T.), 67 pp.

Pembroke (vice-county 45)

West Wales Naturalists' Trust

Among Nature Reserves, all primarily *Bird Reserves*, in this great sea and cliff bird National Park area are Ramsey (SM 7022–7025), Royal Society for the Protection of Birds; Grassholm (SM 5909), R.S.P.B. and W.W.N.T. (great gannetry); Skomer (SM 7209), National Nature Reserve and W.W.N.T., also *Research Station*; Skokholm (SM 7305), Field Studies Council and W.W.N.T., also *Bird Observatory*; and St Margaret's Island (SS 1297), W.W.N.T. *Field Centres* also at Dale Fort (SM 8205), F.S.C.; and at Orielton (SR 9599), where duck decoy and *Ringing Station*. At St David's Head (SM 7227) *Migration Watch Point*

LOCKLEY, R.M. (1947). *Letters from Skokholm*. London, Dent, 243 pp.

LOCKLEY, R.M., INGRAM, G.C.S. and SALMON, H.M. (1949). *The birds of Pembrokeshire*. Haverfordwest, W.W.F.S. (now W.W.N.T.), 71 pp.

BUXTON, [E.J.]M. and LOCKLEY, R.M. (1950). *Island of Skomer*. London and New York, Staples, 164 pp.

LOCKLEY, R.M. (1961). "The birds of the south-western peninsula of Wales", *Nature in Wales* 7: 124–33

Cardigan (vice-county 46)

West Wales Naturalists' Trust

Among W. W. N. T. Nature Reserves in county, Borth Bog (around SN 6391) is importantly a *Bird Reserve*, and Cardigan Island (SN 1651) is also; as are the National Nature Reserves of woodland Coed Rheidol (SN 7177), and great Cors Tregaron (around SN 6863) – Tregaron Bog

PEACH, W.S. and MILES, P.M. (1961). "An annotated list of some birds seen in the Aberystwyth district, 1946–50", *Nature in Wales* 7 : 11–20

PROVINCE NORTH WALES

North Wales Naturalists' Trust
North-Western Naturalists' Union

FORREST, H.E. (1907). *The vertebrate fauna of North Wales*; and (1919) *A handbook of the vertebrate fauna of North Wales.* London, Witherby, 537 and 106 pp.

Montgomery (vice-county 47)

Montgomeryshire Field Club

BARBIER, P.G.R. (1958). "An annotated list of the birds observed in east Montgomeryshire", *Nature in Wales* 4 : 624–8

Merioneth (vice-county 48)

West Wales Naturalists' Trust (shares with N. W. N. T.)

Each of the great series of National Nature Reserves (permits necessary) in this county have importance as *Bird Reserves*: woodland Coed Cymerau (SH 6842), Coed Camlyn (SH 6539), Coed y Rhygen (SH 6836) and Coed Ganllwyd (SH 7224); coastal Morfa Harlech (SH 5535–5633) and Morfa Dyffryn (SH 5525–5623); and montane Rhinog (SH 6530–6727) – which has adjoining National Trust Reserves – and Cader Idris (around SH 7113)

Caernarvon (vice-county 49)

Cambrian Ornithological Society
Friends of Bardsey Observatory

Another fine series of National Nature Reserves all at least quite important as *Bird Reserves*: woodland Coed Gorswen (SH 7571), Coed Dolgarrog (SH 7667) and Coed Tremadoc (SH 5841); montane Cwm Glas (SH 7360), Cwm Idwal (SH 6559) and Y Wyddfa (SH 6054–6149) in the very heart of the Snowdonia National Park; also N. W. N. T. coastal Nature Reserve Morfa Bychan (SH 5436). On Bardsey (SH 1222) flourishing *Bird and Field Observatory*

Thearle, R.F., Hobbs, J.T. and Fisher, J. (1953). "The birds of the St Tudwal Islands", *British Birds* 46 : 182–8

Cowdy, S. (1960). *Bardsey Island and its bird observatory*. Amersham, Bardsey Observatory, 14 pp.

Denbigh (vice-county 50). Embraces Flint Maelor

Cambrian Ornithological Society
Chester Society of Natural Science, Literature and Art
Flintshire Ornithological Society

N.W.N.T.'s Nature Reserve at Cilygroeslwyd Wood (SJ 1255) is a *Bird Reserve*. *Zoo* with birds at Colwyn Bay (SH 8579)

Dobie, W.H. (1893). "Birds of West Cheshire, Denbighshire and Flintshire . . .", *Proceedings C.S.N.S.L.A.* 4 : 282–351
Rutter and others (1964), see vice-county 40 (includes Flint Maelor)

Flint (vice-county 51)

Cambrian Ornithological Society
Chester Society of Natural Science, Literature and Art
Dyserth District Field Club
Flintshire Ornithological Society

Dobie, W.H. (1893), see vice-county 50

Anglesey (vice-county 52)

Cambrian Ornithological Society

Potential *Bird Reserve* at Puffin Island; and N.W.N.T. has Nature Reserve of importance as *Bird Reserve*. The National Nature Reserve of Newborough Warren – Ynys Llanddwyn (SH 4165–3862) is also an important *Bird Reserve*

Tunnicliffe, C.F. (1952). *Shorelands summer diary*. London, Collins, 160 pp.

PROVINCE TRENT

Lincolnshire. Vice-county division is *not* by political boundaries but by River Witham as far up as Lincoln, thence by Foss Dyke to border of Nottinghamshire.

Lincolnshire Naturalists' Union
Lincolnshire Trust for Nature Conservation

Smith, A.E. and Cornwallis, R.K. (1955). *The birds of Lincolnshire*. Lincoln, L.N.U., 136 pp.

South Lincolnshire (vice-county 53)

At least one of several L.T.N.C Nature Reserves in this vice-county is important as a *Bird Reserve*. *Bird Observatory* is operated at Spalding (TF 2422)

North Lincolnshire (vice-county 54)

Humber National *Wildfowl Refuge* on borders of vice-counties 54 and 61 around Read's Island (SE 9622). Of a number of L.N.T. Nature Reserves in vice-county at least 4 are important as *Bird Reserves*. Local Nature Reserve of Skegness – Gibraltar Point (TF 5661–5557) is *Bird Reserve*, with *Bird Observatory* at Gibraltar Point. At North Cotes (TA 3603–3900) and Huttoft Bank (TF 5477) *Migration Watch Points*

Leicestershire and Rutland (vice-county 55)

Leicester Literary and Philosophical Society
Leicestershire and Rutland Ornithological Society
Leicestershire Trust for Nature Conservation
Loughborough Naturalists' Club
Uppingham School Natural History Society

Most of the 6 Nature Reserves of L.T.N.C. are important *Bird Reserves*. Eye Brook Reservoir (SP 8496–8594) is a potential *Wildfowl Refuge*. *Zoo* with some birds at Twycross (SK 3304)

BROWNE, M. (1907). "Birds", *Victoria history of the county of Leicester* 1: 114–57
HAINES, C.R. (1907). *Notes on the birds of Rutland*. London, Porter, 175 pp. (1908) "Birds", *Victoria history of the county of Rutland* 1: 55–76.

Nottinghamshire (vice-county 56)

Collingham and District Bird Watching Group
Nottingham Natural Science and Field Club
Nottinghamshire Trust for Nature Conservation
Trent Valley Bird Watchers

Potential or unofficial *Wildfowl Refuges* in several parts of Trent Valley, in Welbeck Park (around SK 5674) and at Thoresby Lake (SK 6470). Wollaton Park (SK 5339) has corporation *Bird Reserve* and Natural History *Museum*

WHITAKER, J. (1906). "Birds", *Victoria history of the county of Nottingham* 1: 156–76
TRENT VALLEY BIRD WATCHERS (1961). *The birds of Nottinghamshire*. . . Nottingham, T.V.B.W., 32 pp.

Derbyshire (vice-county 57)

Derbyshire Archaeological and Natural History Society
Derbyshire Naturalists' Trust
Derbyshire Ornithological Society
North-Western Naturalists' Union

Several valleys in Peak District National Park deserve Nature or *Bird Reserve* status. Unofficial *Bird Reserves* in estates of Chatsworth (SK 2670), Trent College (SK 4833) and Melbourne Hall (SK 3825). *Zoo* with birds at Ashover (SK 3463)

JOURDAIN, F.C.R. (1905). "Birds", *Victoria history of the county of Derby* 1 : 119–49

EDWARDS, K.C. and others (1962). *The Peak District*. London, Collins *New Naturalist*, 240 pp.

PROVINCE MERSEY

Lancashire and Cheshire Fauna Committee
North-Western Naturalists' Union

COWARD, T.A. (1930). "Aves", pp. 4–16 of *A check list of the fauna of Lancashire and Cheshire*. Arbroath, L.C.F.C., 115 pp.

Cheshire (vice-county 58)

Birkenhead School Natural History and Field Club
Cheshire Conservation Trust
Chester Society of Natural Science, Literature and Art
Liverpool Naturalists' Field Club
Manchester Ornithological Society
Merseyside Naturalists' Association
North of England Zoological Society

Five Nature Reserves of C.C.T. are *Bird Reserves*, including T.A. Coward Memorial Reserves at Cotterill Clough, Bollin Valley (SJ 8083) and Budworth (Marbury) Mere (SJ 6576); and Sandbach Flashes (SJ 7260). Royal Society for the Protection of Birds has a *Bird Reserve* at East Wood, Stalybridge (ST 9797). National Nature Reserve at Rostherne Mere (SJ 7484) is in effect a *Wildfowl Refuge*, with A.W.Boyd Memorial *Observatory*. *Ringing Station* on Hilbre Islands (SJ 1887), which also *Bird Reserve* of Hoylake U.D.C. *Zoo* with fine bird collection at Chester (SJ 4170), of N.E.Z.S.

BOYD, A.W. (1946). *The country diary of a Cheshire man*. London, Collins, 320 pp.; (1951). *A country parish*. London, Collins *New Naturalist*, 278 pp.

EDWARDS, K.C. and others (1962), see vice-county 57

BELL, T.H. (1962). *The birds of Cheshire*. Altrincham, Sherratt, 244 pp.

Lancashire. Vice-county division is River Ribble from mouth to Yorkshire border. All Lancashire north of Morecambe Bay is in vice-county 69

Lancashire Naturalists' Trust

OAKES, C. (1953). *The birds of Lancashire.* Edinburgh and London, Oliver and Boyd, 377 pp.

South Lancashire (vice-county 59)

East Lancashire Ornithologists' Club ·
Liverpool Naturalists' Field Club
Liverpool Ornithologists' Club
Manchester Ornithological Society
Merseyside Naturalists' Association

National *Wildfowl Refuge* at Southport Sanctuary (around SD 3118). *Zoos* with birds at Southport (SD 3418) and Belle Vue, Manchester (SJ 8896)
Bolton *Museums* and Art Gallery; Lord Derby Natural History *Museum*, Liverpool. Manchester *Museum*

HARDY, E. (1941). *The birds of the Liverpool area.* Arbroath, Buncle, 279 pp.
HORAN, M.B. (1949). *The birds and mammals of Bury.* Bury, Bury Times, 72 pp.

Mid Lancashire (vice-county 60)

Lancaster and District Bird Watching Society
North-East Lancashire Naturalists' Union

National *Wildfowl Refuge* at the Wyre–Lune Sanctuary (SD 4254–3448). *Bird Reserve* of the Royal Society for the Protection of Birds at Leighton Moss, Silverdale (SD 4875). *Zoo* with birds at Tower, Blackpool (SD 3036)

PROVINCE HUMBER (Yorkshire)

The boundaries of the 5 vice-counties correspond only partly with those of the three Ridings and the Ainsty of York. Vice-county 61 consists of the East Riding east of the River Ouse; vice-county 62 of the North Riding east of the River Wiske, and the Ainsty of York east of the River Ouse; vice-county 63 of the West Riding north to the Leeds–Liverpool canal and the River Aire below Leeds; vice-county 64 of the Ainsty of York west of the River Ouse and the rest of the West and East Ridings, except for the West Riding north of the east–west line through the Whernside heights of land, which goes to vice-county 65 together with the rest of the North Riding (west of the River Wiske)

Yorkshire Naturalists' Trust
Yorkshire Naturalists' Union (*The Naturalist*)

CHISLETT, R. (1952). *Yorkshire birds*. London and Hull, Brown, 335 pp.

South-east Yorkshire (vice-county 61)

Hull Scientific and Field Naturalists' Club

Potential *Bird Reserves* at Bempton Cliffs (TA 1974–2127) and Hornsea Mere (TA 1947). *Migration Watch Points* at Hornsea Mere (TA 1947) and Flamborough Head (TA 2570). Spurn Point (TA 4115–3910), Nature Reserve of Y.N.T., is *Bird Reserve*; and *Bird Observatory* of Y.N.U. Humber National *Wildfowl Refuge*, see vice-county 54
Museum at Kingston-upon-Hull

CHISLETT, R. and AINSWORTH, G.H. (1958). *Birds on the Spurn Peninsula*, Part I. London and Hull, Brown, 99 pp. (Part II to come)

North-east Yorkshire (vice-county 62)

British Junior Naturalists' Association
Darlington and Teesdale Naturalists' Field Club
Scarborough Field Naturalists' Society

Local Nature Reserve at Farndale (NZ 6102–SE 7187) and Y.N.T. Nature Reserve at Strensall Common (SE 6562–6461) have some importance as *Bird Reserves*. At Redcar (NZ 5528–6124) *Migration Watch Point*. At Hutton Buscel (SE 9784) *Field Centre* of B.J.N.A. At Flamingo Park, Kirby Misperton (SE 7779) *Zoo* with good bird collection
Museum at Scarborough; Yorkshire *Museum* in York

ALMOND, W.E., NICHOLSON, J.B. and ROBINSON, M.G. (1939). "The birds of the Tees Valley", *Transactions Northern Naturalists' Union* 5: 229–51

South-west Yorkshire (vice-county 63)

Barnsley Naturalist and Scientific Society
Doncaster and District Ornithological Society
Leeds and District Bird Watchers' Club

Y.N.T. Nature Reserve at Stocksmoor Common (SE 2714) is educational *Bird Reserve*
Doncaster *Museum* and Art Gallery

Mid-west Yorkshire (vice-county 64)

Leeds and District Bird Watchers' Club

In Yorkshire Dales National Park National Nature Reserves of Ling Gill (SD 7978) and Colt Park Wood (SD 7777) have some interest as *Bird Reserves*, as has Y.N.T.'s Nature Reserve at Askham Bog (SE 5649–5748).

Blubberhouses Moor (around SE 1354), perhaps best grouse moor in the Kingdom, has merit as unofficial moorland *Bird Reserve*. Local Nature Reserve at Fairburn Ings (SE 4527–4726) amounts to a *Wildfowl Refuge*. At Malham Tarn (SD 8967), *Field Centre* of the Field Studies Council; at Knaresborough (SE 3557) *Ringing Station*

North-west Yorkshire (vice-county 65)

Darlington and Teesdale Naturalists' Field Club

National Nature Reserve of Upper Teesdale (NY 8429–8024) has importance as *Bird Reserve*

PROVINCE TYNE

Natural History Society of Northumberland, Durham and Newcastle-upon-Tyne
Northern Naturalists' Union
Northumberland and Durham Naturalists' Trust

Durham (vice-county 66)

Consett and District Naturalists' Field Club
Darlington and Teesdale Naturalists' Field Club
Teesmouth Bird Club
University of Durham Philosophical Society

Marsden Rock (NZ 4064) a potential *Bird Reserve*. Nature Reserves of N.D.N.T. at Hawthorn Dene (NZ 4345), Black Halls Rocks (NZ 4738) and Witton-le-Wear (NZ 1430) have importance as *Bird Reserves*, as has Local Nature Reserve of Castle Eden Denes (NZ 4138–4540). At Hartlepool (NZ 5333) *Migration Watch Point*. At Teesmouth (NZ 5328) *Bird Observatory* of T.B.C.

TEMPERLEY, G.W. (1951). "A history of the birds of Durham", *Transactions N.H.S.N.D.N.-T.* (new series) 9: 296 pp.

Northumberland. Vice-county division is River Coquet, and an approximate line from Linnbriggs (NT 8906) to Carter Fell (NT 6805)

BOLAM, G. (1932). "A catalogue of the birds of Northumberland", *Transactions N.H.S.N.D.N.-T.* (new series) 8: 165 pp.

South Northumberland (vice-county 67)

Consett and District Naturalists' Field Club
Tyneside Bird Club

National Nature Reserve of Coom Rigg Moss (NY 6979) has some importance as *Bird Reserve*; in Gosforth Park (NZ 2570) *Bird Reserve* of

N.H.S.N.D.N.-T. N.D.N.T. also has *Bird Reserve* in this vice-county. At Hauxley (NU 2802) *Migration Watch Point*

Hancock *Museum* at Barras Bridge, Newcastle-upon-Tyne

North Northumberland or Cheviotland (vice-county 68)

Lindisfarne Natural Nature Reserve (NU 0447–1435) is a *Bird Reserve*, and *Migration Watch Point* as are Farne Islands (NU 2539–2037), founded by St Cuthbert as a Nature Reserve in *c.* 676, now National Trust and Farne Islands Association with small *Study Centre*. At Monk's House (NU 2033) *Migration Watch Point*; and World *Bird Research Station* at Glanton (NU 0714)

PERRY, R. (1946). *A naturalist on Lindisfarne*. London, Lindsay Drummond (2nd ed. 1947), 248 pp.

WATT, Grace (1951). *The Farne Islands*. London, Country Life, 236 pp.

ENNION, E.[A.R.] (1960). *The house on the shore*. London, Routledge and Kegan Paul, 200 pp.

PROVINCE LAKES

North-Western Naturalists' Union

Lake District (North Lancashire, Westmorland and Cumberland)

Lake District Naturalists' Trust

STOKOE, Ralph and BLEZARD, E. (1962). *The birds of the Lake counties*. Carlisle, Carlisle Natural History Society, 144 pp.

Westmorland and North Lancashire (vice-county 69)

Ambleside Field Society
Eden Field Club
Kendal Natural History Society
Lancashire Naturalists' Trust

Among National Nature Reserves in vice-county, the following have importance as *Bird Reserves*: Moor House (large area around NY 7729, with Nature Conservancy *Field Station* at NY 7532), Rusland Moss (SD 3388) and Roudsea Wood (around SD 3382). L.D.N.T. has Nature Reserves with importance as *Bird Reserves* at Brantwood (SD 3195), Meathop and Catcrag Mosses (SD 4481), Walney (SD 1873–2361 with Lancs. N.T. neighbouring Reserve) also a *Bird Observatory*, and Foulney (SD 2463). At Merlewood (SD 4079) Nature Conservancy *Research Station*

Cumberland (vice-county 70)

Carlisle Natural History Society

Penrith Natural History Society
Solway Bird Watchers' Society

Parts of Rockcliffe Marsh (NY 3464–3062) are potential *Bird Reserves* or
Wildfowl Refuges. National Trust properties in heights of Lake District
National Park at Kirk and Wasdale Fells (NY 1810–2109) and Sca Fell
(NY 2209–2004) are in effect *Bird Reserves*. Ravenglass and Drigg Dunes
(SD 0497–0795) Nature Reserve of Cumberland C.C. are likewise a
Bird Reserve. At Grune Point (NY 1456) and St Bee's Head (NX 9413)
Migration Watch Points, the former seasonally operated as *Ringing Station*

MACPHERSON, H.A. (1901). "Birds", *Victoria history of the county of
Cumberland* 1 : 179–217

Isle of Man (vice-county 71)

Isle of Man Natural History and Antiquarian Society
Manx Field Club (Field Section of above)
Manx National Trust

M.N.T. has Nature Reserves which are *Bird Reserves* at Maughold Head
(SC 4991) and the Calf of Man (SC 1565) ; latter has been lately operated
also as *Bird Observatory*. *Zoo* with birds at Wildlife Park, the Curraghs
(SC 3695)
Manx *Museum* in Douglas

MADOC, H.W. (1934). *Bird-life in the Isle of Man*. London, Witherby,
199 pp.

SCOTLAND

National Trust for Scotland
Royal Zoological Society of Scotland
Scottish Field Studies Association
Scottish Ornithologists' Club (journal *Scottish Birds*)
Scottish Society for the Protection of Wild Birds
Scottish Wildlife Trust

BAXTER, E.V. and RINTOUL, L.J. (1953). *The birds of Scotland their
history, distribution and migration*. Edinburgh and London, Oliver and Boyd,
2 vols., 816 pp.
RICHMOND, K. (1958). *Wild venture, a bird watcher in Scotland*. London,
Bles, 223 pp.

PROVINCE WEST LOWLANDS

Dumfriesshire and Galloway Natural History and Antiquarian Society
Buteshire Natural History Society
Natural History Society of Glasgow

Dumfries (vice-county 72)

Local Nature Reserve of Castle and High-tae Lochs (NY 0881–0880) is a *Bird Reserve*, as is the great National Nature Reserve of Caerlaverock (NY 0066–0866), in part also a *Wildfowl Refuge*

GLADSTONE, H.S. (1910). *The birds of Dumfriesshire, a contribution to the fauna of the Solway area.* London, Witherby, 482 pp.; (1911). *Addenda and corrigenda to the birds of Dumfriesshire.* Dumfries, D.G.N.H.A.S., 31 pp.; (1912). *A catalogue of the vertebrate fauna of Dumfriesshire.* Dumfries, Maxwell, 80 pp.; (1922). *Notes on the birds of Dumfriesshire. A continuation of the Birds of Dumfriesshire.* Dumfries, D.G.N.H.A.S., 116 pp.

Kirkcudbright (vice-county 73)

National Nature Reserves of Silver Flowe (NX 4684–4781) and Kirkconnell Flow (NX 9769) have some importance as *Bird Reserves*. Loch Ken (NX 6375–6771) is a potential *Wildfowl Refuge*

DUNCAN, A.B. (1947). *List of the birds of the Stewartry of Kirkcudbright.* Transactions D.G.N.H.A.S., 3rd series, 24: 129–43

Wigtown (vice-county 74)

Potential *Bird Reserves* at Mochrum and Castle Lochs (around NX 2953), and on Great Scaur (NX 2533, gannetry)

GRAY, R. and ANDERSON, T. (1869). "On the birds of Ayrshire and Wigtownshire", *Proceedings N.H.S.G.* 1: 269–324

McWILLIAM, J.M. (1945). "Birds of the Scar Rocks. The Wigtownshire gannetry", *Transactions B.N.H.S.* 13: 1–11

Ayr (vice-county 75)

Bird Reserve of Royal Society for the Protection of Birds on Horse Island (NS 2142), and of the S.S.P.W.B. on Lady Isle (NS 2729). Ailsa Craig (NS 0200), with gannetry, a private *Bird Reserve*

PATON, E.R. and PIKE, O.G. (1929). *The birds of Ayrshire.* London, Witherby, 228 pp.

McWILLIAM, J.M. (1936). *The birds of the Firth of Clyde.* London, Witherby, 164 pp.

GIBSON, J.A. (1951). "The breeding distribution, population and history of the birds of Ailsa Craig", *Scottish Naturalist* 63: 73–100, 159–77

Renfrew (vice-county 76)

Castle Semple Loch (NS 6039–5835) is potential *Bird Reserve*

McWILLIAM, J.M. (1936), see vice-county 75

GIBSON, J.A. (1955). "The breeding birds of Renfrewshire", *Glasgow and West of Scotland Bird Bulletin* 4: 28–32

Lanark (vice-county 77). Embraces eastern (detached) Dunbarton

Andersonian Naturalists of Glasgow
Zoological Society of Glasgow and West of Scotland

Possil Marsh (NS 5771–5869) is a *Bird Reserve* of S.S.P.W.B. Hamilton Low Parks Sanctuary (NS 7355) is a Regional *Wildfowl Refuge* of Hamilton Burgh. *Zoo* with birds at Calderpark (NS 6862) of Z.S.G.W.S.

PROVINCE EAST LOWLANDS

Berwickshire Naturalists' Club

EVANS, N.H. (1911). *A fauna of the Tweed area.* Edinburgh, David Douglas, 262 pp.

RINTOUL, L.J. and BAXTER, E.V. (1935). *A vertebrate fauna of Forth.* Edinburgh and London, Oliver and Boyd, 397 pp.

Peebles (vice-county 78)

Selkirk (vice-county 79)

Roxburgh (vice-county 80)

Kelso and District Ornithological Society

BOLAM, G. (1912). *Birds of Northumberland and the Eastern Borders.* Alnwick, Blair, 726 pp.

Berwick (vice-county 81)

Potential *Bird Reserve* at St Abb's Head (NT 9169)

MUIRHEAD, G. (1889–95). *The birds of Berwickshire.* Edinburgh, David Douglas, 2 vols., 334 + 390 pp.

BOLAM, G. (1911), see vice-county 80

East Lothian (vice-county 82)

East Lothian Antiquarian and Field Naturalists' Society

Bird Reserves of Royal Society for the Protection of Birds on Fidra, Eyebroughty and the Lamb Island (NT 4986–5386); Local Nature Reserve at Aberlady Bay (NT 4582–4580), of East Lothian C.C., is also *Bird Reserve*; Bass Rock (NT 6087), with ancient gannetry, is private *Bird Reserve*

TURNBULL, W.P. (1867). *The birds of East Lothian and a portion of the adjoining counties.* Glasgow, A.K. Murray, 48 pp.

HAMILTON, F.D. and MACGREGOR, K.S. (1960). "The birds of Aberlady Bay nature reserve", *Transactions E.L.A.F.N.S.* 8 : 33 pp.

Midlothian (vice-county 83)

Edinburgh Natural History Society
Midlothian Ornithologists' Club
Royal Zoological Society of Scotland

Bird Reserve of Royal Society for the Protection of Birds on Inchmickery (NT 2080); Regional *Wildfowl Refuge* at Duddingston Loch (NT 2872). At Murrayfield (NT 2073) *Zoo*, with fine bird collection, of R.Z.S.S.

In Edinburgh, Royal Scottish *Museum*; and Scottish *Centre for Ornithology* and Bird Protection, 21 Regent Terrace

NASH, J.K. (1935). *The birds of Midlothian.* London, Witherby, 303 pp.

ANDERSON, D.R. and WATERSTON, G. (1961). "The birds of Duddingston Loch, Edinburgh", *Scottish Birds* 1 (special suppl.) : 393–416

West Lothian (vice-county 84)

HIGHLANDS OF SCOTLAND

DARLING, F.Fraser and BOYD, J.Morton (1964). *The Highlands and Islands.* London, Collins *New Naturalist*, 336 pp.

EAST HIGHLANDS

HARVIE-BROWN, J.A. and BUCKLEY, T.E. (1895). *A fauna of the Moray Basin.* Edinburgh, David Douglas, 2 vols., 306 + 309 pp.

SIM, G. (1903). *The vertebrate fauna of Dee.* Aberdeen, 296 pp.

HARVIE-BROWN, J.A. (1906). *A fauna of the Tay Basin and Strathmore.* Edinburgh, David Douglas, 377 pp.

RINTOUL, L.J. and BAXTER, E.V. (1935), see East Lowlands

Fife with Kinross (vice-county 85)

Dunfermline Naturalists' Society
Kirkcaldy Naturalists' Society
Midlothian Ornithologists' Club

Four great National Nature Reserves, all important *Bird Reserves*: Tentsmuir Point (NO 4928), Morton Lochs (NO 4626), Loch Leven (NO 1401) and the Isle of May (NT 6599); at the last a *Bird Observatory* and *Field Station*. At Elie Ness (NT 4999) *Migration Watch Point*; and lighthouses at Bell Rock (NO 7627) and Inchkeith (NT 2982) have been used for this purpose

EGGELING, W.J. (1960). *The Isle of May*. Edinburgh and London, Oliver and Boyd, 280 pp.

GRIERSON, J. (1962). "A check-list of the birds of Tentsmuir, Fife". *Scottish Birds* 2 (special suppl.): 113–64

Stirling (vice-county 86). Part of county north of River Forth to vice-county 87

Part of Loch Lomond National Nature Reserve (NS 4089–4190) in this vice-county is an important *Bird Reserve* (rest in vice-county 99)

LUMSDEN, J. and BROWN, A. (1895). *A guide to the natural history of Loch Lomond and neighbourhood*. Glasgow, Bryce, 103 pp.

BARTHOLOMEW, J. (1955). "The birds of Baldernock parish, West Stirling", *Glasgow and West of Scotland Bird Bulletin* 4: 17–20, 25–8, 37–40

Perth. Vice-county divisions are water-partings of Rivers Forth and Tay between 87 and 88, Rivers Tay and Garry between 88 and 89

Perthshire Society of Natural Science

ALEXANDER, W.B. (1932). "The natural history of the Firth of Tay", *Transactions and Proceedings P.S.N.S.* 9: 35–42

South Perth and Clackmannan (vice-county 87). With small part of Co. Stirling north of River Forth

Nature Reserve of N.T.S. in Dollar Glen (NS 9699) is of importance as *Bird Reserve*

Mid Perth (vice-county 88)

The great, primarily botanical upland, National Nature Reserves of Rannoch Moor (NN 4056–4252). Ben Lawers (NN 6544–6137), Meall nan Tarmachan (NN 5839–5637) and Ben Lui (NN 2627–2725) are also important *Bird Reserves*. In Glen Lyon, Garth *Field Centre* (NN 7547) of Scottish Field Studies Association

North (or *East*) *Perth* (vice-county 89)

Caenlochan (NO 2079–2673), another high National Nature Reserve, partly in vice-counties 90 and 92, is an important *Bird Reserve*. In Strathardle, Kindrogan *Field Centre* (NO 0563) of S.F.S.A.

Angus (vice-county 90)

Two National Nature Reserves, primarily botanical. Caenlochan, see vice-county 89; coastal St Cyrus (NO 7564–7362), partly in vice-county 91, has importance as *Bird Reserve*.

ALEXANDER, W.B. (1932), see Perth

HUNTER, D.G. (1934). *Bird notes in Angus and the far north*. Arbroath, Buncle

Kincardine (vice-county 91). Includes Aberdeen Burgh south of Dee

Nature Reserve of N.T.S. in Crathes Woods (NO 7396) is of importance as *Bird Reserve*. St Cyrus N.N.R., see vice-county 90. At Girdle Ness (NJ 9705) *Migration Watch Point*

Aberdeen. Vice-county 92 is divided from 93 by the water-parting east and west of Inverury

South Aberdeen (vice-county 92)

National Nature Reserve of Cairngorms (NH 9208–NN 9187), the largest in Britain, partly in vice-county 92, is of great importance as *Bird Reserve*. Caenlochan N.N.R., see vice-county 89

North Aberdeen (vice-county 93)

Loch of Strathbeg (NK 0559–0858) is potential *Wildfowl Refuge*; and Sands of Forvie National Nature Reserve (NK 0229–0024) is important *Bird Reserve*. Hatton Castle (NJ 7546) has what may be the largest known rookery

WATSON, A. (1956). "The Hatton Castle rookery", *Scottish Naturalist* 68: 162–64.

Banff (vice-county 94)

EDWARD, Thomas (1877), "Birds of Banff", pp. 394–417 of S. SMILES. *Life of a Scotch naturalist. . . .* London, Murray (5th ed.), 438 pp.

Moray (vice-county 95)

MACDONALD, M. (1934). *Bird watching at Lossiemouth*. Elgin, private publ.

ST JOHN, C. (1882). *Natural history and sport in Moray*. Edinburgh, David Douglas

ST JOHN, H.C. *ed.* (1901). *Charles St John's note books*. Edinburgh, David Douglas, 119 pp.

Inverness. Mainland Inverness is divided between the East Highland province (vice-county 96) and the West Highland province (vice-county 97) by the central water-parting

PERRY, R. (1948). *In the high Grampians*. London, Lindsay Drummond, 173 pp.

Easterness (vice-county 96). East Inverness with Nairn

Inverness Bird Watching Group

Loch Garten (NH 9718–9717) is present headquarters of the recolonized Scottish breeding ospreys, a *Bird Reserve* of the Royal Society for the Protection of Birds. National Nature Reserve at Craigellachie (around NH 8812) is primarily botanical, but has interest as *Bird Reserve*; Achantoul, *Research Station* of Nature Conservancy, is close by. At Pitmain Beag (NH 7400) *Field Centre* of Highland and Overseas Field Holidays. Cairngorms N.N.R., see vice-county 92

St John, H.C. *ed.* (1901), see vice-county 95

Brown, P.[E.] and Waterston, G. (1962). *The return of the osprey.* London, Collins, 223 pp.

Weir, D. (1965). "The birds of Abernethy Forest", *Bird Notes* 31 : 283–88

PROVINCE WEST HIGHLANDS

Harvie-Brown, J.A. and Buckley, Thomas E. (1892). *A vertebrate fauna of Argyll and the Inner Hebrides.* Edinburgh, David Douglas, 262 pp.

Harvie-Brown, J.A. and Macpherson, H.A. (1904). *A fauna of the North-west Highlands and Skye.* Edinburgh, David Douglas, 372 pp.

McWilliam, J.M. (1936). *The birds of the Firth of Clyde.* . . . London, Witherby, 164 pp.

Argyll. The mainland of Argyll is divided into three; that part north of Loch Linnhe joins West Inverness to form vice-county 97, and the remainder is divided at the Crinan Canal to form vice-counties 98 and 101

Westerness (vice-county 97).

West Inverness with North Argyll. National Nature Reserve of Arriundle Oakwood (NM 8464) has importance as *Bird Reserve*, as have some ancient stands of Caledonian Pine such as that at Ardgour (around NM 9963) which are potential Nature Reserves

Hamilton, F.D., Macgregor, K.S. and Zamboni, R.C.F. (1954). "Notes on the birds of Glen Moidart, Inverness-shire", *Scottish Naturalist* 66: 89–93

Murray, W. (1961). "Bird life in a Highland glen", *Bird Notes* 29: 231–35

Goodfellow, P.F. (1961). "The birds of Corrour deer forest, Inverness-shire", *S.N.* 70: 48–59

Argyll (Main) (vice-county 98)

Recreational Area of Glencoe (NN 1358–1851), National Trust for Scotland, has some importance as *Bird Reserve*, as has National Nature Reserve of Ben Lui (NN 2626), partly in vice-county 88, which see. Ancient Caledonian forest of Black Mount (around NN 2842) is potential Nature Reserve and *Bird Reserve*

Dunbarton (*West*) (vice-county 99)

Part of Loch Lomond National Nature Reserve (NS 4089–4388) in this vice-county is an important *Bird Reserve* (rest in vice-county 86)

LUMSDEN, J. and BROWN, A. (1895), see vice-county 86

CRUM, F.M. (1956). "The birds of Rosneath", *Glasgow Bird Bulletin* 5: 13–19, 30–34, 37–40

Clyde Isles (vice-county 100). The administrative county of Bute.

Buteshire Natural History Society

MCWILLIAM, J.M. (1927). *The birds of the island of Bute.* London, Witherby, 128 pp.: (1938). "The birds of Inchmarnock, a Clyde island", *Transactions B.N.H.S.* 12: 5–20

GIBSON, J.A. and GORDON, C.J. (1952). "The breeding birds of Inchmarnock", *Glasgow and West of Scotland Bird Bulletin* 2: 54–57

BAGENAL, T.B. and MILLAR, R.H. (1954). "A list of the birds of the Great Cumbrae". *G.W.S.B.B.* 3: 33–36

GIBSON, J.A. (1954). "The breeding birds of Pladda", *Glasgow Bird Bulletin* 3: 55–56; (1956). "The birds of the Island of Arran". Rothesay, Bute Newspapers, revised ed. from paper (1955). *Transactions B.N.H.S.* 14

Cantire (*Kintyre*) (vice-county 101)

GREENLEES, J. (1953). "The birds of Southend, Argyll", *Glasgow Bird Bulletin* 2: 33–37

GIBSON, J.A. (1956). "The breeding birds of Sanda, Sheep Island and Glunimore", *Glasgow Bird Bulletin* 5: 5–12, 20–21

South Ebudes (*Inner Hebrides*) (vice-county 102). Includes Scarba

Among several potential Nature Reserves: on Colonsay, Kiloran (NR 3996), in effect *Bird Reserve*; and on Islay Loch Gruinart (NR 3073–2867) – *Wildfowl Refuge*, and coast of the Oa (around NR 2641) – *Bird Reserve*

ROSS, A. (1913). "Birds of Islay"; and (1915). "Additional notes on the birds of Islay", *Glasgow Naturalist* 6: 7–32; 7: 97–101

LODER, J. de V. (1935). *Colonsay and Oronsay in the Isles of Argyll. . . .* Edinburgh and London, Oliver and Boyd, 472 pp.

MEIKLEJOHN, M.F.M. and STANFORD, J.K. (1954). "June notes on the birds of Islay", *Scottish Naturalist* 66: 129–45

Mid Ebudes (*Inner Hebrides*) (vice-county 103)

Private Nature Reserve of Treshnish Isles (NM 3044–2337) is important *Bird Reserve*. Staffa (NM 3235) is potential Nature and *Bird Reserve*

GRAHAM, H.D. (1890). *The birds of Iona and Mull*. Edinburgh, David Douglas, 279 pp.

TOMISON, J. (1907). "Bird-life as observed at Skerryvore lighthouse", *Annals of Scottish Natural History* 16 : 20–31

BOYD, J. Morton (1958). "The birds of Tiree and Coll", *British Birds* 51 : 41–56, 103–18

North Ebudes (*Inner Hebrides*) (vice-county 104)

Whole island of Rhum (around NM 3698) is National Nature Reserve with importance as *Bird Reserve*, as potentially are parts of neighbouring islands of Canna, Sanday and Eigg

MACPHERSON, H.A. (1888). "The birds of Skye, . . .", *Proceedings of the Royal Physical Society of Edinburgh* 9 : 118–43

NASH, J.K. (1914). "Bird life on the island of Eigg", *Zoologist* (series 4) 18 : 226–34

PEACOCK, A.D., SMITH, E.P. and DAVIDSON, C.F. (1934–5). "The natural history of South Rona", *Scottish Naturalist 1934* : 113–27, 149–63; *1935* : 3–10

TEMPERLEY, G.W. (1938). "Notes on the bird life of the island of Raasay, Inner Hebrides", *S.N. 1938* : 11–27

CARRICK, R. and WATERSTON, G. (1939). "The birds of Canna", *S.N. 1939* : 5–22

GORDON, S. (1942). *In search of northern birds*. London, Royal Society for the Protection of Birds, 224 pp.

ATKINSON, R. (1949). *Island going*. . . . London, Collins, 384 pp.

BOURNE, W.R.P. (1957). "The birds of the island of Rhum", *S.N.* 69 : 21–31

WILLIAMSON, K. and BOYD, J. Morton (1963). *A mosaic of islands*. Edinburgh and London, Oliver and Boyd, 183 pp.

PROVINCE NORTH HIGHLANDS

HARVIE-BROWN, J.A. and BUCKLEY, T.E. (1887). *A vertebrate fauna of Sutherland, Caithness and West Cromarty*. Edinburgh, David Douglas, 344 pp. : (1895), see East Highlands Province

HARVIE-BROWN, J.A. and MACPHERSON, H.A. (1904), see West Highlands Province

WILLIAMSON, K. and BOYD, J. Morton (1963). *A mosaic of islands*. Edinburgh and London, Oliver and Boyd, 183 pp.

Ross. Vice-county division by central water-parting

West Ross (vice-county 105)

Large National Nature Reserves of Inverpolly (NC 0519–1605) and Beinn
Eighe (NG 9767–9656) are important *Bird Reserves*. Ristol and the Summer
Isles (NB 9712–9101) are private Nature Reserves of *Bird Reserve* or
Wildfowl Refuge status. National Trust for Scotland's Recreational Areas
of Balmacara (NG 8034–8126) and Kintail (NH 0126–NG 9913) contain
effective *Bird Reserves*. By Beinn Eighe N.N.R., Anancaun *Field Station*
(NM 0263) of Nature Conservancy

FISHER, J. (1949). "Natural history of Inverpolly Forest", *Bird Notes* 23:
253–60 (also papers by J.A.HARVIE-BROWN and others); (1886).
Transactions Norfolk and Norwich Naturalists' Society 4: 310–15; (1894).
Proceedings Royal Physical Society of Edinburgh 12: 377–415; (1896, 1898).
Annals of Scottish Natural History 1896: 93–97; *1898*: 65–75

East Ross (vice-county 106)

At Tarbat Ness (NH 9487) *Migration Watch Point*

Sutherland. Vice-county division by central water-parting

ST JOHN, C. (1849). *A tour in Sutherlandshire.* . . . London, John Murray,
2 vols. (new ed. 1884), 296+288 pp.

East Sutherland (vice-county 107)

Potential *Bird Reserve* at Dunrobin (NC 8500)

West Sutherland (vice-county 108)

At Cló Mór (NC 2973–3272), Faraid Head to Smoo (NC 3971–4167) and
Eilean Bulgach or Am Balg (NC 1866), potential *Bird Reserves* for sea
birds. National Nature Reserves of Invernaver (NC 6762–7059), Strathy
Bog (NC 7953) and Inchnadamph (NC 2521–2617), primarily botanical,
have some interest as *Bird Reserves*. Handa (NC 1447) is a magnificent
island *Bird Reserve* of the Royal Society for the Protection of Birds

ATKINSON, R. (1949), see vice-county 104
FISHER, J. and PIERCY, K. (1950). "Notes on Eilean Bulgach, Suther-
land", *Scottish Naturalist* 62: 26–30
PENNIE, I.D. (1951). "The Cló Mór bird cliffs", *S.N.* 65: 26–32

Caithness (vice-county 109)

No nature reserves; but some sea cliffs and parts of the Berriedale woodland

Handa: the Great Stack of this noble sandstone island off Sutherland, a
Bird Reserve of the Royal Society for the Protection of Birds. Drawing from
A Fauna of the North West Highlands, by J.A. Harvie-Brown.

(around ND 1122) are potential *Bird Reserves*. At Ness Head (ND 3855)
Migration Watch Point

BAXTER, E.V. and RINTOUL, L.J. (1931). "Some notes on Caithness
birds", *S.N. 1931*: 133–39

PROVINCE NORTH ISLES

Outer Hebrides (vice-county 110)

All National Nature Reserves in this area of marvellous sea-bird colonies,
rarities and migrant flyways are *Bird Reserves*: North Rona (HW 8132)
and Sula Sgeir (HW 6130), the remotest (gannetry on S.S.); St Kilda
(around NA 0900) the greatest and grandest of all (Britain's largest
fulmary and puffinry; the world's largest northern gannetry, etc.) has

St Kilda. Bird fowling on the Dún in 1876, from a drawing by J. Sands. Five miles away, Boreray houses the world's largest gannet colony. The whole archipelago is now a National Nature Reserve.

been manned as *Migration Watch Point*; and Loch Druidibeg (NF 7540–8037). Other inaccessible or uninhabited islands are natural nature reserves, and *Bird Reserves* also, indeed, notably the Flannan Isles (NA 7246) whose lighthouse is Britain's remotest inhabited spot (has been used as *Migration Watch Point*); Gasker (NA 8711); the Shiant Islands (NG 4197), a private reserve in fact; Haskeir (NF 6182–5980); Heisker *or* Monach Islands (around NF 6361); and Berneray and Mingulay (around NL 5582). Rockall, 191 miles west of St Kilda, the remotest islet in the North Atlantic, is visited by birds. *Bird Reserves* are also proposed on Balranald Marshes (NF 7170) and Wiay (around NF 8746), and the only strong woodland bird fauna of the Long Isle, around Lews Castle, Stornoway (NB 4133) deserves special conservation. Among potential wader and *Wildfowl Refuges* are Melbost Sands (around NB 4534), Traighs Seilebost and Luskentyre (around NG 0798), and Loch Bee (around NF 7743). *Migration Watch Points* at Butt of Lewis (NB 5166) and in neighbourhood of Gallan Head (NB 0539) in west Lewis

HARVIE-BROWN, J.A. (1879). "The Shiant Islands and their bird life", *Transactions of the Norfolk and Norwich Naturalists' Society* 3 : 49–60

HARVIE-BROWN, J.A. and BUCKLEY, T.E. (1885). *A vertebrate fauna of the Outer Hebrides*. Edinburgh, David Douglas, 279 pp.

MACRURY, J. (1894, 1898). "The birds of the island of Barra", *Annals of Scottish Natural History* 3 : 140–45; 7 : 75–77

HARVIE-BROWN, J.A. (1903). "On the avifauna of the Outer Hebrides", *A.S.N.H.* 12 : 7–22

CLYNE, R. (1911, 1915). ". . . birds . . . at the Butt of Lewis", *A.S.N.H.* 20: 65–70 and *Scottish Naturalist 1915*: 29–37, 77–81

BEVERIDGE, F.S. (1919). "The birds of North Uist", *S.N. 1919*: 17–24

STEWART, M. (1933). *Ronay*. . . . London, Oxford University Press, 73 pp.

FORREST, J.E., WATERSTON, A.R. and WATSON, E.V. (1936). "The natural history of Barra, Outer Hebrides. . . .", *Proceedings of the Royal Physical Society of Edinburgh* 22: 241–96

ELTON, C. (1938). "Notes on the ecological and natural history of Pabbay, and other islands in the Sound of Harris, Outer Hebrides", *Journal of Ecology* 26: 275–97

DARLING, F.Fraser (1939). *A naturalist on Rona essays of a biologist in isolation*. Oxford, Clarendon Press, 137 pp.

ATKINSON, R. (1949), see vice-county 104

MACGREGOR, A.A. (1949). *The Western Isles*. London, Robert Hale, 366 pp.

SERGEANT, D.E. and WHIDBORNE, R.F. (1951). "Birds on Mingulay in the summer of 1949", *S.N.* 63: 8–25

ATKINSON, R. and ROBERTS, B. (1952). "Notes on the islet of Gasker", *S.N.* 64: 129–37

ALLAN, R.M. (1955). "Observations on the fauna of Heisker or Monach Isles, Outer Hebrides", *S.N.* 67: 3–8

ROBERTS, B. and ATKINSON, R. (1955). "The Haskeir Rocks, North Uist", *S.N.* 67: 9–18

FISHER, J. (1956). *Rockall*. London, Bles, 200 pp.

WILLIAMSON, K. and BOYD, J.Morton (1960). *St Kilda summer*. London, Hutchinson, 224 pp.; (1963). *A mosaic of islands*. Edinburgh and London, Oliver and Boyd, 183 pp

ANDERSON, A., BAGENAL, T.B., BAIRD, D.E. and EGGELING, W.J. (1961). "A description of the Flannan Isles and their birds", *Bird Study* 8: 71–88

Orkney (vice-county 111)

Eynhallow (HY 3629) is a private *Bird Reserve*. Areas patrolled by Royal Society for the Protection of Birds, and with some *Bird Reserve* status, include Papa Westray (HY 5055–4849), Eday and the Calf of Eday (HY 5640–5528), Gairsay and its holms (HY 4322–4520) and large parts of Mainland. The gannetry of Sule Stack (HX 5617) is a *Bird Reserve* by virtue of inaccessibility. The west cliffs of Hoy (HY 1904–1700) deserve nature reserve status. At North Ronaldsay (HY 7856–7651) and Burray (ND 5096) *Migration Watch Points*; and Sule Skerry (HX 6224), Auskerry (HY 6715), Graemsay (HY 2406) and Pentland Skerries (ND 4678) lighthouse stations have been used as such

BUCKLEY, T.E. and HARVIE-BROWN, J.A. (1891). *A vertebrate fauna of the Orkney Islands.* Edinburgh, David Douglas, 314 pp.

TOMISON, J. (1904). "Sule Skerry, Orkney, and its bird life", *Annals of Scottish Natural History* 13 : 16–26, 91–98

SERLE, W. (1934). "Note on the breeding birds of the island of Hoy, Orkney", *Scottish Naturalist 1934* : 129-36

MEINERTZHAGEN, R. (1939). "A note on the birds of Hoy, Orkney", *Ibis* (series 14) 3 : 258–64

MARWICK, J.C. (1940). "Some Orkney birds", pp. 197–205 of J. GUNN. *Orkney the magnetic north.* London, etc., Nelson, revised ed.

LACK, David (1942–3). "The breeding birds of Orkney", *Ibis* (series 14) 6 : 461–84; 85 : 1–27

DUFFEY, E. (1955). "Notes on the natural history of Eynhallow', *S.N.* 67 : 40–51

Shetland (vice-county 112)

Friends of Fair Isle

National Nature Reserves are important *Bird Reserves* : Hermaness (HP 6120–5912), the northernmost point of the kingdom, with gannetry, on the isle of Unst – a useful *Migration Watch Point* also the isle of Haaf Gruney (HU 6398); Ronas Hill (around HU 3083); Noss (HU 5440), with gannetry. Patrolled by Royal Society for Protection of Birds are some of above, Fetlar (HU 5792) and Spiggie (HU 3717). The remote inhabited island of Foula (HT 9738) is an often-manned *Migration Watch Point*, as is sometimes also Sumburgh Head (HU 4007). The Fair Isle (HZ 2272), most remarkable migration station in Europe, with famous *Bird Observatory*, is a National Trust for Scotland *Bird Reserve* in effect, too

PERRY, R. (1948). *Shetland sanctuary birds on the isle of Noss.* London, Faber and Faber, 300 pp.

INKSTER C. (1951). "Some notes on the birds of Yell", *Bird Notes* 24 : 227–31, 270–73

VENABLES, L.S.V. and VENABLES, U.M. (1955). *Birds and mammals of Shetland.* Edinburgh, Oliver and Boyd, 385 pp.

MITCHELL, D.R. (1956). "The birds of Unst", *B.N.* 27 : 84–89

DICKENS, R.F. and WILSON, D.R. (1957). "A list of birds recorded on Foula, Shetland. . . .", *Fair Isle Bird Observatory Bulletin* 3 : 187–92

WILLIAMSON, K. and BOYD, J.Morton (1963). *A mosaic of islands.* Edinburgh and London, Oliver and Boyd, 183 pp.

WILLIAMSON, K. (1965): *Fair Isle and its birds.* Edinburgh, Oliver and Boyd, 311 pp.

IRELAND

Wild animals and plants know nothing of the partition of Ireland; accordingly zoologists and botanists use a vice-comital system, based on the late R. Lloyd Praeger's *Irish topographical botany* of 1901, that takes no account in its order and ecological logic of the ancient Provinces of Ireland, or (needless to say) of the present boundaries of the Free State and Northern Ireland. Scientists and conservationists are oblivious of the border in the sharing of work and the exchanging of experience. The national organisations of the two countries are therefore grouped together here

An Taisce (the National Trust for Ireland)
Bord Failte Eireann (Irish Tourist Board; gives information and advice)
Committee for Nature Conservation in Northern Ireland
Irish Ornithologists' Club (publishes *Irish Bird Report*)
Irish Society for the Protection of Birds
National Trust (for England, Wales and Northern Ireland)
Royal Irish Academy
Royal Zoological Society of Ireland
· Ulster Game and Wild Fowl Preservation Society
Ulster Society for the Protection of Birds

Journals: of some of the above and the *Irish Naturalists' Journal*

Conservation in Ireland is progressing rapidly under both governments, and the fact that there is no National Park yet in the island, and less than a couple of dozen Nature Reserves, by no means reflects a lack of sophistication among the Irish on conservation issues or in biological prowess. It reflects, quite simply, the state of human population pressure on Ireland's wild life, which compares quite well with that in Great Britain a century ago. Such pressure, now increasing, must eventually bring a reserve network into being throughout Ireland, with the advantage that it can be planned with more care and time than the somewhat over-complex network that has been hastily improvised in England and Wales, and more carefully evolved in Scotland, in the last couple of decades. The bird places selected for attention under the vice-county headings that follow, then, are often *potential* bird reserves and wildfowl refuges, which I have called "strongholds" of sea birds, water birds (including wildfowl) or land birds. Most contain birds of no very great global rarity, but of great interest to the student of Irish bird fauna which, compared with that of Great Britain, is rather impoverished. Nevertheless, Ireland is a paradise of birds, with its rugged Atlantic coast and countless islets, its maze of loughs and waterways, its moors and bogs and ancient relict woodland. Many good bird areas, especially the wintering places of wildfowl, are so large that only a two-figure grid reference is necessary – to a square of side 10 kilometres. Some four-figure references give the centre of largish areas. The Irish National Grid (on which all references are made) is available on the one-inch sheets published by the Ordnance Survey of Northern Ireland in Belfast, and on the half-inch (not the one-inch) sheets published by the Ordnance Survey of Ireland in Dublin

DEANE, C.D. (1934). "Handbook of the birds of Northern Ireland", *Bulletin of the Belfast Museum* 1 : 120–90

KENNEDY, P.G., RUTTLEDGE, R.F., SCROOPE, C.F. and HUMPHREYS, G.R. (1954). *The birds of Ireland: an account of the distribution migrations and habits as observed in Ireland.* Edinburgh and London, Oliver and Boyd, 437 pp.

O'RUADHAIN, M. (1956). "The position of nature protection in Ireland in 1956", *Irish Naturalists' Journal* 12 : 81–104

RUTTLEDGE, R.F. and WATT, R.Hall (1958). The distribution and status of wild geese in Ireland", *Bird Study* 5 : 22–33

ARMSTRONG, E.A. (1940). *Birds of the grey wind.* London, etc., Oxford University Press, 228 pp. New eds. 1944, 1947

Kerry. The vice-county divide follows the south and west boundaries of the the old baronies of Magunihy and Trughanacmy. This is not on modern maps, but runs approximately from the Cork boundary at Coomagearlahy (W 1077) and west via Mangerton Mountain (V 9880), crossing Upper Lake Killarney at V 9081 and turning thence north on the east side of Purple Mountain to Lough Leane at Cullinagh (V 9287). From the exit of the River Laune at V 9091 the line then sweeps west south of the Laune, to reach the Castlemaine Estuary at Illaunstookagh (V 6896) opposite Inch. Inch and the Dingle Peninsula belong to vice-county 1, the division continuing from Aughils (Q 7202) across Baurtregaum (Q 7507) to Derrymore (Q 7511) in Inner Tralee Bay[1]

South Kerry (vice-county 1)

Water-bird stronghold at Tralee Bay (around Q 7612). Many sea-bird strongholds from Brandon Point (Q 5216) to Scariff Island (V 4455), including Inish Tearaght (V 1794–1894) a useful *Migration Watch Point*, Great Blasket (V 2594–2696), Little Skellig (V 2611) with huge gannetry and Great Skellig (V 2460)

ALEXANDER, S.M.D. (1954). "The birds of the Blasket Islands", *Bird Study* 1 : 148–68

[1] This is the most bothersome vice-county boundary. As stable boundaries are essential for biological records, if not human life, a large-scale vice-county map would be a great boon.

MUNNS, D.J. (1956). "Further notes on the birds of the Blasket Islands", *B.S.* 3: 248–50

HARROP, J.M. (1959). "Birds of the Great Skellig, Co. Kerry", *Irish Naturalists' Journal* 13: 17–18

North Kerry (vice-county 2)

A chain of water-bird strongholds from the Shannon Estuary (Q 0049) to Castlemaine Harbour (Q 7200), including the Feale (or Cashen) Estuary (Q 8738), Akeragh Lough (Q 7526) and Tralee Bay (Q 7612). Sea-bird strongholds on several cliffs from Leck Point (Q 8644) to Kerry Head (Q 6730). The Bourn Vincent Memorial Park, Killarney (around V 98) is a Nature Reserve and *Bird Reserve*; and there is a small Nature Reserve on Ross Island (V 9488)

Cork. Another complex division. West Cork is separated from Mid Cork by a line from Milstreet (W 2692) through Macroom (W 3373) to Bandon (W 4955), the boundary being completed by the Killarney Railway in the north, and the River Bandon in the south. Mid Cork is separated from East Cork by the Great Southern and Western Railway from Charleville (R 5522) to Cork (W 6872), thence by the River Lee and the western shore of Cork Harbour to the sea

Cork Historical and Archaeological Society

West Cork (vice-county 3)

A chain of sea-bird strongholds from the Bull and Cow Rocks (V 4039, 4239) – with gannetry on the Bull, to the Old Head of Kinsale (W 6339), including Bantry Bay (V 95), Roaringwater Bay (W 03) and Cape Clear Island (V 9621), where also *Bird Observatory*. A small Nature Reserve on Garnish Island (Ilnacullin) near Glengarriff (V 9354)

Mid Cork (vice-county 4)

A sea-bird stronghold at Reanies (W 7451), and water-bird stronghold in Cork Harbour (W 7566, with vice-county 5)

East Cork (vice-county 5)

Water-bird stronghold at Ballymacoda (X 0672). Sea-bird stronghold at Power Head (W 8859)

Waterford (vice-county 6)

Sea-bird strongholds from Ardmore Head (X 1676) to Dunmore East (S 6900), including Helvick Head (X 3188) and Great Newtown Head

(X 5798). Water-bird strongholds from Dungarvan Harbour (X 2792) to Waterford Harbour (S 70), including Carrick-on-Suir (S 4021) and Back Strand, Tramore (S 6101)

South Tipperary (vice-county 7)

Water-bird stronghold in the Suir Valley, from Templemore (S 1270) to Camus (S 0443)

Limerick (vice-county 8)

Water-bird stronghold in the Shannon Estuary, especially near Mellon (R 4458)

Clare and Aran Islands (vice-county 9)

Sea-bird strongholds from Loop Head (Q 6947) to Inishmore, Aran Islands (L 7811), including Kilkee Cliffs (Q 8357–8559) and Cliffs of Moher (R 0189–0594). Water-bird strongholds from the Shannon Estuary (as vice-county 8) to Lough Bunny near Gort (R 3797), including Baltard (Q 96), Mattle (Q 9772) and Mutton (Q 9774) Islands, and the Corrofin – Ruan area (R 28–38)

ARMSTRONG, E.A. (1957). "Birds of the Aran Islands", *Irish Naturalists' Journal* 12: 207–08

BARRETT, J.N. (1958). "Birds seen on Inishmore, Aran Islands, 1957", *I.N.J.* 12: 314–16

North Tipperary (vice-county 10)

Water-bird stronghold in Shannon Valley, see vice-county 18

Kilkenny (vice-county 11)

Water-bird stronghold at Ballyragget (S 46)

Wexford (vice-county 12)

Sea-bird strongholds from Carnivan Head (S 7802) to Lady's Island Lake (T 1006), including Great Saltee (X 9496), where gannetry, and Tacumshin Lake (T 0506). Water-bird strongholds from Bannow Bay (S 8108) to Wexford Harbour whose famous goose "slobs" lie to south (around T 0716) and north (around T 0825); including the Cull at Duncormick (S 9206) and Kilmore Quay (S 9603). Great Saltee (X 9496) is *Bird Reserve*; has had *Bird Observatory*; another important *Migration Watch Point* is Tuskar Rock (T 2267)

MASON, A.G. (1944). "Birds of the Saltees", *Irish Naturalists' Journal* 8: 143–45 (several other papers in this journal)

BYRNE, L.H. (1964). "Ornithological notes from S.E. Wexford, autumn, 1963", *I.N.J.* 14: 271–74

Carlow (vice-county 13)

Laoighis (Leix, once Queen's County; vice-county 14)

Galway. The West Galway (Connemara) vice-county is divided from North-east Galway by Lough Corrib and the River Corrib; South-east Galway from North-east Galway by the Midland Great Western Railway from Oranmore (M 3825) to Ballinasloe (M 8532). West Galway includes Inishark (L 4864), and Inishbofin (L 5467), from Co. Mayo

RUTTLEDGE, R.F. (1950). "A list of the birds of the counties of Galway and Mayo", *Proceedings of the Royal Irish Academy* 52B: 315–81

South-east Galway (vice-county 15)

Sea-bird stronghold (inland cormorants) at Lough Cutra (R 4798). Water-bird strongholds in Shannon Valley, see vice-county 18 and on River Suck north of Ballyforan (with vice-county 25)

West Galway (vice-county 16)

Sea-bird strongholds on Inishshark (L 4864) and Inishbofin (L 5467); and on Mutton Island (M 2923). Water-bird stronghold on Inishbroon off Rinvyle (L 8364), and official *Wildfowl Refuge* at Lough Rusheen (L 7931)

RUTTLEDGE, R.F. (1957). "The birds of Inishbofin, Co. Galway, with some notes on those of Inishshark", *Bird Study* 4: 71–80

North-east Galway (vice-county 17)

Water-bird stronghold near Tuam (M 45).

Offaly (once King's County, vice-county 18)

Water- and land-bird strongholds at Charleville (N 3123) and in Shannon Valley area (M 91, 92, N 01, 02) on borders of vice-counties 10, 15 and 25

Kildare (vice-county 19)

The Curragh, large Native Flora Reserve (around N 7713) has some interest as a *Bird Reserve*

Wicklow (vice-county 20)

Sea-bird strongholds at Wicklow Head (T 3492) and Bray Head (O 2817).

Water-bird strongholds at Broad Lough (T 3097–3194) and Poulaphouca Reservoir (around O 0010). Land-bird strongholds at Russborough (N 9511) and Powerscourt (O 2116)

Dublin (vice-county 21)

Dublin Naturalists' Field Club
Royal Dublin Society

Sea-bird strongholds from Howth (O 2936–2939) to Rockabill (O 3262) including Ireland's Eye (O 2841) and Lambay (O 3151–3250). Water-bird strongholds from Dublin Bay (O 23) to the Swords Estuary at Malahide (O 2247), including Booterstown Marsh (O 1830), the official *Wildfowl Refuge* of the North Bull (O 2236) and Baldoyle Bay (O 2441). Land-bird stronghold in Phoenix Park (O 1334), where also Native Flora Reserve and *Zoo* with good bird collection. Native Flora Reserve of interest as *Bird Reserve* also at the Botanic Gardens, Glasnevin (O 1537) In Dublin, the National *Museum*

KENNEDY, P.G. (1953). *An Irish sanctuary: birds of the North Bull.* Dublin, at the Sign of the Three Candles, 168 pp.

MITCHELL, A.F. (1953). "Bird notes from inner Dublin", *Irish Naturalists' Journal* 11 : 66–70

JACKSON, R.D. (1955). "A list of birds of the West Pier, Dun Laoghaire, Co. Dublin", *I.N.J.* 11 : 271–79

Meath (vice-county 22)

Water-bird stronghold in Boyne Estuary (O 1376), with vice-county 31

Westmeath (vice-county 23)

Water-bird stronghold around River Inny headwaters and lakes up to Lough Sheelin (around N 4282) and south to Lough Ennell (around N 4047). Around Lough Ree (N 0252) land-bird woodland stronghold, shared with vice-counties 24 and 25

Longford (vice-county 24)

Lough Ree, see vice-county 23. At mouth River Inny (N 1055) a water-bird stronghold

Roscommon (vice-county 25)

Lough Ree, see vice-county 23. Water-bird strongholds of Shannon Valley shared with vice-counties 15 and 18, which see

Mayo. East Mayo is divided from West Mayo by Lough Musk and the River Ayle, thence by the T40 to Castlebar, whence down the River

Clydagh, Lough Cullin and the River Moy to the Sligo border near the sea

The Red-necked Phalarope Bird Sanctuary is a *Bird Reserve* of the Irish Society for the Protection of Birds in Co. Mayo

RUTTLEDGE, R.F. (1950), see Galway

East Mayo (vice-county 26)

Water-bird stronghold on River Moy by Foxford (G 2404) shared with vice-county 27

West Mayo (vice-county 27)

Sea-bird strongholds all round the coast from Inishturk (L 5975–6275) to Downpatrick Head (G 1242), including Clare Island (L 6484–6988), the Bills of Achill (L 5493), Black Rock (F 4815), Inishkea Islands (around F 5622), Kid Island and Rinnaglana (F 7843–7942), Benwee Head (F 8144), the Stags of Broadhaven (F 8448), Portacloy to Laghtmurragha (F 8444–9342), and Lough Carrowmore (F 8329). Water-bird strongholds from Derrycraff River (around M 0072) to Broad Haven (around F 7737), including Clare Island, islands in Clew Bay (L 89–99), Achill Sound (F 7401), Inishgalloon (F 6203), Inishkea Islands and the Mullet (F 6222) and Blacksod Bay (around F 7025)

RUTTLEDGE, R.F (1951). "Some notes on Achill birds", *Irish Naturalists' Journal* 10: 205–07
CABOT, D.B. (1963). "The breeding birds of Inishkea Islands, Co. Mayo", *I.N.J.* 14: 113–15

Sligo (vice-county 28)

Sea-bird strongholds from Aughris Head (G 4936) to Skerrydoo (G 7457), including Inishmurray (G 5653) and Mullaghmore (G 7058). Water-birds strongholds from Sligo Bay (around G 6040) to Lough Mullaghmore (G 7257), including Drumcliff Bay (G. 6243), Lissadell (G 6244) and Bunduff Lough (G 7155)

RUTTLEDGE, R.F. (1956). "An ornithological visit to Inishmurray", *Irish Naturalists' Journal* 12: 28–29
CABOT, D.B. (1962). "An ornithological expedition to Inishmurray, Co. Sligo", *I.N.J.* 14: 59–61

Leitrum (vice-county 29)

Water-bird stronghold at Lough McNean, see vice-county 33

Cavan (vice-county 30)

Water-bird stronghold at Lough McNean, see vice-county 33. Near Killashandra (H 30) a stronghold of woodland land birds, and of water birds in the maze of the River Erne

Louth (vice-county 31)

Boyne Estuary, see vice-county 22. At Bellurgan Park (J 0909) land-bird stronghold

Monaghan (vice-county 32)

Fermanagh (vice-county 33)

Water-bird strongholds around Upper Lough McNean (H 0339) with vice-counties 29 and 30, and Lower Lough McNean (H 1037). The Lower Lough Erne woodlands (H 15) harbour a land-bird stronghold, with some official Nature Reserves, including *Bird Reserves*[1] on islands near Castlecaldwell (around H 0260). Castlecoole (H 2543) is a *Bird Reserve*, in effect, of the National Trust

Donegal. East Donegal is officially separated from West Donegal by a line dividing the baronies of Raphoe and Boylagh from those of Inishowen and Kilmacrennan, forgotten on modern maps. The approximate boundary from south to north is the River Eske, Lough Eske and a line winding through the hills a mile or more west of longitude 8°W (or easting 200 on the Irish National Grid) to the L 74 near Meenirroy Hill (B 9706), whence north-east to the source of the River Swilly and down it to the sea

East Donegal (vice-county 34)

Sea-bird strongholds from Rinulla to Stookaruddan (C 4558–4955), at Slievebane and Rossnabartan (C 4258) and on Inishtrahull (C 4865), which also is a *Migration Watch Point*, as is Malin Head (C 3959) which now has official *Bird Observatory* (C 4057). Water-bird strongholds at Rossnowlagh (G 8668), Lough Swilly (around C 3020), with vice-county 35, and Trawbreaga Bay (around C 4549)

STELPOX, A.W. (1940). "Inishtrahull, Co. Donegal: a preliminary survey", *Irish Naturalists' Journal* 7: 238–43

---

[1] The expression *Bird Reserves* as I use it for vice-counties in Northern Ireland includes official Provincial "Wild Bird Sanctuaries".

West Donegal (vice-county 35)

Sea-bird strongholds all along coast from Inishduff (G 6472) to Breaghy
Head (C 0855), including Slieve League (G 5578), Tormore Point
(G 5590), Roaninish (B 6502), Illancrone (B 6910), Aranmore (B 6418),
Tory Island (B 8646–8745) where *Bird Observatory*, and Horn Head
(B 9940–C 0340). Water-bird strongholds at Inishduff, Aranmore and
Sheep Haven (C 0836)

CABOT, D.B. (1961). "Birds on Roaninish, Co. Donegal", *Irish Naturalists'*
Journal 13: 238–39; (1962). "Birds on Inishduff, Co. Donegal", *I.N.J.*
14: 36–37

Tyrone (vice-county 36)

Water-bird strongholds at Loughs Brantry (H 7453), Eskragh (H 7761)
and Ballysaggart (H 7961), and at Ardboe Point (H 9675). Land-bird
strongholds at Drumlea (H 5486) and Boorin (H 5085) Woods, Barons-
court (H 3682), Lislap Forest (H 4882), Drum Manor (H 7677) and
Caledon (H 7443)

Armagh (vice-county 37)

Armagh Field Naturalists' Society

Water-bird strongholds at Caledon Decoy (H 7442), Lough Castledillon
(H 9048) and on Annagh and Brackagh Mosses (J 0152–0250). Land-bird
stronghold at Drumbanagher (J 0536). Official *Bird Reserves* at Drum-
man Lakes (H 8947) and Fathom Wood (J 1020); also at Acton Lake
(Lough Shark J 0641) shared with Co. Down

PETERS, J.V. (1957). "Birds observed at Annagh and Brackagh Mosses,
Co. Armagh", *Irish Naturalists' Journal* 12: 168–71
NESBITT, L. (1964). "Wildfowl count on Castledillon Lake, Co. Armagh,
1960–63", *I.N.J.* 14: 274–76

Down (vice-county 38)

Sea-bird strongholds at Carlingford Loch (J 2509 and 2411), Killard Point
(J 6143), Strangford Lough (around J 5560), Burial Island (J 6663),
Ballywalter Pier (J 6369), Bangor Harbour (J 5082) and the Copeland
Islands (J 5985) where *Bird Observatory*. Strangford Lough, with Quoile
(J 4946) is also a water-bird stronghold, and has 17 official *Bird Reserves*;
other water-bird strongholds are on Downpatrick Marshes (around
J 4743) and around Dundrum Inner Bay (J 4137). Tollymore Forest Park
(J 3532) is a land-bird stronghold (with a nature trail and trailside
museum), as are the National Trust Reserves of Castleward (J 5749),

Rowallane (J 4057), Mount Stewart (J 5569) and Scrabo (J 4772); all these could rate as *Bird Reserves*. Besides these are official *Bird Reserves* at Craigavard (J 4381), Stormont Castle (J 4074), Hillsborough (J 2458) Magheratimpany (J 3848), Ballyward Lake (J 2637) and Lough Shark (see Armagh). At St John's Point (J 5233) a *Migration Watch Point*

Antrim (vice-county 39)

Belfast Natural History and Philosophical Society
Belfast Naturalists' Field Club

Sea-bird strongholds from White Head (J 4690) along coast to White Rocks (C 8940), including the Gobbins (J 4897–4898), the Maidens (D 4511), Rathlin Island (D 1547–0851) where is also a *Bird Observatory*, Larry Bane and Sheep Island (D 0445–0644), White Park Bay (D 0044–0244), where also a Nature Reserve of National Trust, partly a *Bird Reserve*; and Giant's Causeway (around C 9444). Water-bird strongholds at Belfast Lough (around J 3678); Larne Lough (around D 4200) where small *Wildfowl Refuge* on Islandmagee and official *Bird Reserve* on Swan Island (J 4299); and along east and north shore of Lough Neagh from Hog Park Point (J 0768), through Lough Beg and down River Bann to Portglenone (C 9703) – an area of general biological interest. Official *Bird Reserves* also at Ballymena (D 1003), Jordanstown (J 3584) and in Belfast. *Zoo* with birds at Bellevue (J 3280)
Museum in Belfast

PORT, L.N. (1959). "A population and distribution sketch of birds on Rathlin I., July, 1958", *Irish Naturalists' Journal* 13: 92–99.

HILDITCH, W.G. (1963). "Duck conservation at the Loughins, Island-magee, Co. Antrim", *I.N.J.* 14: 167–71

Derry (vice-county 40)

Limavady Naturalists' Field Club
Londonderry Naturalists' Field Club

Sea-bird strongholds from Castlerock (C 7255) to Binevenagh (C 6850), some inland. Water-bird strongholds in Bann Estuary (mouth C 7836), on Magilligan Strand (around C 6936) and in Lough Foyle (River Foyle mouth C 4823)

DOVE, R.S. (1956). "Birds of Magilligan Strand", *Irish Naturalists' Journal* 12: 52–55

CHAPTER 12

The Shell List of British and Irish Birds

At their Annual General Meeting on 15 May 1878 our senior learned ornithological body, the British Ornithologists' Union, decided to make the first official List of British Birds. P. L. Sclater, N. T. Wharton and six other committee members got to work, and eventually published (in 1883) a document based on records to 1880.

Since then several revisions and refinements have been published. The last B. O. U. *Check-List of the Birds of Great Britain and Ireland* considered records to 31 July 1950, was compiled by the late W. E. Glegg and others, and was published in 1952. No new Official List has been issued since then, though the Records Sub-committee of the Union has published additions and amendments in its journal *The Ibis*, the latest in 1960. With the rise of field ornithology, and the increase in the spate of rarity records, British material for the season 1958 onwards has been published in the scientific journal *British Birds* after vetting and editing by this admirable journal's Rarities Committee, which keeps close liaison with the B. O. U.'s Records Committee and publishes no new "first record" for Britain and Ireland not also passed by the B. O. U. Ireland now "looks after its own" but with continued close liaison with the B. O. U. and *British Birds*, and now publishes an excellent annual *Irish Bird Report*.

The present list is compiled entirely on my own responsibility but with full regard to the succession of publications in *British Birds* on rarities, the last available to me at the time of press being the 1964 season report and some other material published in 1965. I have included no species new to Britain or Ireland, or records of rare species, that occurred since 1964. I believe the only species I have included (not in square brackets) that the Union or the Rarities Committee may still be disposed to reject is the mandarin duck, which has been truly feral in England for enough years surely to qualify for list status. It is as true a British bird now as the accepted Canada goose, in my opinion and that of many better qualified to judge. Though this species may be officially *sub judice* this present list is, after all, *un*official.

Besides *British Birds* I have (like everybody else) found valuable mines of accurate information in P. A. D. Hollom's *Popular Handbooks* (Witherby) of

British Birds and *Rarer British Birds*. Transatlantic land-bird records were valuably discussed by W. B. Alexander and R. S. R. Fitter in *British Birds* in 1955, and many of the "doubtfuls" (square brackets) in the present list derive from their paper. Fitter's *The Ark in our Midst* (Collins 1959) contains much scholarly information on introduced species which has also helped me to decide just which of the 70 or so candidates for the British List, offered here and there in the literature but not yet accepted, should be mentioned in square brackets here.

As a consequence of the paper by E. M. Nicholson and I. J. Ferguson-Lees in *British Birds* for 1962 all birds reputed to have been collected (and some reputed to have been seen) between 1892 and 1930 in the Hastings area (see p. 74) of east Sussex and west Kent have been excluded from consideration. This means that 6 species in the B. O. U. *Check-List* of 1952, of which no other or later approvable records exist, have been relegated to square brackets (doubtful) – grey-rumped sandpiper, slender-billed curlew, black lark, masked shrike, Rüppell's warbler and snow finch. The B. O. U. British Records Committee has also relegated the meadow bunting for other reasons. All these species remain as *possible* candidates for the British List, but must stay in square brackets until better evidence that a wild individual has reached Britain or Ireland has satisfied the Union.

In my opinion, which I would not proffer were it not shared by some greater scholars of the records, 30 other species have been worth appending to the list, and these I have entered also as square-bracket doubtfuls. About half are American birds whose records were rejected before the chances of migratory land birds being driven across the Atlantic in westerly gales, and living to tell the tale to a collector or bird-watcher, were fully realised. Doubtless some may again be considered by the B. O. U., as may as many of putative vagrants from our own Palearctic bird fauna (that of Europe, North Africa and northern Asia), notably the black woodpecker, which many believe has been black-balled from the club too often. Of course in listing these square-bracket species I am celebrating the care which must be taken before a record can be admitted. No equivocation can be allowed, under the rules. I am *not* celebrating any disagreement with the Union.

The systematic arrangement of orders, families and subfamilies follows my own and Roger Tory Peterson's *The World of Birds* (Macdonald 1964). Within these groups the arrangement usually follows Charles Vaurie's scholarly *The Birds of the Palearctic Fauna* (Witherby 1959, 1965) with such minor revisions as appear to me to have been justified by later authoritative works, among them recent volumes of Peters's *Check List of Birds of the World* (Harvard Museum of Comparative Zoology). I follow Vaurie in regarding Audubon's shearwater (B18) as a race of the little shearwater (B17). In 1956 the B.O.U. List Committee held that the black-winged pratincole (B191) was a colour-phase of the collared pratincole (B190), that the spotted sandpiper (B160) was a race of the common sandpiper (B159), and that the hooded crow (B281) was a race of the carrion crow. Vaurie's later volumes uphold the last but not the first two of these "lumpings", and I agree.

This is the first full list of British birds which includes fossil records, and I have summarised all those known to me, rejecting all about which the slightest doubt was expressed by those who identified them. The stages of the Pleistocene period and the Prehistoric Ages following it are shown in the diagram on pp. 22–23, and for shortness I use "Ice Age" for the Pleistocene Ice Ages. Thus Early Ice Age means Lower Pleistocene; Mid Ice Age, Middle Pleistocene; Late Ice Age, Upper Pleistocene. I have mentioned only the first and last fossil horizons from which bones of a species have been identified; for instance the cormorant, as "Fossil from Early Ice Age to Dark Ages ESI [England, Scotland, Ireland]" has been, to my knowledge, recorded from the mid Lower Pleistocene of Norfolk; the late Lower Pleistocene of Somerset; the mid Middle Pleistocene of Essex; the late Upper Pleistocene of Co. Clare; the Middle Stone Age of Yorkshire; the New Stone Age of Argyll, Caithness and Orkney; the Bronze Age of Co. Antrim; the Late Bronze Age of Shetland; the Iron Age of Somerset; the (Broch) Iron Age of Orkney; and the Dark Ages of Co. Meath (Celtic) and Shetland (Viking and Norse). It will be understood that the fossil citation in the list can be a condensation of records, just as the distributional citation is a sweeping condensation of the historical records.

The sign † represents an order, family or species known only as fossil: E represents England; W, Wales; S, Scotland; I, Ireland. The B numbers are those of the B.O.U. *Check-List* of 1952. The number of records cited for rare species is the number regarded as acceptable by B.O.U. and *British Birds* records and rarities committees, to the best of my researches, and excluding such scholars' pests as the "Hastings Rarities". The word "record", means a sighting or a collecting at one place and period. Thus a flock seen together means one record: an individual bird seen over a period of several days or weeks means one record; if the bird is obviously joined by a new one within that period this means a second record. For rare birds I cite the year of the first acceptable record, e.g. red-flanked bluetail "4 or 5 records, since 1903". For others I cite the earliest year for a record I have been able to find, e.g. black redstart "records from 1743"; these years often represent the date of writing or publication of some document or book, but represent the actual year of a certain sighting or collecting if it antedates the earliest literary date I know of. Of early poems containing bird records *Beowulf* and *The Seafarer* are held to date, as regards the birds they mention, from the late seventh century, the *Riddles*, some other poems in the *Exeter Book* and a Latin to Anglo-Saxon vocabulary in Corpus Christi College, Cambridge (Parker XCLIV) from the eighth century.

In the analysis of the British–Irish bird fauna that follows I have used only the primary status of each species, by which I mean the first item in the distributional summary, which I so place as the most *presently* important. The black redstart is *now*, for instance "resident and summer visitor E[ngland]; passage and winter visitor E[ngland] W[ales] and I[reland]; passage visitor S[cotland]." In the analysis it is treated as 'a resident.

The British–Irish avifauna; records to 1964

General status	No. species	Breeding species	
		Past or irregular	Regular
Vagrant, under 21 records	133	1	
Vagrant, over 20 records	79	13	
Vagrant, total	→212	→ 14	
	—	—	
Winter visitors	25	4	
Passage visitors	28	11	
Non-breeding summer visitors[1]	3	1	
Breeding summer visitors	54		54
Visitors, total	→ 322		
	—		
Residents	133		133
Former resident, now extinct as species[2]	1	1	
	—		—
Species of the historical fauna (neospecies)[3]	456[4]		187
Neospecies known only as fossil[5]	3	2 →	33
	—		—
Neospecies, total	459	total, have bred	220
			—
Purely fossil species (paleospecies)	20		
	—		
Avifauna, species total	479		
	—		

[1] Great and sooty shearwaters, breed southern hemisphere; and spoonbill, bred EW in past.

[2] Great auk.

[3] It is useful to regard species living after 1600 as neospecies; species extinct by then as paleospecies, Some workers even take Linnaeus's year 1758 as the threshold. It is true that by an historian's definition, historical times begin far earlier; but the historical times of birds, in the scientific sense, did not flourish until some time after the Renaissance. I have classed the Roman, Dark Ages and Medieval fossil record with that of the earlier Stone, Bronze and Iron Ages, as Prehistoric in this sense.

[4] With a simplest breakdown of 243 "regular" species (118 water birds, 125 wholly land birds), 1 extinct and 212 vagrant (of which 48 from North America).

[5] Wandering albatross, Dalmatian pelican, hazel grouse. The pelican and hazel grouse were doubtless indigenous breeders.

THE SHELL LIST OF BRITISH AND IRISH BIRDS

Order †Hesperornithiformes
  Family †Enaliornithidae
        †*Enaliornis barretti*
          Fossil in the Lower Cretaceous of Cambs.
        †*Enaliornis sedgwicki*
          Fossil in the Lower Cretaceous of Cambs.

Order Gaviiformes
  Family Gaviidae, divers or loons
        †*Colymboides anglicus*
          Fossil in the Upper Eocene of Hants.
    B4 Red-throated diver *Gavia stellata*
          Fossil from Late Ice Age to Dark Ages ESI. Resident SI; also
          winter visitor EWSI. Records from 1771
    B1 Black-throated diver *Gavia arctica*
          Resident S; also winter visitor EWSI. Records from 1743
    B2 Great northern diver *Gavia immer*
          Fossil from after Ice Age to Iron Age SI. Winter visitor EWSI.
          Records from 1634
    B3 White-billed diver *Gavia adamsii*
          About 19 records, since 1829

Order Podicipediformes
  Family Podicipedidae, grebes
    B9 Dabchick *Podiceps ruficollis*
          Fossil from Late Ice Age to Iron Age EI. Resident EWSI; also
          winter visitor. Records from *c.* 998
    B8 Black-necked grebe *Podiceps nigricollis*
          Summer visitor EW; irregular SI; also winter visitor and passage
          migrant EWSI. Records from 1666
    B7 Slavonian grebe *Podiceps auritus*
          Fossil in Dark Ages S. Resident S; also winter visitor and passage
          migrant EWSI. Records from 1776
    B6 Red-necked grebe *Podiceps griseigena*
          Winter visitor EW; rare SI. Records from 1787
    B5 Great crested grebe *Podiceps cristatus*
          Fossil from Late Ice Age to Dark Ages EI. Resident EWSI.
          Records from VIIIc.
        Pied-billed grebe *Podilymbus podiceps*
          1 record in 1963; from America

Eider

Woodpigeon

Pied wagtail

Starling

Lesser white-fronted goose

Bean goose

The big National Nature Reserve of Caerlaverock in Dumfries county is a great
refuge for wintering Iceland whoopers, pinkfeet and grey lags, and Spitsbergen
barnacle geese (in foreground). The wispy flight is a pack of arctic-breeding knot.
Donald Watson

Donald Watson — 1964

Pink-footed goose

Gadwall

Smew

Redshank

Bar-tailed godwit

Puffin

Order Procellariiformes
   Family Diomedeidae, albatrosses
      †*Diomedea anglica*
         Fossil from Upper Pliocene to Early Ice Age of Suffolk
         Wandering albatross *Diomedea exulans*
         Fossil in the Mid Ice Age of Essex; the only British record
      B10 Black-browed albatross *Diomedea melanophris*
         4 records, since 1897
         [Yellow-nosed albatross *Diomedea (chrysostoma) chlororhynchos*
         Doubtful]

   Family Procellariidae, petrels and shearwaters
      B26 Fulmar *Fulmarus glacialis*
         Fossil in the Viking Dark Ages of St Kilda. Resident E W S I
         coasts, after sensational spread; dispersive. Records from 1697
         [Cape pigeon *Daption capensis*
         Doubtful]
      B23 Kermadec petrel *Pterodroma neglecta*
         1 record in 1908
      B25 Diablotin *or* capped petrel *Pterodroma hasitata*
         1 record in 1850
      B24 Gould's *or* collared petrel *Pterodroma leucoptera*
         1 record in 1889
      B22 Bulwer's petrel *Bulweria bulwerii*
         3 records, since 1837
      B20 Cory's shearwater *Procellaria (Calonectris) diomedea*
         Autumn visitor, coasts E S I. Records from 1906
      B19 Great shearwater *Puffinus gravis*
         Summer non-breeding visitor, coasts E S I. Records from 1839
      B21 Sooty shearwater *Puffinus griseus*
         Summer non-breeding visitor, coasts E W S I. Records from 1828
      B16 Manx shearwater *Puffinus puffinus*
         Fossil (probably this species) in Iron Age E S. Resident E W S I
         coasts; dispersive. Records from 1660
   { B17 Little (including Audubon's) shearwater *Puffinus assimilis*
   { B18 9 records, since 1853

   Family Hydrobatidae, storm petrels
      B11 Wilson's storm petrel *Occanites oceanicus*
         About 11 records, since 1838
      B15 Frigate (*or* white-faced storm) petrel *Pelagodroma marina*
         2 records, since 1890

B14 British storm petrel *Hydrobates pelagicus*
    Fossil in Iron Age of Shetland. Resident coasts EWSI; dispersive. Records from 1676
B12 Leach's storm petrel *Oceanodroma leucorhoa*
    Fossil in Dark Ages of Shetland. Resident O. Hebrides, Shetland, has bred I; dispersive EWSI coasts. Records from 1818
B13 Madeiran storm petrel *Oceanodroma castro*
    2 records, since 1911

Order Pelecaniformes
  Family Phaëthontidae, tropic birds
        †*Prophaethon shrubsolei*
        Fossil in the Lower Eocene of Kent

  Family Pelecanidae, pelicans
        Dalmatian pelican *Pelecanus (roseus) crispus*
        Fossil from New Stone or Bronze Age to Iron Age, Yorks., Norfolk, Cambs. and Soms.

The only British pelican records positively identified apart from dubious records, doubtless "escapes"; though some scholars have understood pelicans from descriptions of Fen birds in the MS. *Book of Ely* written in the mid XIIc. Although the VI to XIc. Anglo-Saxons had, according to the glossarists, dufedoppa, pellican, stangella (?) and wanfota as words (at least in some contexts) for pelican, all the passages that I can find them in may derive from the Scriptures

  Family Sulidae, gannets and boobies
    B27 North Atlantic gannet *Sula bassana*
        Fossil from Mid or Late Ice Age to Dark Ages EWSI. Resident coasts EWSI. Records from *Beowulf*, late VIIc.

  Family †Elopterygidae
        †*Argillornis emuinus*
        Fossil in the Lower Eocene of Kent

  Family Phalacrocoracidae, cormorants
        †*Actiornis anglicus*
        Fossil in the Upper Eocene of Hants.
    B28 Cormorant *Phalacrocorax carbo*
        Fossil from Early Ice Age to Dark Ages ESI. Resident coasts EWSI. Records from 1382

B29 Shag *Phalacrocorax arisiotelis*
Fossil from New Stone Age to Dark Ages S. Resident coasts
EWSI. Records from VIIIc.

Family Fregatidae, frigate birds
Magnificent frigate bird *Fregata magnificens*
1 record in 1953, 1 probably this species 1960

Order †Odontopterygiformes
Family †Odontopterygidae
†*Odontopteryx toliapica*
Fossil in the Lower Eocene of Kent

Order Ciconiiformes
Family Ardeidae, herons
†*Proherodius oweni*
Fossil in the Lower Eocene of London
B38 Bittern *Botaurus stellaris*
Fossil from New Stone Age to Dark Ages ES. Resident E; has
bred I; also winter visitor EWSI. Records from VIIIc.
B39 American bittern *Botaurus lentiginosus*
Rare vagrant, since 1804; from America
B37 Little bittern *Ixobrychus minutus*
Annual passage vagrant E; rare WSI; may have bred E.
Records from 1666
[Green heron *Butorides virescens*
Doubtful; from America]
B36 Night heron *Nycticorax nycticorax*
Annual passage vagrant E; rare WSI; "escaped" breeders S.
Records from 1782
B34 Squacco heron *Ardeola ralloides*
Rare vagrant, since 1775
B35 Cattle egret *Ardeola (Bubulcus) ibis*
4 records, since 1805
B33 Great egret *Egretta alba*
About 10 records, since 1824
B32 Little egret *Egretta garzetta*
Fossil in New Stone or Bronze Age London. Annual summer
vagrant E; rarer WSI. Records from 1826
B30 Heron *Ardea cinerea*
Fossil from Early Ice Age to Dark Ages ESI. Resident EWSI.
Records from VIIIc.

B31 Purple heron *Ardea purpurea*
    Annual vagrant E; rare WSI. Records from 1787

Family Ciconiidae, storks
  B40 White stork *Ciconia ciconia*
      Fossil from Bronze Age to Roman ES. Bred S XVc. Rare
      vagrant EWSI. Records from *c.* 992
  B41 Black stork *Ciconia nigra*
      Rare vagrant, since 1814

Family Threskiornithidae, ibises and spoonbills
      †*Ibidopsis hordwelliensis*
      Fossil in the Upper Eocene of Hants.
  B43 Glossy ibis *Plegadis falcinellus*
      Irregular autumn passage visitor EI; rare WS. Records from
      1787
  B42 Spoonbill *Platalea leucorodia*
      Bred EW to XVIIIc. Non-breeding (mostly summer) visitor E;
      rare WSI. Records from mid XIIc.

Order Phoenicopteriformes
  Family † Agnopteridae
      †*Agnopterus hantoniensis*
      Fossil in the Upper Eocene of Hants. and the Lower Oligocene
      of the Isle of Wight

Family Phoenicopteridae, flamingos
      †*Elornis anglicus*
      Fossil in the Upper Eocene of Hants.
  B44 Greater flamingo *Phoenicopterus ruber*
      Rare vagrant, since 1881

Order Anseriformes
  Family Anatidae, wildfowl
    B84 Mute swan *Cygnus olor*
        Fossil from Late Ice Age to Roman EI. Resident EWSI.
        Records from VIIIc.
    B85 Whooper swan *Cygnus cygnus*
        Fossil from Mid Ice Age to Dark Ages ESI. Winter visitor
        EWSI; irregular breeder S. Records from *Beowulf*, late VIIc.
    B86 Bewick's swan *Cygnus (columbianus) bewickii*
        Fossil from New Stone Age to Dark Ages EI. Winter visitor
        EWSI. Records from 1824

B75 Grey lag goose *Anser anser*
> Fossil from Early Ice Age to Medieval ESI. Resident S, formerly EI; feral E; winter visitor EWSI. Records from VIIIc. (domestic *c.* 692)

B76 White-fronted goose *Anser albifrons*
> Fossil from Late Ice Age to Dark Ages I. Winter visitor EWSI. Records from 1186

B77 Lesser white-fronted goose *Anser erythropus*
> Vagrant, now annual, since 1886

B78 *Anser fabalis*
> Fossil from Mid Ice Age to Bronze Age ES

> Bean goose *Anser fabalis fabalis*
> Winter visitor ES; scarce WI. Records from 1678

> Pink-footed goose *Anser fabalis brachyrhynchus*
> Winter visitor EWSI. Records from 1638

B79 Snow goose (including blue colour-phase) *Anser caerulescens*
> Vagrant, since 1871; from America

B82 Canada goose *Branta canadensis*
> Resident EWSI; introduced from America. Records from 1676

B81 Barnacle goose *Branta leucopsis*
> Fossil in the Dark Ages of Ireland. Winter visitor ESI; rare W. Records from VIIIc.

B83 Red-breasted goose *Branta ruficollis*
> About 20 records, since 1776

B80 Brent goose *Branta bernicla*
> Fossil in Early Ice Age E. Winter visitor coasts EWSI. Records from 1508

> [Egyptian goose *Alopochen aegyptiacus*
> Feral E after aviculture, but not to extent yet warranting British–Irish List status]

B74 Ruddy shelduck *Tadorna ferruginea*
> Rare vagrant EWSI, since 1776

B73 Shelduck *Tadorna tadorna*
> Fossil from Late Ice Age to Dark Ages ESI. Resident EWSI. Records by 1450

> Mandarin duck *Aix galericulata*
> Now feral E and recorded S; introduced from Asia. Records (aviculture) from 1745. Not on official lists.

B45 Mallard *Anas platyrhynchos*
> Fossil from Early Ice Age to Dark Ages EI. Resident EWSI. Records from VIIIc.

Black duck *Anas rubripes*
1 record in 1954; from America

B46 Teal *Anas crecca*
Fossil from Late Ice Age to Dark Ages E S I. Resident E W S I.
Records from 1275
Baikal teal *Anas formosa*
2 records, since 1954

B49 Gadwall *Anas strepera*
Resident E S I; visitor W. Records from 1666

B50 Wigeon *Anas penelope*
Fossil from Late Ice Age to Dark Ages E S I. Resident S;
irregular breeder E W I; passage and winter visitor E W S I.
Records from 1508

B51 American wigeon *Anas americana*
About 18 records, since 1838; from America

B52 Pintail *Anas acuta*
Fossil from Late Ice Age to Dark Ages I. Resident E S; irregular
breeder I; passage and winter visitor E W S I. Records from
1672

B47 Garganey *Anas querquedula*
Fossil from Bronze Age to Dark Ages E I. Summer visitor E; has
bred W S I. Records from 1662

B48 Blue-winged teal *Anas discors*
16 or more records, since 1858; from America

B53 Shoveler *Anas clypeata*
Fossil from Early Ice Age to Dark Ages E S. Resident E W S I;
also passage and winter visitor. Records from *c.* 1460

B54 Red-crested pochard *Netta rufina*
Annual vagrant E; rare W S I. Records from 1818

B57 Pochard *Aythya ferina*
Fossil from Late Ice Age to Iron Age E I. Resident E W S;
irregular breeder I. Records from 1544 (? this or B56 *c.*
998)

B58 Ferruginous white-eye *Aythya nyroca*
Annual vagrant E; rare W S I. Records from 1806
Ring-necked duck *Aythya collaris*
5 or 6 records, since 1955; from America

B56 Tufted duck *Aythya fuligula*
Fossil from Late Ice Age to Dark Ages E S I. Resident E W S I.
Records from 1662
[Lesser scaup *Aythya affinis*
Doubtful; from America]

B55 Scaup *or* greater scaup *Aythya marila*
Fossil from Late Ice Age to Dark Ages E I. Passage and winter visitor E W S I; irregular breeder S. Records from 1672

B67 Eider *Somateria mollissima*
Fossil from Late Ice Age to Dark Ages S I. Resident E S I; visitor W. Records from mid XIIc., though believed known on Farnes VIIc.

B68 King eider *Somateria spectabilis*
Vagrant E S I. Records from 1832

B66 Steller's eider *Polysticta stelleri*
5 records, since 1830

B65 Harlequin duck *Histrionicus histrionicus*
6 records, since 1862

B61 Long-tailed duck *Clangula hyemalis*
Fossil in Late Ice Age S. Winter visitor E W S I; has bred S. Records from 1694

B62 Velvet scoter *Melanitta fusca*
Fossil in Dark Ages S. Passage and winter visitor E W S; rare I; also summer visitor S, where may have bred. Records from 1676

B63 Surf scoter *Melanitta perspicillata*
Fossil in Late Ice Age E S. Annual vagrant S, rare E I, since 1846

B64 Common scoter *Melanitta nigra·*
Fossil from Late Ice Age to New Stone Age E S I. Resident S I; winter visitor E W S I. Records from 1537

B60 Goldeneye *Bucephala clangula*
Fossil from Middle Stone Age to Dark Ages E I. Winter and passage visitor E W S I; has bred E. Records from 1555
[Barrow's goldeneye *Bucephala islandica*
Doubtful]

B59 Bufflehead *Bucephala albeola*
6 records, since 1830; from America

B72 Hooded merganser *Mergus cucullatus*
5 records, since 1831; from America

B71 Smew *Mergus albellus*
Fossil from Late Ice Age to Bronze Age E I. Winter visitor E; irregular W S I. Records from 1666

B69 Red-breasted merganser *Mergus serrator*
Fossil from Late Ice Age to Dark Ages E S I. Resident E W S I; winter visitor E W. Records from *c.* 998

B70 Goosander *Mergus merganser*
Resident E S; winter visitor E W; irregular I. Records from 1622

Order Falconiformes
  Family Cathartidae, New World vultures
      † *Lithornis vulturinus*
        Fossil in the Lower Eocene of Kent

  Family Accipitridae, hawks and eagles
      † *Palaeocircus cuvieri*
        Fossil in the Upper Eocene of Hants.
      [Black-winged kite *Elanus caeruleus*
        Doubtful]
      [Swallow-tailed kite *Elanoïdes forficatus*
        Doubtful; from America]
  B98 Honey buzzard *Pernis apivorus*
        Summer visitor E ; has bred S ; irregular passage visitor E W S I.
        Records from 1675
  B95 Red kite *Milvus milvus*
        Fossil from Middle Stone Age to Iron Age E. Resident W,
        formerly E S where now rare vagrant. Records from VIIIc.
  B96 Black kite *Milvus migrans*
        5 records, since 1866 – though it is conceivable that the
        scavenging kites of XVc. London were black, not red
      [Bald eagle *Haliaeetus leucocephalus*
        Doubtful; from America]
  B97 White-tailed eagle *Haliaeetus albicilla*
        Fossil from Early Ice Age to Dark Ages ESI. Vagrant E,
        rare WSI; formerly bred ESI. Records from *c.*'662
  B94 Goshawk *Accipiter gentilis*
        Fossil in Iron Age E. Annual vagrant E, rare WSI; formerly
        bred E, and may still. Records from *c.* 998
  B93 Sparrow hawk *Accipiter nisus*
        Fossil in Prehistoric I. Resident EWSI. Records from VIIIc.
      [Red-tailed hawk *Buteo jamaicensis*
        Doubtful; from America]
  B92 Rough-legged buzzard *Buteo lagopus*
        Winter visitor ES, rare WI. Records from 1792
  B91 Buzzard *Buteo buteo*
        Fossil from Early Ice Age to Dark Ages ESI. Resident EWS,
        formerly I where now annual vagrant. Records from XIc.
      [Red-shouldered hawk *Buteo lineatus*
        Doubtful; from America]
  B90 Great spotted eagle *Aquila clanga*
        About 14 records, since 1845

B89   Golden eagle *Aquila chryaëtos*
Fossil in New Stone Age W. Resident S, formerly E WI; has bred again lately EI; rare vagrant W. Records from *c.* 998

B87   Egyptian vulture *Neophron percnopterus*
2 records, since 1825

B88   Griffon vulture *Gyps fulvus*
3 records, since 1843

It is conceivable that a vulture was a member of the Dark Ages English fauna and attended the aftermath of Anglo-Saxon battles. But the five Anglo-Saxon words which have been referred to "vulture" in Anglo-Saxon glossaries from VIIIc. can all be shown to have been employed in works based on the Mediterranean classics or the Scriptures – including *ultur* in King Alfred's translation of Boëthius (*c.* 897)

B100   Hen harrier *Circus cyaneus*
Resident SI; winter and passage visitor EW, where has bred occasionally. Records from 1544

B101   Pallid harrier *Circus macrourus*
4 records, since 1931

B102   Montagu's harrier *Circus pygargus*
Summer visitor E and irregularly WI; rare vagrant S. Records from 1802

B99   Marsh harrier *Circus aeruginosus*
Summer visitor E, irregularly W, formerly also SI where now rare vagrant. Records from 1544

Family Pandionidae, osprey

B103   Osprey *Pandion haliaetus*
Fossil in Late Ice Age E. Summer visitor S after late recolonisation, formerly also bred E; passage visitor ES; vagrant WI. Records from X or XIc.

Family Falconidae, falcons

B106   Gyrfalcon *Falco rusticolus*
Annual vagrant ES, rare WI. Records from VIII to XIc. (possibly some wild) otherwise from 1803

B105   Peregrine *Falco peregrinus*
Fossil from Late Ice Age to Dark Ages ESI. Resident EWSI; also passage visitor. Records from VIIIc.

B104   Hobby *Falco subbuteo*
Summer visitor E, and has bred WS where (with I) generally rare vagrant. Records from 1186

B107 Merlin *Falco columbarius*
    Resident EWSI; also passage visitor. Records from 1186
B108 Red-footed kestrel *Falco vespertinus*
    Annual vagrant, since 1830
B109 Lesser kestrel *Falco naumanni*
    13 records, since 1867
B110 Kestrel *Falco tinnunculus*
    Fossil from Late Ice Age to Iron Age EI. Resident EWSI;
    also passage visitor. Records from VIIIc.

Order Galliformes
  Family Tetraonidae, grouse
    B111 Red grouse *Lagopus lagopus scoticus*
        Fossil (of this race or ancestral willow grouse *L. lagopus*) from
        Mid Ice Age to Roman ESI. Resident EWSI. Records from
        VIIIc.

    B112 Ptarmigan *Lagopus mutus*
        Fossil from Mid to Late Ice Age ES. Resident S. Records from
        1599

      Hazel grouse *Tetrastes bonasia*
        Fossil in the Late Ice Age of Devon, the only British record
    B113 Black grouse *Tetrao (Lyrurus) tetrix*
        Fossil from Mid Ice Age to Dark Ages EWS. Resident EWS.
        Records from 1427
    B114 Capercaillie *Tetrao urogallus*
        Fossil in Late Ice Age E. Resident S after re-introduction;
        formerly bred ESI and probably W. Records from 1186

  Family Phasianidae, pheasants, fowl, partridges and quail
    B115 Red-legged partridge *Alectoris rufa*
        Resident EWS after XVII–XVIIIc. introductions. Records
        from 1673
    B116 Partridge *Perdix perdix*
        Fossil from Late Ice Age to Medieval ESI. Resident EWSI.
        Records from 1059
    B117 Quail *Coturnix coturnix*
        Fossil from Late Ice Age to Prehistoric EI. Summer visitor
        EWSI. Records from *c.* 700
    B118 Pheasant *Phasianus colchicus*
        Fossil in Roman E. Probably not feral until around Norman
        invasion. Resident EWSI. Records from 1059 (earlier Anglo-
        Saxon references seem to be from Mediterranean literary
        sources)

[Golden pheasant *Chrysolophus pictus*

Amherst pheasant *Chrysolophus amherstiae*

> Feral E after aviculture, particularly the latter, but not to an
> extent yet warranting British–Irish List status]

Order Gruiformes

Family Gruidae, cranes

> †*Palaeogrus hordwelliensis*
>
>> Fossil in the Upper Eocene of Hants.
>
> †*Geranopsis hastingsiae*
>
>> Fossil in the Upper Eocene of Hants.

B119 Crane *Grus grus*

> Fossil from Late Ice Age to Dark Ages EI. Lately annual
> vagrant E, vagrant S, rare WI; previously rarer; but to
> XVIIIc. winter visitor, and to XVIc. bred at least E. Records
> from *c.* 570

Family Rallidae, rails

B120 Water rail *Rallus aquaticus*

> Fossil from Late Ice Age to New Stone Age ESI. Resident
> EWSI; also passage and winter visitor. Records from 1450

B121 Spotted crake *Porzana porzana*

> Rare summer visitor E, has bred WSI; irregular passage
> and winter visitor EWSI. Records from 1766

B122 Sora *Porzana carolina*

> 5 records, since 1864; from America

B124 Little crake *Porzana parva*

> Rare vagrant EWSI. Records from 1813

B123 Baillon's crake *Porzana pusilla*

> Rare vagrant EWSI, has bred E. Records from 1819

B125 Corncrake *Crex crex*

> Fossil from Late Ice Age to Dark Ages EI. Summer visitor
> EWSI, decreasing EW. Records from XIc.

B126 Moorhen *Gallinula chloropus*

> Fossil from Late Ice Age to Dark Ages EI. Resident EWSI.
> Records from *c.* 998

American purple gallinule *Porphyrula martinica*

> 1 record in 1958; from America

B127 Coot *Fulica atra*

> Fossil from Late Ice Age to Dark Ages EWI. Resident EWSI.
> Records from *c.* 998

Family Otididae, bustards
   B128 Great bustard *Otis tarda*
           Rare vagrant E W S I; formerly bred E S. Records since *c.* 1460
   B129 Little bustard *Otis tetrax*
           Rare vagrant E W S I. Records from 1751
   B130 Houbara *Chlamydotis undulata*
           5 records, since 1847

Order †Diatrymiformes
   Family †Gastornithidae
           †*Gastornis klaasseni*
               Fossil in the Upper Paleocene of London
           †*Dasornis londinensis*
               Fossil in the Lower Eocene of Kent
           †*Macrornis tanaupus*
               Fossil in the Upper Eocene of Hants.

Order Charadriiformes
   Family Haematopodidae, oystercatchers
   B131 Oystercatcher *Haematopus ostralegus*
           Fossil from New Stone Age to Dark Ages E S. Resident E W S I;
           and winter visitor. Records from 1527

Family Charadriidae, plovers and turnstones
   B134 Ringed plover *Charadrius hiaticula*
           Fossil from Early Ice Age to New Stone Age E S. Resident
           E W S I; also winter and passage visitor. Records from
           1525
   B135 Little ringed plover *Charadrius dubius*
           Summer visitor (recent colonist) E; vagrant W S. Records
           from 1850
   B137 Killdeer *Charadrius vociferus*
           13 records, since 1859; from America
   B136 Kentish plover *Charadrius alexandrinus*
           Rare passage visitor E, formerly bred; vagrant W S I. Records
           from 1802
   B138 Caspian plover *Charadrius asiaticus*
           1 record in 1890
   B142 Dotterel *Eudromias morinellus*
           Summer visitor S, possibly still E; scarce passage visitor E W S,
           rare I. Records by 1450 ·

B140 Golden plover *Pluvialis apricaria*
> Fossil from Early Ice Age to Roman EI. Resident EWSI; also passage and winter visitor. Records from *c.* 998

B141 Lesser golden plover *Pluvialis dominica*
> 8 records, since 1870

B139 Grey plover *Pluvialis squatarola*
> Fossil from Late Ice Age to Roman ESI. Winter and passage visitor EWSI. Records from 1523

B132 Sociable lapwing *Vanellus gregarius*
> 8 records, since *c.* 1860

B133 Lapwing *Vanellus vanellus*
> Fossil from Late Ice Age to Bronze Age ESI. Resident EWSI; also summer, passage and winter visitor. Records from VIIIc.

B143 Turnstone *Arenaria interpres*
> Winter and passage visitor EWSI; some stay summer. Records from 1676

Family Scolopacidae, sandpipers, snipe, etc.

B180 Semipalmated sandpiper *Calidris pusillus*
> 3 records, since 1953; from America
> Western sandpiper *Calidris mauri*
> 2 records, since 1956; from America

B171 Little stint *Calidris minuta*
> Passage visitor EWSI. Records from 1776

B173 Temminck's stint *Calidris temminckii*
> Scarce passage visitor ES, has bred; vagrant WI. Records from 1832

B172 Least sandpiper *Calidris minutilla*
> 7 records, since 1853; from America

B174 Baird's sandpiper *Calidris bairdii*
> 9 records, since 1903; from America

B175 White-rumped sandpiper *Calidris fuscicollis*
> Rare vagrant, since 1836; from America

B176 Pectoral sandpiper *Calidris melanotos*
> Annual vagrant EWSI; from America. Records from 1830

B177 Sharp-tailed sandpiper *Calidris acuminata*
> 7 records, since 1848

B170 Purple sandpiper *Calidris maritima*
> Passage and winter visitor EWSI. Records from 1798

B178 Dunlin *Calidris alpina*
> Resident EWSI; also passage and winter visitor. Records from 153?

B179 Curlew sandpiper *Calidris ferruginea*
Passage visitor EWSI. Records from 1786

B169 Knot *Calidris canutus*
Fossil in Late Ice Age E. Passage and winter visitor EWSI. Records from 1452

B181 Sanderling *Calidris alba*
Passage and winter visitor EWSI. Records from XVIc.

B184 Ruff *Philomachus pugnax*
Passage and winter visitor EWSI. Formerly bred E and may have lately. Records from 1465

B183 Broad-billed sandpiper *Limicola falcinellus*
Rare vagrant, since 1836

B149 Upland sandpiper (or "plover") *Bartramia longicauda*
15 records, since 1851; from America

B182 Buff-breasted sandpiper *Tryngites subruficollis*
Annual vagrant, ESI since 1826; from America
Long-billed dowitcher *Limnodromus scolopaceus*

B144 Short-billed dowitcher *Limnodromus griseus*
Annual vagrants; EWSI from America. Some early dowitcher records, since 1801, are not specifically distinguishable; of the 64 records of the genus 25 are determinable – 14 of them long-billed

B162 Spotted redshank *Tringa erythropus*
Passage visitor ES, rarer WI. Records from 1771

B163 Greater yellowlegs *Tringa melanoleuca*
About 13 records, since 1906; from America

B161 Redshank *Tringa totanus*
Fossil in Late Ice Age I. Resident EWSI; also passage and winter visitor. Records from 1500

B164 Lesser yellowlegs *Tringa flavipes*
Annual vagrant EWSI, since 1854; from America

B166 Marsh sandpiper *Tringa stagnatilis*
About 15 records, since 1887

B165 Greenshank *Tringa nebularia*
Summer visitor S; passage visitor EWSI; some winter EWI. Records from 1678

B156 Green sandpiper *Tringa ochropus*
Fossil in Late Ice Age E. Passage visitor EWSI; has bred ES; some winter I. Records from 1676

B158 Solitary sandpiper *Tringa solitaria*
8 records, since before 1870

B157 Wood sandpiper *Tringa glareola*
Passage visitor ES, where has bred; irregular WI. Records from 1784

[B167 Grey-rumped sandpiper *Tringa brevipes*
Doubtful, "Hastings"]

B159 Common sandpiper *Tringa hypoleucos*
Summer visitor EWSI; also passage visitor; some winter EWI. Records from 1544

B160 Spotted sandpiper *Tringa (hypoleucos) macularia*
At least 7 records, since 1866; from America

B168 Terek sandpiper *Tringa (Xenus) terek*
5 records, since 1951. *Xenus cinereus* becomes its Linnean name if placed in genus *Xenus*

Stilt sandpiper *Micropalama himantopus*
4 records, since 1954; from America

B154 Black-tailed godwit *Limosa limosa*
Summer visitor E; has bred S; passage and winter visitor EWSI. Records from 1384

B155 Bar-tailed godwit *Limosa lapponica*
Fossil from Late Ice to Bronze Age E. Passage and winter visitor EWSI. Records from 1520

B150 Curlew *Numenius arquata*
Fossil from Late Ice Age to Dark Ages ES. Resident EWSI; also summer, passage and winter visitor. Records from XIc.

[B153 Slender-billed curlew *Numenius tenuirostris*
Doubtful, "Hastings"]

B151 Whimbrel *Numenius phaeopus*
Fossil from Early to Late Ice Age E. Summer visitor S; passage visitor EWSI. Records from *The Seafarer*, late VIIc.

B152 Eskimo curlew *Numenius borealis*
7 records, since 1852; from America

B148 Woodcock *Scolopax rusticola*
Fossil from Late Ice Age to Roman EI. Resident EWSI; also summer and winter visitor. Records from VIIIc.

B145 Snipe *Gallinago gallinago*
Fossil in Late Ice Age EI. Resident EWSI; also winter visitor. Records from VIIIc.

B146 Great snipe *Gallinago media*
Scarce visitor E; vagrant WSI. Records from 1776

B147 Jack snipe *Lymnocryptes minimus*
Fossil in Late Ice Age E. Winter and passage visitor EWSI. Records from XVIc.

Family Recurvirostridae, stilts and avocets

B186 Black-winged stilt *Himantopus himantopus*
> Rare vagrant E, where has bred; also records WSI. Records from 1684

B185 Avocet *Recurvirostra avosetta*
> Summer visitor E while some winter; rare vagrant WSI; has bred I. Records from *c.* 1600

Family Phalaropodidae, phalaropes

B187 Grey phalarope *Phalaropus fulicarius*
> Passage visitor EWSI. Records from 1757

B188 Red-necked phalarope *Phalaropus lobatus*
> Summer visitor SI; also passage visitor EWSI. Records from 1676

> Wilson's phalarope *Phalaropus tricolor*
> 17 records, since 1954, annual lately; from America

Family Burhinidae, thick-knees

B189 Stone curlew *Burhinus oedicnemus*
> Summer visitor E, where may winter; rare vagrant WSI. Records from 1666

Family Glareolidae, coursers and pratincoles

B192 Cream-coloured courser *Cursorius cursor*
> Rare vagrant, since 1785

B190 Collared pratincole *Glareola pratincola*
> Rare vagrant, since 1809

B191 Black-winged pratincole *Glareola (pratincola) nordmanni*
> 6 records, since 1909

Family Stercorariidae, skuas

B194 Great skua *Stercorarius skua*
> Resident S; dispersive passage visitor ESWI. Records from 1666

B195 Pomarine skua *Stercorarius pomarinus*
> Passage visitor ES, scarce WI. Records from 1819

B193 Arctic skua *Stercorarius parasiticus*
> Summer visitor S; passage visitor EWSI. Records from 1713

B196 Long-tailed skua *Stercorarius longicaudus*
> Scarce passage visitor E, rare WSI. Records from 1832

Family Laridae, gulls and terns

> †*Halcyornis toliapicus*
> Fossil in the Lower Eocene of Kent

B204 Great black-headed gull *Larus ichthyaëtus*
    5 records, since 1859

B205 Mediterranean (black-headed) gull *Larus melanocephalus*
    Annual vagrant E, rare WSI, since 1866

B206 Bonaparte's gull *Larus philadelphia*
    About 15 records, since 1848; from America

B207 Little gull *Larus minutus*
    Passage and winter visitor ES, scarce WI. Records from 1813

B208 Black-headed gull *Larus ridibundus*
    Fossil in Dark Ages S. Resident and dispersive EWSI. Records from 1536

    Slender-billed gull *Larus geneï*
    2 records, since 1960

B199 Lesser black-backed gull *Larus fuscus*
    Fossil in Late Ice Age I. Summer visitor EWSI, some resident. Records from 1802

B200 Herring gull *Larus argentatus*
    Fossil from New Stone Age to Dark Ages S. Resident EWSI, dispersive; also winter visitor E. Records from VIIIc. (or close species)

B203 Iceland gull *Larus glaucoides*
    Scarce winter visitor EWSI. Records from 1823

B202 Glaucous gull *Larus hyperboreus*
    Winter visitor EWSI. Records from 1822

B198 Great black-backed gull *Larus marinus*
    Fossil from Iron Age to Dark Ages ES. Resident coasts EWSI, dispersive; also winter and summer visitor. Records from 1678

B201 Common gull *Larus canus*
    Fossil from Early Ice Age to Roman EI. Resident ESI, dispersive; also winter and passage visitor EWSI. Records by 1450

B209 Sabine's gull *Larus sabini*
    Scarce passage and winter visitor EWSI. Records from 1822

B211 Kittiwake *Rissa tridactyla*
    Fossil in Dark Ages S. Resident coasts EWSI, dispersive; and winter visitor. Records from *The Seafarer*, late VIIc.

B210 Ross's gull *Rhodostethia rosea*
    4 records, since 1847

B197 Ivory gull *Pagophila eburnea*
    Rare vagrant, since 1822

B212 Black tern *Chlidonias niger*
    Passage visitor EWSI; formerly bred E. Records since 1544

B213 White-winged black tern *Chlidonias leucopterus*
    Annual vagrant E, rare WSI. Records from 1841

B214 Whiskered tern *Chlidonias hybrida*
    Rare vagrant, since 1836

B215 Gull-billed tern *Gelochelidon nilotica*
    Annual vagrant E, where has bred; rare WSI. Records from before 1813

B216 Caspian tern *Hydroprogne tschegrava*
    Rare vagrant, since 1825

B223 Sandwich tern *Sterna sandvicensis*
    Summer visitor EWSI; also passage visitor. Records from 1671
    Royal tern *Sterna maxima*
    1 record in 1954

B217 Common tern *Sterna hirundo*
    Fossil from Late Ice Age to New Stone Age ES. Summer visitor EWSI. Records from *The Seafarer*, late VIIc. (or next species)

B218 Arctic tern *Sterna paradisaea*
    Summer visitor EWSI; also passage visitor. Records from 1819

B219 Roseate tern *Sterna dougallii*
    Summer visitor EWSI. Records from 1813

B220 Sooty tern *Sterna fuscata*
    About 17 records, since 1852

B221 Bridled tern *Sterna anaethetus*
    4 records, since 1931

B222 Little tern *Sterna albifrons*
    Summer visitor EWSI. Records from 1671
    [Noddy *Anoüs stolidus*
    Doubtful]

Family Alcidae, auks

B226 Little auk *Plotus alle*
    Fossil from Late Ice Age to New Stone Age ESI. Irregular winter visitor EWSI. Records from 1676

B234 Razorbill *Alca torda*
    Fossil from New Stone Age to Bronze Age ESI. Resident coasts EWSI, dispersive. Records from 1661

B225 Great auk *Pinguinus impennis*
    Fossil from New Stone Age to Dark Ages ESI. Formerly bred S, probably Isle of Man, recorded I; was dispersive. Records from *c*. 1652; last S record *c*. 1840; species became extinct (last Iceland) 1844

B227 Common guillemot *Uria aalge*
    Fossil from Late Ice Age to·Dark Ages WSI. Resident coasts
    EWSI, dispersive. Records from mid XIIc.
B228 Arctic (Brünnich's) guillemot *Uria lomvia*
    4 records, since 1908
B229 Black guillemot *or* tystie *Cepphus grylle*
    Resident coasts ESI, vagrant W. Records from 1661
B230 Puffin *Fratercula arctica*
    Fossil from Late Ice Age to Dark Ages ES. Resident coasts
    EWSI, dispersive. Records from 1337

Order Columbiformes
  Family Pteroclidae, sand grouse
    B231 Pallas's sand grouse *Syrrhaptes paradoxus*
        Irregular invader (has bred) ES 1859–1909, has reached WI

  Family Columbidae, pigeons
    B234 Woodpigeon *Columba palumbus*
        Fossil from Late Ice Age to Bronze Age EI. Resident EWSI.
        Records from *c.* 685
    B232 Stock dove *Columba oenas*
        Fossil in Late Ice Age E. Resident EWSI. Records by 1450
    B233 Rock dove *Columba livia*
        Fossil in Late Ice Age EI. Resident coasts EWSI, though EW
        populations mixed with domestic stock. Records from *c.* 998
      [Passenger pigeon *Ectopistes migratorius*
        Doubtful; from America; species became extinct (last
        Cincinatti Zoo) 1914]
      Collared dove *Streptopelia decaocto*
        Resident EWSI, after invasion beginning 1952
    B235 Turtle dove *Streptopelia turtur*
        Summer visitor EWS, has bred I; also passage visitor EWSI.
        Records from *c.* 975
    B236 Rufous turtle dove *Streptopelia orientalis*
        3 records, since 1889

Order Cuculiformes
  Family Cuculidae, cuckoos
    B237 Cuckoo *Cuculus canorus*
        Summer visitor EWSI. Records from *c.* 699
    B238 Great spotted cuckoo *Clamator glandarius*
        10 records, since 1842

B239 Yellow-billed cuckoo *Coccyzus americanus*
　　　Rare vagrant, since 1825; from America
B240 Black-billed cuckoo *Coccyzus erythopthalmus*
　　　4 records, since 1871; from America

Order Strigiformes
　Family Tytonidae, barn owls
　　B241 Barn owl *Tyto alba*
　　　　　Fossil from Late Ice Age to Dark Ages EI. Resident EWSI.
　　　　　Records from *c.* 1225

　Family Strigidae, typical owls
　　B244 Snowy owl *Nyctea scandiaca*
　　　　　Fossil in Late Ice Age E. Vagrant EWSI, since 1808
　　B243 Eagle owl *Bubo bubo*
　　　　　Fossil in Early Ice Age E. Records (possibly native) VIII to XIc.,
　　　　　otherwise rare vagrant, since *c.* 1768
　　B248 Long-eared owl *Asio otus*
　　　　　Fossil in Late Ice Age E. Resident EWSI; also passage visitor.
　　　　　Records from 1544
　　B249 Short-eared owl *Asio flammeus*
　　　　　Fossil in Late Ice Age E. Resident EWS, has bred I; also
　　　　　winter and passage visitor EWSI. Records from 1678
　　B242 Scops owl *Otus scops*
　　　　　Rare vagrant, since 1805
　　B250 Tengmalm's owl *Aegolius funereus*
　　　　　Rare vagrant, since 1812
　　B246 Little owl *Athene noctua*
　　　　　Fossil in Late Ice Age E. Resident EWS, vagrant I, after
　　　　　successful introduction 1889. Some records from 1808
　　B245 Hawk owl *Surnia ulula*
　　　　　9 records, since 1830
　　B247 Tawny owl *Strix aluco*
　　　　　Resident EWS. Records from VIIIc.

Order Caprimulgiformes
　Family Caprimulgidae, nightjars
　　B251 Common nighthawk *Chordeiles minor*
　　　　　2 records, since 1927; from America
　　B252 Nightjar *Caprimulgus europaeus*
　　　　　Summer visitor EWSI. Records from *c.* 998

B253 Red-necked nightjar *Caprimulgus ruficollis*
    1 record in 1856
B254 Egyptian nightjar *Caprimulgus aegyptius*
    1 record in 1883

Order Apodiformes
  Family Apodidae, swifts
    B257 White-throated needle-tailed swift *Hirundapus caudacutus*
      4 records, since 1846
    B255 Swift *Apus apus*
      Fossil in Early Ice Age E. Summer visitor EWSI. Records
      from 1544
    B256 Alpine swift *Apus melba*
      Annual vagrant E; rare WSI, since 1829

Order Coraciiformes
  Family Alcedinidae, kingfishers
    [Belted kingfisher *Ceryle alcyon*
      Doubtful; from America]
    B258 Kingfisher *Alcedo atthis*
      Resident EWSI. Records from VIIIc.

  Family Meropidae, bee eaters
    B259 Bee eater *Mcrops apiaster*
      Vagrant EWSI, has bred ES. Records from 1794
      Blue-cheeked bee eater *Merops superciliosus*
      1 record in 1951

  Family Coraciidae, rollers
    B260 Roller *Coracias garrulus*
      Vagrant EWSI. Records from 1644

  Family Upupidae, hoopoe
    B261 Hoopoe *Upupa epops*
      Passage visitor EWSI, has bred EW. Records from *c.* 1600

Order Piciformes
  Family Picidae, woodpeckers
    B265 Wryneck *Jynx torquilla*
      Summer visitor E, has bred WS; vagrant SI. Records from
      1544
    B262 Green woodpecker *Picus viridis*
      Resident EWS; 3 records I. Records from VIIIc.

[Black woodpecker *Dryocopus martius*
Doubtful. May be admitted to British List on re-assessment of some records]

B263 Great spotted woodpecker *Dendrocopos major*
Fossil in Late Ice Age E I. Resident E WS; irregular I. Records from *c.* 998

B264 Lesser spotted woodpecker *Dendrocopos minor*
Resident E W; vagrant S. Records from 1666
[Three-toed woodpecker *Picoïdes tridactylus*
Doubtful]

Order Passeriformes

Family Alaudidae, larks

B269 Short-toed lark *Calandrella cinerea*
Annual vagrant, since 1841
Lesser short-toed lark *Calandrella rufescens*
4 records, since 1956

B267 Calandra lark *Melanocorypha calandra*
1 record in 1961
Bimaculated lark *Melanocorypha bimaculata*
1 record in 1962

B268 White-winged lark *Melanocorypha leucoptera*
4 records, since 1869

[B266 Black lark *Melanocorypha yeltoniensis*
Doubtful, "Hastings"]

B273 Shore lark *Eremophila alpestris*
Winter visitor E S; vagrant I. Records from 1830

B270 Crested lark *Galerida cristata*
11 or more records, since before 1845

B271 Wood lark *Lullula arborea*
Resident E W; rare visitor S; vagrant I, where has bred. Records from 1544

B272 Skylark *Alauda arvensis*
Fossil from Early to Late Ice Age E I. Resident E WS I; also passage and winter visitor. Records from VIIIc.

Family Hirundinidae, swallows

[Tree swallow *Tachycineta bicolor*
Doubtful; from America]
[Purple martin *Progne subis*
Doubtful; from America]

B277 Sand martin *Riparia riparia*
Summer visitor E WS I. Records from VIIIc.

B274 Swallow *Hirundo rustica*
Fossil in Late Ice Age E I. Summer visitor E W S I. Records from *c.* 685

B275 Red-rumped swallow *Hirundo daurica*
12 records, since 1906

B276 House martin *Delichon urbica*
Fossil from Late Ice Age to Prehistoric E I. Summer visitor E W S I. Records from VIIIc.

Family Motacillidae, wagtails and pipits

B374 Richard's pipit *Anthus novaeseelandiae*
Annual vagrant, since 1812

B375 Tawny pipit *Anthus campestris*
Annual vagrant E, rare W S I, since 1858

B376 Tree pipit *Anthus trivialis*
Summer visitor E W S, also passage visitor; vagrant I. Records from 1738

B377 Pechora pipit *Anthus gustavi*
About 20 records, since 1925

B373 Meadow pipit *Anthus pratensis*
Fossil from Late Ice Age to Prehistoric E I. Resident E W S I; also summer, passage and winter visitor. Records from 1544

B378 Red-throated pipit *Anthus cervinus*
Vagrant, since 1854

B379 *Anthus spinoletta*
Fossil in Late Ice Age E.
American pipit *Anthus spinoletta rubescens*
Rare vagrant S; from America
Water pipit *Anthus spinoletta spinoletta*
Rare winter visitor E W I
Rock pipit *Anthus spinoletta petrosus* etc.
Resident coasts E W S I. Records from 1766

B382 Yellow wagtail *Motacilla flava*
Summer visitor E W S; passage visitor I, where formerly bred. Records from *c.* 1600
Citrine wagtail *Motacilla citreola*
7 records, since 1954

B381 Grey wagtail *Motacilla cinerea*
Resident E W S I. Records from 1678

B380 *Motacilla alba*
Fossil in Late Ice Age E I.

Pied wagtail *Motacilla alba yarrellii*
>Resident EWSI; also summer visitor. Records from VIIIc.

White wagtail *Motacilla alba alba*
>Passage visitor EWSI; has bred

[Masked wagtail *Motacilla alba personata*
>Doubtful, "Hastings"]

Family Pycnonotidae, bulbuls
>[Common bulbul *Pycnonotus capensis* (?*barbatus*)
>Doubtful]

Family Laniidae, shrikes
B388 Red-backed shrike *Lanius collurio*
>Fossil in Late Ice Age E. Summer visitor E, formerly W; passage visitor S; vagrant I. Records from VIIIc.

[B387 Masked shrike *Lanius nubicus*
>Doubtful, "Hastings"]

B386 Woodchat shrike *Lanius senator*
>Annual vagrant, since 1769

B385 Lesser grey shrike *Lanius minor*
>Rare vagrant, since 1851

B384 Great grey shrike *Lanius excubitor*
>Fossil in Late Ice Age E. Winter and passage visitor ES; vagrant WI. Records since 1544

Family Bombycillidae, waxwings
B383 Waxwing *Bombycilla garrulus*
>Winter visitor EWSI, irregularly invasive. Records from 1662

Family Cinclidae, dippers
B300 Dipper *Cinclus cinclus*
>Fossil in Late Ice Age E. Resident EWSI. Records from 1544

Family Troglodytidae, wrens
B299 Wren *Troglodytes troglodytes*
>Fossil in Late Ice Age E. Resident EWSI. Records from VIIIc.

Family Prunellidae, accentors
B372 Alpine accentor *Prunella collaris*
>Rare vagrant, since 1817

B371 Dunnock *or* hedge sparrow *Prunella modularis*
>Fossil from Late Ice Age to Roman E. Resident and passage visitor EWSI. Records from VIIIc.

Family Muscicapidae, Subfamily Turdinae, thrushes

B353 Rufous bush robin *Cercotrichas (Agrobates) galactotes*
    8 records, since 1854

B325 Robin *Erithacus rubecula*
    Fossil from Early to Late Ice Age E I. Resident E W S I; also summer, passage and winter visitor. Records from *c.* 530

B323 Thrush nightingale *Erithacus (Luscinia) luscinia*
    3 records, since 1911

B322 Nightingale *Erithacus (Luscinia) megarhynchos*
    Fossil in Late Ice Age E. Summer visitor E W; vagrant S I. Records from *c.* 685

    [Siberian rubythroat *Erithacus (Luscinia) calliope*
    Doubtful]

B324 Bluethroat *Erithacus (Luscinia) svecica*
    Passage visitor E S, vagrant W I. Records from 1826

B319 Red-flanked bluetail *Erithacus (Tarsiger) cyanurus*
    4 or 5 records, since 1903

B321 Black redstart *Phoenicurus ochruros*
    Summer visitor E; passage and winter visitor E W I; passage visitor S. Records from 1743

B320 Redstart *Phoenicurus phoenicurus*
    Summer visitor E W S; irregular I; also passage visitor. Records from VIIIc.

B318 Whinchat *Saxicola rubetra*
    Fossil in Late Ice Age E I. Summer visitor E W S I; also passage visitor. Records from 1678

B317 Stonechat *Saxicola torquata*
    Resident E W S I; also summer and passage visitor. Records from XIc.

B315 Isabelline wheatear *Oenanthe isabellina*
    1 record in 1887

B311 Wheatear *Oenanthe oenanthe*
    Fossil from Early to Late Ice Age E. Summer visitor E W S I; also passage visitor. Records from XIc.

B312 Desert wheatear *Oenanthe deserti*
    15 records, since 1880

B313 Black-eared wheatear *Oenanthe hispanica*
    16 records, since 1875

B314 Pied wheatear *Oenanthe pleschanka*
    3 records, since 1909

B316 Black wheatear *Oenanthe leucura*
    5 records, since 1912

B310 Rock thrush *Monticola saxatilis*
    7 records, since 1843
    Siberian thrush *Zoothera sibirica*
    1 record in 1954
B309 Golden mountain thrush *Zoothera dauma*
    Rare vagrant, since 1828
    Grey-cheeked thrush *Catharus minimus*
    3 records, since 1953; from America
    Swainson's *or* olive-backed thrush *Catharus ustulatus*
    1 record in 1956; from America
B307 Ring ouzel *Turdus torquatus*
    Summer visitor EWSI; also passage visitor. Records from 1450
B308 Blackbird *Turdus merula*
    Fossil from Early to Late Ice Age E. Resident EWSI; also
    summer, passage and winter visitor. Records from VIIIc.
    Eyebrowed thrush *Turdus obscurus*
    3 records in 1964
B306 Black-throated thrush *Turdus ruficollis (atrogularis)*
    3 records, since 1868
B305 Naumann's (dusky) thrush *Turdus naumanni (eunomus)*
    3 records, since 1905
B302 Fieldfare *Turdus pilaris*
    Fossil in Late Ice Age EI. Winter visitor EWSI; also passage
    visitor. Records from XIc.
B304 Redwing *Turdus iliacus*
    Fossil from Early to Late Ice Age EI. Winter visitor EWSI;
    breeds sometimes S; also passage visitor. Records from *c.* 1600
B303 Song thrush *Turdus philomelos*
    Fossil from Early Ice Age to Roman EI. Resident EWSI;
    also summer, passage and winter visitor. Records from VIIIc.
B301 Mistle thrush *Turdus viscivorus*
    Fossil in Late Ice Age EI. Resident EWSI; also summer,
    passage and winter visitor. Records from VIIIc.
    American robin *Turdus migratorius*
    9 records, since 1891; from America

Subfamily Panurinae, bearded tit and parrotbills
    B295 Bearded tit *Panurus biarmicus*
        Resident E, also winter vagrant; vagrant W. Records from 1662

Subfamily Sylviinae, Old World warblers and gnatwrens
    B326 Cetti's warbler *Cettia cetti*
        2 records, from 1961

B329 Savi's warbler *Locustella luscinioides*
    Former summer visitor E, extinct *c.* 1885; records from 1835.
    Since 1960 again rare summer visitor E
    River warbler *Locustella fluviatilis*
    1 record in 1961

B330 Pallas's grasshopper warbler *Locustella certhiola*
    3 records, since 1908

B327 Grasshopper warbler *Locustella naevia*
    Summer visitor EWSI; also passage visitor. Records from 1678

B328 Lanceolated warbler *Locustella lanceolata*
    11 records, since 1909

B331 Moustached warbler *Lusciniola melanopogon*
    3 records, since 1946 when bred E

B338 Aquatic warbler *Acrocephalus paludicola*
    Annual vagrant, since 1853

B337 Sedge warbler *Acrocephalus schoenobaenus*
    Summer visitor EWSI; also passage visitor. Records from
    1766

B336 Paddy-field warbler *Acrocephalus agricola*
    2 records, since 1925

B335 Blyth's reed warbler *Acrocephalus dumetorum*
    6 records, since 1910

B334 Marsh warbler *Acrocephalus palustris*
    Summer visitor E; vagrant W (has bred) and S. Records
    from 1871

B333 Reed warbler *Acrocephalus scirpaceus*
    Summer visitor EW; passage visitor E; vagrant I (has bred)
    and S. Records from 1676

B332 Great reed warbler *Acrocephalus arundinaceus*
    Annual vagrant, since 1847
    Thick-billed reed warbler *Acrocephalus aedon*
    1 record in 1955

B340 Icterine warbler *Hippolais icterina*
    Annual vagrant, since 1848; has bred E

B339 Melodious warbler *Hippolais polyglotta*
    Annual vagrant, since 1897

B341 Olivaceous warbler *Hippolais pallida*
    6 records, since 1951

B342 Booted warbler *Hippolais caligata*
    2 records, since 1936

B344 Barred warbler *Sylvia nisoria*
    Annual vagrant, since before 1879

B345 Orphean warbler *Sylvia hortensis*
  2 records, since 1848
B346 Garden warbler *Sylvia borin*
  Summer and passage visitor EWSI. Records from 1676
B343 Blackcap *Sylvia atricapilla*
  Summer and passage visitor EWSI; some also winter. Records from *c.* 998
B347 Whitethroat *Sylvia communis*
  Fossil in Late Ice Age E. Summer visitor EWSI; also passage visitor. Records from 1544
B348 Lesser whitethroat *Sylvia curruca*
  Summer visitor EW; passage visitor S, where has bred, and E; vagrant I. Records from *c.* 1780
[B349 Rüppell's warbler *Sylvia rüppelli*
  Doubtful, "Hastings"]
B350 Sardinian warbler *Sylvia melanocephala*
  1 record in 1955
B351 Subalpine warbler *Sylvia cantillans*
  Rare vagrant, since 1894
B352 Dartford warbler *Sylvia undata*
  Resident E; vagrant I. Records from 1773
B354 Willow warbler *Phylloscopus trochilus*
  Summer visitor EWSI. Records from 1718
B356 Chiffchaff *Phylloscopus collybita*
  Summer visitor EWSI, also some winter EWI. Records from 1678
B358 Bonelli's warbler *Phylloscopus bonelli*
  15 records, since 1948
B357 Wood warbler *Phylloscopus sibilatrix*
  Summer visitor EWS; has bred I; also passage visitor ES. Records from 1676
B362 Dusky warbler *Phylloscopus fuscatus*
  3 records, since 1913
B363 Radde's willow warbler *Phylloscopus schwarzi*
  5 records, since 1898
B360 Yellow-browed warbler *Phylloscopus inornatus*
  Annual vagrant, since 1838
B361 Pallas's leaf warbler *Phylloscopus proregulus*
  14 records, since 1896
B359 Arctic warbler *Phylloscopus borealis*
  Rare vagrant, since 1902

B355 Greenish warbler *Phylloscopus trochiloides*
      Rare vagrant, since 1896

Subfamily Regulinae, goldcrests
  B364 Goldcrest *Regulus regulus*
        Resident E W S I; also passage visitor. Records from 1544
  B365 Firecrest *Regulus ignicapillus*
        Winter visitor E W; vagrant S I; now breeds E. Records from
        1832
        [Golden-crowned kinglet *Regulus (ignicapillus) satrapa*
        Doubtful; from America]
        [Ruby-crowned kinglet *Regulus calendula*
        Doubtful; from America]

Subfamily Muscicapinae, Old World flycatchers and fantails
  B368 Pied flycatcher *Ficedula hypoleuca*
        Summer visitor E W S; also passage visitor E W S I. Records
        from 1676
  B369 Collared flycatcher *Ficedula albicollis*
        5 records, since 1947
  B370 Red-breasted flycatcher *Ficedula parva*
        Annual vagrant, since 1863
  B366 Spotted flycatcher *Muscicapa striata*
        Summer visitor E W S I; also passage visitor. Records from 1662
  B367 Brown flycatcher *Muscicapa latirostris*
        2 records, since 1956

Family Paridae, titmice
  B294 Long-tailed tit *Aegithalos caudatus*
        Resident E W S I. Records from VIIIc.
  B292 Marsh tit *Parus palustris*
        Resident E W S I. Records from 1678 (? this or B293 X or XIc.)
  B293 Willow tit *Parus montanus*
        Resident E W S. Records from 1897
  B291 Crested tit *Parus cristatus*
        Resident S; rare vagrant E. Records from 1678
  B290 Coal tit *Parus ater*
        Resident E W S I. Records from *c.* 998
  B289 Blue tit *Parus caeruleus*
        Resident E W S I; also passage visitor. Records from VIIIc.
  B288 Great tit *Parus major*
        Fossil in Late Ice Age E. Resident E W S I; also passage visitor.
        Records from VIIIc.

Family Sittidae, nuthatches
> B296 Nuthatch *Sitta europaea*
>> Fossil in Late Ice Age E. Resident EW; vagrant S. Records by
>> 1450
> B297 Wallcreeper *Tichodroma muraria*
>> 4 records, since 1872

Family Certhiidae, creepers
> B298 Tree creeper *Certhia familiaris*
>> Fossil in Late Ice Age E. Resident EWSI. Records from XIc.

Family Emberizidae, Subfamily Emberizinae, buntings and American
sparrows
>> Slate-coloured junco *Junco hyemalis*
>>> 1 record in 1905; from America
>> [White-crowned sparrow *Zonotrichia leucophrys*
>>> Doubtful; from America]
>> White-throated sparrow *Zonotrichia albicollis*
>>> 2 records, since 1909; from America
>> Song sparrow *Passerella (Melospiza) melodia*
>>> 2 records, since 1959; from America
>> Fox sparrow *Passerella iliaca*
>>> 1 record in 1961; from America
> B422 Lapland bunting *Calcarius lapponicus*
>> Passage visitor ESI, also winter visitor; vagrant W. Records
>> from 1826
> B423 Snow bunting *Plectrophenax nivalis*
>> Resident S; winter visitor EWSI. Records from 1678
> B410 Corn bunting *Emberiza calandra*
>> Fossil in Late Ice Age E. Resident EWSI. Records by 1450
> B409 Yellowhammer *Emberiza citrinella*
>> Fossil in Late Ice Age EI. Resident EWSI; also passage and
>> winter visitor. Records from VIIIc.
> B411 Pine bunting *Emberiza leucocephala*
>> 2 records, since 1911
> B417 Rock bunting *Emberiza cia*
>> 3 records, since 1902
> [B418 Meadow bunting *Emberiza cioides*
>> Doubtful]
> B416 Ortolan *Emberiza hortulana*
>> Annual vagrant, since before 1776

B415 Cirl bunting *Emberiza cirlus*
    Resident E W; vagrant S I. Records from 1800
B420 Little bunting *Emberiza pusilla*
    Annual vagrant, since 1864
B419 Rustic bunting *Emberiza rustica*
    Annual vagrant, since 1867
B414 Yellow-breasted bunting *Emberiza aureola*
    19 records, since 1905
B412 Black-headed bunting *Emberiza melanocephala*
    About 11 records, since 1868
B413 Red-headed bunting *Emberiza bruniceps*
    1 record in 1931; records since are classed doubtful
    owing to prevalence of "escapes", though some possibly of
    wild birds
B421 Reed bunting *Emberiza schoeniclus*
    Resident E W S I; also summer, passage and winter visitor.
    Records from *c.* 1460

Subfamily Cardinalinae, cardinals, etc.
    Rose-breasted grosbeak *Pheucticus ludovicianus*
        1 record in 1957; from America
    [Painted bunting *Passerina ciris*
        Doubtful; from America]

Subfamily Tanagrinae, tanagers
    Summer tanager *Piranga rubra*
        1 record in 1957; from America

Family Parulidae, wood warblers
    Black-and-white warbler *Mniotilta varia*
        1 record in 1936; from America
    Yellow warbler *Dendroica petechia*
        1 record in 1964; from America
    Myrtle warbler *Dendroica coronata*
        2 records, since 1955; from America
    [Blackburnian warbler *Dendroica fusca*
        Doubtful; from America]
    Northern waterthrush *Seiurus noveboracensis*
        1 record in 1958; from America
    Yellowthroat *Geothlypis trichas*
        1 record in 1954; from America

Family Vireonidae, vireos
> Red-eyed vireo *Vireo olivaceus*
>> 2 records, since 1951; from America

Family Icteridae, icterids
> [Rusty blackbird *Euphagus carolinus*
>> Doubtful; from America]'
> Baltimore oriole *Icterus galbula*
>> 3 records, since 1958; from America
> [Eastern meadowlark *Sturnella magna*
>> Doubtful; from America]
> Bobolink *Dolichonyx oryzivorus*
>> 1 record in 1962; from America

Family Fringillidae, finches
> B407 Chaffinch *Fringilla coelebs*
>> Fossil in Late Ice Age EI. Resident EWSI; also passage and winter visitor. Records from *c*. 685
> B408 Brambling *Fringilla montifringilla*
>> Winter visitor EWSI; has bred S. Records from 1544
> B399 Citril finch *Serinus citrinella*
>> 1 record in 1904
> B400 Serin *Serinus serinus*
>> Annual vagrant (increasing E), since 1852
> B392 Greenfinch *Carduelis chloris*
>> Fossil from Early to Late Ice Age EI. Resident EWSI; also passage and winter visitor. Records from 1532
> B394 Siskin *Carduelis spinus*
>> Resident EWSI; winter and passage visitor. Records from 1369
> B393 Goldfinch *Carduelis carduelis*
>> Resident EWSI. Records from VIIIc.
> [American goldfinch *Carduelis tristis*
>> Doubtful; from America]
> B396 Twite *Acanthis flavirostris*
>> Resident ESI, has bred W; also winter visitor. Records from 1562
> B395 Linnet *Acanthis cannabina*
>> Fossil in Late Ice Age EI. Resident EWSI; also summer, passage and winter visitor. Records from VIIIc.
> B397 Redpoll *Acanthis flammea*
>> Resident EWSI; also summer, passage and winter visitor. Records from 1678

B398 Arctic redpoll *Acanthis* (*?flammea*) *hornemanni*
> Rare vagrant, since 1855

B402 Scarlet grosbeak *or* common rose finch *Carpodacus erythrinus*
> Annual vagrant, since 1869

B403 Pine grosbeak *Pinicola enucleator*
> About 4 records, since 1890

B405 Parrot crossbill *Loxia pytyopsittacus*
> Rare vagrant, since 1818. Invasion of winter 1962–63 raised records from 9 to well over the score. The Scottish race of the crossbill, below, has been referred to this species but is held in *L. curvirostra* by the authorities I follow

B404 Crossbill *Loxia curvirostra*
> Records from 1251. Scottish race *Loxia curvirostra scotica* resident S. Continental race *Loxia curvirostra curvirostra* resident E and has bred W I following, and refreshed by, periodic invasions from Continent

B406 White-winged crossbill *Loxia leucoptera*
> Irregular vagrant, since 1802

> [Long-tailed rose finch *Uragus sibiricus*
> Doubtful]

B401 Bullfinch *Pyrrhula pyrrhula*
> Fossil from Late Ice Age to Prehistoric I. Resident EWSI; also winter visitor. Records from 1369

B391 Hawfinch *Coccothraustes coccothraustes*
> Fossil from Late Ice Age to Prehistoric EI. Resident EWS; vagrant I, where may have bred. Records from 1666

Family Ploceidae, weavers and true sparrows

B424 House sparrow *Passer domesticus*
> Fossil from Late Ice Age to Prehistoric EI. Resident EWSI; also winter and passage visitor E. Records from *c.* 731

B425 Tree sparrow *Passer montanus*
> Resident EWSI; also winter and passage visitor. Records from 1713

[B426 Snow finch *Montifringilla nivalis*
> Doubtful, "Hastings"]

Family Sturnidae, starlings

B390 Rosy starling *Sturnus roseus*
> Irregular vagrant EWSI. Records from 1743

B389 Starling *Sturnus vulgaris*
> Fossil in Late Ice Age EI. Resident EWSI; also winter visitor. Records from VIIIc.

Family Oriolidae, Old World orioles
> B278 Golden oriole *Oriolus oriolus*
>> Passage visitor E W, has bred; vagrant S I. Records from 1743

Family Corvidae, crows
> B286 Jay *Garrulus glandarius*
>> Fossil from Late Ice Age to Roman E I. Resident E W S I; also
>> winter visitor E. Records from 1382
> B284 Magpie *Pica pica*
>> Fossil from Late Ice Age to Dark Ages S I. Resident E W S I.
>> Records from *c.* 998
> B285 Nutcracker *Nucifriga caryocatactes*
>> Rare vagrant, since 1753
> B287 Chough *Pyrrhocorax pyrrhocorax*
>> Fossil from Late Ice Age to Dark Ages E W I. Resident E W S I.
>> Records from *c.* 998
> B283 Jackdaw *Corvus monedula*
>> Fossil from Late Ice Age to Roman E I. Resident E W S I; also
>> winter visitor. Records by 1150
> B282 Rook *Corvus frugilegus*
>> Fossil from Late Ice Age to Medieval E I. Resident E W S I;
>> also winter and passage visitor. Records from VIIIc.
> Crow *Corvus corone*
>> Fossil from Early Ice Age to Dark Ages E S I. Records from
>> *c.* 676. Hybridisation zone of races around south S
> B280 Carrion crow *Corvus corone corone*
>> Resident E W S, has bred I; also winter visitor
> B281 Hooded crow *Corvus corone cornix*
>> Resident S I, has bred E W; also winter visitor
> B279 Raven *Corvus corax*
>> Fossil from Early Ice Age to Dark Ages E S I. Resident E W S I;
>> also winter visitor. Records from *c.* 699.

Index

Page references in **bold** type refer to illustrations

339

Reference to National and Irish Grid

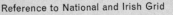

HL	HM	HN	HO	HP	JL
HQ	HR	HS	HT	HU	JQ
HV	HW	HX	HY	HZ	JV
NA	NB	NC	ND	NE	OA
NF	NG	NH	NJ	NK	OF
NL	NM	NN	NO	NP	OL
NQ / NR	NS	NT	NU	OQ	
NX	NY	NZ	OV		
SC	SD	SE	TA	TB	
SH	SJ	SK	TF	TG	
SN	SO	SP	TL	TM	
SR	SS	ST	SU	TQ	TR
SV	SW	SX	SY	SZ	TV

Irish grid letters: A B C D / F G H J / L M N O / Q R S T / V W X Y / SM / SQ